Antiquities under Siege

Antiquities under Siege

*Cultural Heritage Protection
after the Iraq War*

EDITED BY LAWRENCE ROTHFIELD

ALTAMIRA
PRESS

A Division of
ROWMAN & LITTLEFIELD PUBLISHERS, INC.
Lanham • New York • Toronto • Plymouth, UK

ALTAMIRA PRESS
A division of Rowman & Littlefield Publishers, Inc.
A wholly owned subsidiary of The Rowman & Littlefield Publishing Group, Inc.
4501 Forbes Boulevard, Suite 200, Lanham, MD 20706
www.altamirapress.com

Estover Road, Plymouth PL6 7PY, United Kingdom

British Library Cataloguing in Publication Information Available

Library of Congress Cataloging-in-Publication Data

Antiquities under siege : cultural heritage protection after the Iraq war / edited by Lawrence Rothfield.
    p. cm.
Includes bibliographical references and index.
ISBN-13: 978-0-7591-1098-4 (cloth : alk. paper)
ISBN-10: 0-7591-1098-0 (cloth : alk. paper)
ISBN-13: 978-0-7591-1099-1 (pbk. : alk. paper)
ISBN-10: 0-7591-1099-9 (pbk. : alk. paper)
    1. Iraq War, 2003– —Destruction and pillage. 2. Archaeological thefts—Iraq. 3. Iraq—Antiquities. 4. Cultural property—Protection—Iraq. I. Rothfield, Lawrence, 1956–

DS79.76.A584 2008
363.6'909567—dc22
2007043447

Printed in the United States of America

∞™ The paper used in this publication meets the minimum requirements of American National Standard for Information Sciences—Permanence of Paper for Printed Library Materials, ANSI/NISO Z39.48-1992.

For Hannah

Contents

Figures and Tables

Acknowledgments

THIS VOLUME IS THE WORK OF MANY HANDS. FROM THE VERY BEGINNING AND throughout, McGuire Gibson has helped fuel and guide our efforts. Equally valuable has been the advice provided by Patty Gerstenblith, who took a lead role in organizing the February 2006 convening held at the University of Chicago Law School at which we broached the legal issues involved in wartime heritage looting. At that conference, Patrick Boylan and Jan Hladik helped us recognize the historical and legal contexts within which international legal instruments have evolved, and colleagues Eric Posner and Kenneth Dam provided canny and sharp-edged outsiders' views of the issues.

The Cultural Policy Center is deeply grateful to the Smart Family Fund, the Franke Institute for the Humanities, the Otto L. and Hazel T. Rhoades Fund, and Dean Saul Levmore of the Law School for underwriting the Law School meeting. Dean Gil Stein and the Oriental Institute provided canny advice, technical support, and timely funding help for this meeting and for the project as a whole. The logistics were handled with grace and efficiency by Jennifer Chang and Charlotte Toolan. Additional thanks are owed to the Council on Foreign Relations, Saving Antiquities for Everyone, and Ms. Jamee Rosa for their support. Special thanks to my codirector at the Cultural Policy Center, Carroll Joynes, for all his help in garnering support and seeing the big picture.

The follow-up meeting in August 2006 brought together a wider range of stakeholders, many of whom had never met before. The participants, many of whom are contributors to this book, shaped the thoughts and recommendations that emerge throughout these pages. They include John Alexander, J.

Holmes Armstead, Col. Matthew Bogdanos, Mounir Bouchenaki, Bonnie Burnham, Guido Carducci, John Curtis, Kenneth Dam, Col. Scott Feil, Lamia al-Gailani Werr, Patty Gerstenblith, McGuire Gibson, Katharyn Hanson, Col. Christopher Herndon, Christopher Hoh, Richard Jackson, Carroll Joynes, Lt. Col. Joris Kila, James McAndrew, Col. Michael Meese, Sultan Muhesen, Wendy Norris, Abby O'Neil, Robert Perito, Timothy Potts, John M. Russell, Stephen Urice, and Maj. Corine Wegener. These intense discussions constitute an enormous step forward for cultural heritage protection because of the combined expertise of these individuals, their desire to share it, and their willingness to carefully consider views other than their own. This meeting could not have been such a success without the assistance of Joseph Collins and Arthur Houghton, who provided invaluable advice about whom to invite and how to frame the discussions. Following the meeting, Elizabeth Stone and Joanne Farchakh generously shared information and images that helped clarify the dynamics and extent of the looting.

The difficult issues being grappled with demanded a secluded venue and one that would encourage informal give-and-take beyond the scheduled sessions. No place is better for this purpose than the Pocantico Conference Center of the Rockefeller Brothers Fund, which kindly agreed to host our meeting. Our sincere thanks to Charles Granquist and Judy Clark for their marvelous hospitality. Crucial funding for this meeting and for the preparation of the book was provided by the Harris School of Public Policy Studies. We are grateful beyond words for the steadfast support provided by Dean Susan Mayer and Raja Kamal.

We wish to thank our editors at AltaMira, Serena Krombach, Claire Rojstaczer, and Janice Braunstein, for seeing the value of this project, for their guidance in helping us pull it together, and for their patience as we did so. At the Cultural Policy Center, Laura Page and Katharyn Hanson provided able assistance in vetting chapters and preparing the manuscript, and Eleanor Cartelli lent an eagle eye in compiling and editing the references. But it is to Wendy Norris, associate director of the center, and to our editor, John Whitman, that I owe the deepest debt. Tirelessly and with aplomb, they managed a lengthy manuscript generated by dozens of contributors, while also shaping the substance of the book in myriad ways.

Lastly, I wish to thank my wife, Penelope, for permitting me to continue working on this project even after the hotel in Jordan, where we originally had planned to meet, was bombed.

Introduction

IN THE FIRST HEADY DAYS IMMEDIATELY FOLLOWING THE FALL OF BAGHDAD, WITH the airwaves saturated with video of Saddam's statue being toppled, another story began to emerge of other, more ancient statues being pulled down from pedestals and walls in the Iraq Museum. This wasn't captured in the news footage, but the sacking of the world's most important repository of Mesopotamian antiquities was dramatic enough to grab headlines worldwide, at least for a few days. Secretary of Defense Donald Rumsfeld and Secretary of State Colin Powell were questioned about how the military could have permitted such a thing to happen, and the president himself was said to be concerned about the museum's fate. But public attention, and the interest of policymakers, soon turned to other matters, and the museum's losses—numbering in the range of fifteen thousand artifacts—were soon forgotten.

Horrendous as these depredations were, they would soon be dwarfed by losses from unconstrained looting at thousands of archaeological sites around the country. Illegal digging on a massive scale continues to this day, virtually unchecked, with Iraq's ten thousand officially recognized sites being destroyed at a rate of roughly 10 percent per year. In part because it is a slow-motion disaster, in part because reporters trying to cover it risk being kidnapped or killed, this part of the story has gone almost totally untold. And as was the case with the museum, no one is being held accountable for what has gone wrong.

The absence of detailed oversight makes it easy to dismiss the looting as just another manifestation of the mishandling of U.S. prewar planning for the occupation of Iraq. But that would be an oversimplification. As James Fallows's overview of prewar planning efforts notes in passing, failure took a distinct form in the case of cultural heritage. In other sectors such as health, environment, and education, the problem was one primarily of implementation. Under State Department auspices, plans were drawn up—though not executed by the military—to secure hospitals, schools, and other socially vital institutions; humanitarian nongovernmental organizations, joined by officials from the relevant government agencies, met repeatedly with Pentagon planners, at the Pentagon's request, to voice their concerns—though most went unheeded—about the dangers to their sectors that lay ahead. International institutions weighed in repeatedly before the start of the war with concerns and offers of help. By contrast, the intergovernmental and nongovernmental organizations responsible for cultural heritage preservation generally did not succeed in getting to the table with postwar planners at the Pentagon, who were never contacted by officials from any other government agency on this matter. For its part, the Pentagon neglected to include culture in the list of things that would need to be cared for once the regime had fallen, even though its officials had previously experienced the embarrassment of museum looting on their watch. Immediately after the United States and United Kingdom delineated a no-fly zone in parts of northern Iraq in 1992, looting broke out in nearly all the museums within these boundaries. And the State Department did no better, belatedly establishing a working group on cultural heritage when the invasion was just six weeks away.[1]

The disaster that has befallen Iraq's cultural heritage, in short, has complex roots, involving a range of institutions and bodies cutting across many divides—military and civilian, legislative and executive, domestic and international, governmental and extragovernmental. One might have expected this set of policy players to be able to meet the challenge of safeguarding the priceless remnants of the earliest known civilization on earth. Yet the array of laws and international conventions, the advocacy efforts of cultural heritage organizations, the military planning and implementation of cultural protection operations all failed, and continue to fail, to prevent the debacle in Iraq.

Iraq publicly and prominently exposed a serious structural problem in the field of heritage preservation. Once relatively rare, antiquities looting in the aftermath of war has become commonplace in the last twenty years. Why did the military not learn any lessons about cultural looting from its earlier experience in Iraq, or from the war-related pillaging of Cambodia's Angkor Wat, Bosnia's churches, or Karwar (often described as Afghanistan's "Pompeii")? Why did the State Department's Middle East experts, and the Iraqi exile groups with which they were working to create a blueprint for postwar Iraq, completely disregard the need to protect Babylon, Ur, Nineveh, Nippur, and other fabled cities that dated to the beginnings of civilization? Why did those whom one might have expected to collaborate on anti-looting plans—archaeologists, antiquities collectors, museum directors, foundation officers, on the one hand, governmental postwar planners, on the other—produce no plans? Why did those one might have expected to pressure the authorities to implement effective security measures fail, for the most part, to get the ear of war planners? Why did those who *did* manage to place their concerns before officials fail to get governments to take the necessary steps? And why did international legal instruments designed to protect cultural heritage have so little impact?

These are not simply academic questions. If military planners in the United States and elsewhere do not address them head-on, they risk making the Iraq war a precedent-setting case. If this happens, we all take the chance that we will once again witness irrevocable damage to the repository of human history. Complaining about the Bush administration's failure to secure sites and museums is no substitute for the kind of policy-analytic thinking needed to ensure it does not happen again. It makes sense for those who are concerned about antiquities in Syria, Iran, and elsewhere to prepare contingency plans in advance, so as to be ready to move quickly and forcefully if the need arises. We need to establish a planning process, produce realistic and well-structured policy options, and develop advocacy strategies to ensure that such plans are not merely accepted by governments (if governments must be involved for them to succeed), but fully implemented as well. But to do this properly, we need to learn the lessons Iraq offers about cultural heritage protection.

This book seeks to further these objectives, taking Iraq as a case study in what can go wrong, and a point of departure for developing forward-looking policy options. To ensure that policymakers understand the field in which they are—or should be—acting, we begin by reviewing the prewar planning process within the United States insofar as it touched on questions of cultural heritage protection. The story that emerges is one of mixed motives, mixed signals, and missed opportunities, involving a cast of characters that includes archaeologists, collectors, cultural bureaucrats, Pentagon war planners, ambassadors, military targeting experts, antiquities officials, and dozens of others. All were acting within institutional frameworks that constrained what they could do, and what they could imagine themselves doing.

The remaining chapters in part I shift the perspective from meeting rooms and offices to shattered display cases and beyond—to the pockmarked landscape of devastated archaeological sites that supply the stream of cylinder seals, cuneiform tablets, vases, and statuary for the global antiquities market, and feed the demand of the small core of high-end collectors whose appetite is served by auction houses and antiquities dealers. Donny George Youkhanna and McGuire Gibson provide a view from inside the Iraq Museum, where curatorial staff instructed by the Ministry of Culture took desperate steps to brace for the chaos they knew was coming. Matthew Bogdanos clarifies the complex situation faced on the ground by U.S. combat forces left without policy guidance or adequate support, and the equally complex situation inside the museum, where clues indicate that artifacts were stolen by at least three different kinds of looters. Joanne Farchakh-Bajjaly takes us out into the countryside to introduce us to the poverty-stricken men who eke out a living destroying their country's cultural patrimony in search of an artifact that might bring them a few dollars. The same artifact, as Neil Brodie shows, disappears into the shadowy world of middlemen and smugglers, reappearing only in the case of lucky seizures. (Of the 5,000 items recovered from the Iraq Museum looting, 1,000 were seized in the United States, 700 in Jordan, 500 in France, and 250 in Switzerland.) As Bogdanos elaborates, a global black market for antiquities that has long included some of the world's major institutional and individual collectors has grown to include some middlemen who aim to finance terrorism and the Iraqi insurgency.

Having described in part I what has not been done in Iraq to prevent looting, we turn in the remainder of the volume to the question of how, having learned from the past, we can avoid being condemned to repeat it. The lessons of Iraq are not the same for all constituencies, so we have chosen to address sections to specific stakeholders. Congress and other legislative bodies face challenges in ratifying and implementing international treaties, as Patty Gerstenblith and Guido Carducci explain. Lawmakers also need to consider ways of crafting more effective domestic legislation and in exercising tighter oversight over the executive branch and the military's chain of command, according to Patty Gerstenblith, Katharyn Hanson, and J. Holmes Armstead, Jr. For their part, war planners need to think about the nuts and bolts of cultural policing: What forces can be formed or mobilized to provide security, using what equipment, deployed according to what strategy? And how can civil affairs and law-enforcement agencies contribute to this effort? Michael Dziedzic and Christine Stark discuss the use of military policing units such as those operated by the Italian Carabinieri, while Matthew Bogdanos, Corine Wegener, and Joris Kila speak to the role of Interpol, customs officers, and civil-military affairs advisors, and John Alexander describes the wide range of flexible technologies available to them.

The "hard" forms of power—law, armed forces, and their auxiliaries—must be focused on the problem of looting if we hope to be more successful in preventing it in the next war. But "soft" power also has a crucial role to play, and so in the last three sections of this volume we address those who exercise this power. These stakeholders include, first and foremost, those in foreign services or international organizations who work regularly with the military before, during, and after combat, often taking a lead role in reconstruction efforts. The need for such organizations to include cultural heritage protection on their agenda is clear; the question we address is how this can be done. State Department officer Christopher Hoh and former UNESCO official Mounir Bouchenaki describe their organizations' efforts to date and suggest improvements that could be made. One enormous stumbling block in cultural heritage protection as in other areas of postwar reconstruction planning has been the difficulty of organizing an operation that involves multiple agencies acting in synchrony. Scott Feil analyzes the problem of coordination and suggests a possible solution to achieve the unity of effort needed.

The softest power of all is exercised by those who have the greatest interest in cultural heritage protection: cultural ministries and antiquities boards, on the one hand, and nongovernmental groups devoted to preserving the past, on the other. We conclude with chapters that address these stakeholders. Nancy Wilkie, a member of the president's Cultural Property Advisory Committee, surveys the U.S. governmental landscape to identify the often obscure offices that perform at least some of the functions that in other countries are consolidated in ministries of culture. The policy challenges facing cultural bureaucrats in a country engaged in planning for an invasion, of course, are quite distinct from those facing their counterparts in a country at risk of being invaded. Archaeologist McGuire Gibson and former Iraq Museum director Donny George Youkhanna speak to what can and should be done in-country to harden, as much as possible, vulnerable sites and museums and to safeguard holdings. Bonnie Burnham and Stephen Urice explain how the nonprofit cultural sector can strengthen their role in cultural heritage protection by coordinated international engagement in research and education, advocacy, and fund-raising.

Each contributor in part II offers proposals for changes in policy based on his or her own expertise. In appendix C, we supplement these with a summary of policy recommendations arrived at jointly by participants in two working meetings that gave rise to the idea for this book. Those meetings in themselves constituted a policy innovation. This was the first time that representatives from archaeological associations, the museum world, preservation advocacy groups, national antiquities agencies, U.S. Departments of Defense and State and the uniformed military, UNESCO and NATO, and academia all sat down together for extended discussions. Beyond the specific recommendations generated by these discussions, these meetings reduced to one degree of separation what had been an abyss separating preservationists from policymakers in the government and the military. And with one participant, Col. Michael Meese, having been tapped to oversee reconstruction efforts in Baghdad, heritage protection advocates have a pipeline to at least one high-level official who has been educated about what is at stake and what might be done at this late date, after the looting of the museum, after the decimation of myriad archaeological sites, after the failure to adequately support Iraq's own efforts to develop site policing forces.

The recommendations we lay out in this book are not aimed at putting Humpty Dumpty together again, however. They are, rather, prospective. We hope they will lead to real changes in the way in which countries preparing for war recognize and take responsibility for averting the threat of untrammeled looting of the cultural patrimony of mankind in the wake of war.

NOTE

1. James Fallows, "Blind into Baghdad," *The Atlantic Monthly* 293, no. 1 (January/ February 2004), http://www.epic-usa.org/Default.aspx?tabid=185.

Part I

THE CASE OF IRAQ AND THE CONTEXT OF LOOTING

THE LOOTING OF IRAQ'S MUSEUM IN APRIL 2003, AND THE CONTINUING DEVASTATION of archaeological sites throughout the country, reflect a major policy failure that occurred despite the efforts of multiple stakeholders both within and outside governments. (For a chart of those involved in efforts to protect Iraq's cultural heritage in the 2002–2003 period, see the following pages.) In this section we clarify the causes of this failure by laying out the history of prewar planning with regard to Iraq's cultural heritage. The steps taken, and not taken, by policymakers in the United States and within Iraq determined in part what took place on the ground in the chaos following the invasion. Without the disregard of policymakers, the opportunity to break into the museum or to bulldoze ancient mounds with impunity would not have arisen. The looting was also determined by the existence of an international market for Mesopotamian antiquities—one that links poverty-stricken peasants with millionaire collectors and museum directors through a network of smugglers and dealers.

Policy Stakeholders Involved in Cultural Heritage Protection Efforts in Iraq, 2002-2003

NGOs and Nonprofits

U.S. Professional Associations
- American Coordination Committee of Iraqi Cultural Heritage (ACCICH)*
- American Anthropological Association
- American Oriental Society
- Archaeological Institute of America
- Association of Art Museum Directors (AAMD)
- College Art Association
- Society for American Archaeology
- Society for Historical Archaeology

University-based Research Institutions
- British School of Archaeology in Iraq
- Cambridge University [UK]
  - McDonald Institute for Archaeological Research
  - Illicit Antiquities Research Centre
- English Heritage [UK]
- SUNY-Stony Brook
- University of Chicago
  - Oriental Institute
- University of Michigan
- University of Pennsylvania

Government Organizations

United States Government
- **Central Intelligence Agency**
- **Department of Homeland Security**
  - Immigration and Customs Enforcement (ICE)
- **Department of Justice**
  - FBI
- **Department of State**
  - Bureau of Educational and Cultural Affairs
    - *Cultural Heritage Center*
  - Bureau of International Narcotics and Law Enforcement Affairs

- **Department of State (cont.)**
  - Bureau of Near East Affairs
  - Bureau for Population, Migration, and Refugees
  - Future of Iraq Project *[at Middle East Institute]*
  - U.S. Agency for International Development (USAID)
    - *Disaster Assistance Response Team (DART)*
- **Library of Congress**
- **National Security Council**
- **NEA and NEH**
- **White House Office of Science and Technology Policy**

Military and Police

U.S. Military and Police Forces
- **Department of Defense**
  - Assistant Secretary of Defense for Special Operations and Low-Intensity Conflict
  - Defense Intelligence Agency
    - *Operational Environ-mental Analysis Division*

- Military Departments
- Office of the Deputy Secretary of Defense
  - *General Counsel's Office*
- Office of the Joint Chiefs of Staff

* The ACCICH is comprised of representatives from the other professional associations listed here, as well as individual scholars

NGOs and Nonprofits

Museums
- British Museum [UK]
- Getty Conservation Institute
- International Council of Museums (ICOM)*
- Iraqi National Museum
- Metropolitan Museum of Art [NY]
- Smithsonian Institution

U.S. Philanthropists
- **Foundations**
  - Packard Humanities Institute; Getty; Mellon; Pew; Rockefeller
- **Corporations**
  - American Express
- **Individuals**

U.S. Collectors/Dealers
- American Council for Cultural Policy (ACCP)

International Organizations
- International Committee of the Blue Shield (ICBS)
- International Council on Monuments and Sites (ICOMOS)‡
- Saving Antiquities for Everyone (SAFE)
- World Monuments Fund (WMF)

Government Organizations

Foreign Governments
- **British Government**
  - Department of Media, Culture, and Sport
  - Parliamentary Archaeology Group
- **Iraqi Government**
  - Facility Protection Service
  - Iraqi National Congress (in exile)
  - Ministry of Culture
    - State Board of Antiquities and Heritage (SBAH)

International Governmental Organizations (IGOs)
- **United Nations**
  - Department of Peacekeeping Operations
  - United Nations Educational, Scientific and Cultural Organization (UNESCO)

Military and Police

- **Department of Defense (cont.)**
  - USCENTCOM
    - Coalition Forces Land Component Command (CFLCC)
      + 352nd Civil Affairs Command
    - Office of Reconstruction and Humanitarian Assistance (ORHA)

Foreign and International Military and Police
- **Carabinieri per la Tutela del Patrimonio Culturale [Italy]**
- **Ministry of Defence [UK]**
- **Interpol§**
- **NATO**
  - Civil Military Co-operation/ Cultural Affairs (CIMIC/CA) Unit [The Netherlands]

* ICOM is an international organization comprised of national museum associations
‡ ICOMOS is comprised of national associations for monuments and sites
§ Interpol facilitates coordination between the police organizations of 186 member countries

CHAPTER 1

Preserving Iraq's Heritage from Looting

What Went Wrong
(within the United States)

LAWRENCE ROTHFIELD

WITHIN THE VAST PANORAMA OF FUTILITY AND ANARCHY THAT IS CONTEMPORARY Iraq, the looting of Iraq's cultural heritage is a relatively insignificant issue that has received little attention from chroniclers, despite the flurry of media attention that greeted the news of the looting of the Iraq Museum. Perhaps this is because it seems a simple tale, and an outrageous one: invading American troops supposedly stood by while one of the world's major museums was looted. People ask, rhetorically, How could such a thing have happened?

But the question is not just rhetorical. What led up to the disaster at the museum—and to the much less well-reported, but far more devastating ongoing looting of thousands of archaeological sites—was not a moral failure alone. It was also, and more complicatedly, a failure of policy within the cultural sector as well as the government and the military. Leadership was part of the problem, but there were also serious shortcomings in the chain of command, in coordination of efforts, in advocacy, and in capabilities. All contributed, and continue to contribute, to the debacle.

To learn from what went wrong, we need to understand what these policy flaws were. This history seeks to help readers do that.

SITE POLICING DURING THE PREWAR PERIOD

One of the first countries in the Middle East to establish a professional antiquities ministry, Iraq had a long and honorable history of preserving its archaeological heritage from the ravages of looting. The Baath Party continued this tradition, and Saddam, who took a personal interest in these matters, viewed

Iraq's pre-Islamic Mesopotamian past as reflecting glory on his present-day secular tyranny, added the deterrence of terror. As one museum official put it after the 2003 invasion, "'In Saddam Hussein's time, if they caught you looting, they did this,' he said, making a slicing motion at this throat."[1]

The 1991 Persian Gulf War took a major toll on Iraq's Ministry of Culture and on the country's cultural heritage. In the uprisings following the establishment of no-fly zones, eleven regional museums were looted. Over the course of the decade, haphazard looting of archaeological sites throughout the country evolved into regularized operations, fueled by the desperate living conditions of Iraqis under UN sanctions, combined with a surge in international demand from collectors, especially for tiny, easily smuggled, and valuable cuneiform tablets and cylinder seals.[2]

Iraqi antiquities professionals could do little to respond to the rising tide of looting. Their budget had been slashed to the point that the ministry could no longer provide the vehicles needed for local antiquities authorities to monitor their sites. Even when they learned of looting, however, they could no longer expect help from the Iraqi National Police, which had itself been forced into petty corruption by neglect after the 1991 war.[3] Moreover, the establishment of no-fly zones meant that remote sites could no longer be quickly reached by helicopter with forces capable of driving off looters. The only bulwark against looting, under these circumstances, was the moral force of local elders, to whom guards—mostly unarmed and lacking in authority or even basic security training—often turned for help in getting items returned.

The surge in cultural looting in the Iraqi countryside during the 1990s provided a preview of what would happen if central authority were destroyed, and highlighted the need for peacekeeping forces in postwar Iraq. That need had been amply demonstrated, of course, by the Persian Gulf War, Bosnia, and Kosovo. Yet the Pentagon never developed policing forces of any kind, or even budgeted for them. As Robert Perito notes, the United States "simply had not adopted postconflict stability as a core mission."[4] In an effort to grapple with this problem, the Clinton administration had set up a Peacekeeping Core Group. But this interagency group was abolished, along with all others, in Bush's first national security directive, reflecting the incoming administration's disdain for nation building.

The member states of the European Union did maintain experienced peacekeeping forces. Moreover, they also had more specialized paramilitary units trained to deal with cultural heritage protection, in particular the Italian Carabinieri, NATO's smaller CIMIC Group North Cultural Affairs unit, and national reservist teams from the Netherlands and Poland. These assets, however, would remain untapped until well after the disaster in Iraq unfolded.[5]

"NOBODY THOUGHT OF CULTURE": CULTURAL PROTECTION IN THE POSTWAR PLANNING PROCESS

In May of 2002, Ashton Hawkins, former general counsel for the Metropolitan Museum of Art in New York and president of the American Council for Cultural Policy (ACCP)—a group committed to the idea that, as Hawkins put it, "legitimate dispersal of cultural material through the market is one of the best ways to protect it"—contacted the group's vice president, Arthur Houghton. Hawkins asked Houghton to nose around Washington to find out what communications might be taking place between the U.S. government and the archaeological and cultural heritage community on the question of Iraq.

In an earlier epoch, someone like Houghton—an old State Department hand who also had served as curator of the Getty, a scion of the American aristocracy who was Harvard-educated, urbane, and well-connected—might have been able to bring the concerns of Hawkins and others to the attention of policymakers at the highest level simply by calling a few friends in the power elite. But the old-boy network was a thing of the past, and it took some time before Houghton discovered that working groups of Iraqi exiles convened by the State Department were developing plans for postwar Iraq. The Future of Iraq Project, which aimed at uniting fractious exile parties, kept a deliberately low profile to avoid unwanted attention from congressional backers of the Iraqi National Congress. So effective was this effort that no one from the cultural heritage community knew that the project existed—or that none of the fifteen working groups focused on the country's cultural sector.

On the face of it, this was an odd lacuna. After all, these were highly cultivated current and former State Department hands, working together with experts from Iraqi exile groups who cared deeply about their homeland, and who brought expertise on a variety of topics, ranging from transitional justice to water, agriculture, and the environment. And Iraq was, after all, the cradle of civilization. Yet, as Houghton eventually discovered, "nobody thought of quote *culture* as being an independent stand-alone issue that needed to be looked into."[6] According to McGuire Gibson, professor of Mesopotamian archaeology, Near Eastern languages, and civilizations at the University of Chicago Oriental Institute, none of the Iraqi exiles was an expert on cultural heritage, nor did any expect an escalation in looting after Saddam's fall. And their State Department hosts were oblivious to culture as an object of policy concern—perhaps because it is not, in fact, recognized in the United States as such. The United States' officially stated position on cultural policy is that it has no cultural policy, a view reflected in the absence of a cabinet-level position or ministry. Responsibility for various aspects of culture is divvied up among a number of uncoordinated offices and institutions with limited mandates, all of which failed to take the initiative in reaching out to war planners, even within the same agency. (For instance, the State Department's Bureau of Educational and Cultural Affairs (ECA) did not communicate with the State Department's Future of Iraq Project until January 2003.)

Even in the absence of cultural bureaucrats to champion their cause, archaeological and preservationist NGOs could have pushed for inclusion in the umbrella group of one hundred and fifty or so humanitarian NGOs, called InterAction, that met repeatedly with the Pentagon and the U.S. Agency for International Development (USAID) in the run-up to the war. Humanitarian NGOs operating in-theatre had developed working relationships with U.S. planners during the Afghan war, where the destruction of the Bamiyan statues should have provided an opening for cultural protection NGOs. But their efforts in Afghanistan appeared on no one's radar screen, and they remain relatively ineffectual even today in that still-dangerous country, whose heritage is in dire straits.[7] Looting in the Afghan countryside remains completely out of control: between 2004 and 2006, the British government seized three to four tons (!) of plundered items.[8]

One stumbling block in the way of archaeological NGO involvement in militarized activities in both Afghanistan and Iraq was undoubtedly that flagship cultural heritage NGOs are oriented toward peacetime conservation, not toward injecting units into unstable situations in which their lives might be at risk.[9] There is a single potential exception to this general rule about cultural heritage NGOs, one organization focused on cultural heritage protection in militarized situations: the Blue Shield, an international consortium of national committees describing itself as the cultural equivalent of the Red Cross. But, incomprehensibly, in 2002–2003 the Blue Shield had no U.S. committee, and its comatose international body would not have been welcomed by U.S. war planners, who have long resisted working with groups affiliated with international organizations. UNESCO, for instance, had made several attempts to go into Iraq after the 1991 Persian Gulf War, but the United States vetoed the requests.

Consequently, as war clouds began to gather in the spring and summer of 2002, no one from either inside or outside the government was speaking about the danger of cultural looting to those beginning to draw up plans for postcombat Iraq.

This planning was taking place in at least three different places: the State Department, the military, and the Pentagon. In the Pentagon, William Luti, the senior aide to Douglas Feith, the under secretary of defense for policy, sought to create a cadre of lightly armed Iraqis to serve as "scouts, advisers, and experts on civil affairs"[10]—including, one must assume, the policing of museums and archaeological sites. Later, as it became clear that these troops were not going to be ready, Secretary of Defense Donald H. Rumsfeld suggested that the United States approach Muslim nations to guard Iraq's religious sites. That the Muslim nations the United States could ask to supply guards were Sunni, while the religious shrines to be protected were mostly Shiite, apparently had not occurred to the defense secretary.

The attitude of the uniformed military toward the Pentagon's postcombat security plan is well summed up by Army General Tommy R. Franks's comment to Feith after one of Luti's presentations: "I don't have time for this fucking bullshit."[11] At the U.S. Army's Central Command (CENTCOM), as Bernard Trainor reports, "the plan was to use members of the Iraqi Regular Army who had capitulated to control the country's borders and take on other security tasks that the overstretched allied troops would be faced with after the war."[12]

CENTCOM also would have a Civil Affairs Command officer advising Gen. Franks on general policy matters and requirements, doubled one level down on the Army Central Command's primary staff, and below that civil affairs teams disseminated all the way down to the maneuver brigade level. Civil affairs officers include experts in a variety of areas, including, at least in principle, cultural heritage. An armored brigade commander would, according to Maj. Chris Varhola of the Army's 352nd Civil Affairs Battalion, ideally "have a civil affairs guy whispering in his ear saying, 'Hey, don't forget, in your sector you have the museum, based on the 1991 experiences where all of Nasiriyah was looted, down to the traffic lights, you should watch out for the museum.'"[13]

That was the theory. In reality, Civil Affairs had on its several-thousand-strong roster only two low-ranking archaeologist officers, neither of whom had any access to Gen. Franks. Moreover, because planners overburdened Civil Affairs with threats to be addressed, these few experts were reassigned by field commanders to whatever the commander deemed more pressing problems. As a result, according to Varhola, some civil affairs officers—and consequently, some field commanders—"didn't even know they had a museum in their sector." And civil affairs officers untrained in cultural heritage were unlikely to think museums important enough to warrant interfering with a tank commander in the middle of combat operations. As one targeting civil affairs officer told Varhola: "When you have an armor battalion commander . . . on the ground in central Baghdad, even though the museum is being looted, [civil affairs officers] are not going to intervene. They are not going to tell that battalion commander to protect the museum because that's undermining his unity of effort, undermining his command, [and] undermining his authority."

At the other end of the chain of command, Gen. Franks could not have relied on his civil affairs officer to provide information on cultural issues, since

Civil Affairs, technocratic in orientation, does not require its officers to be educated in foreign cultures. Franks would have had to turn instead to foreign affairs officers assigned to CENTCOM. There is no evidence that he ever did so, or that any foreign affairs officer brought up the matter with him.

Once combat operations had concluded, the military planned to turn responsibility over to a civilian interagency humanitarian aid and reconstruction effort coordinated by Elliott Abrams (of Iran-Contra infamy, but now a senior National Security Council official) and budget official Robin Cleveland.[14] In the immediate aftermath, Abrams was to dispatch a disaster relief team to "enter liberated areas of Iraq in coordination with U.S. military forces," managing relief activities, and liaising with the military, other donors, NGOs, and international organizations.[15] Unfortunately, cultural disaster did not fall under the rubric of a humanitarian emergency, and no experts were solicited from the Institute of Museum and Library Services (IMLS), the National Endowment for the Arts (NEA), or any other cultural agency.

Abrams's other nexus of postwar reconstruction planning was located two layers under Luti, in Joseph Collins's Office of Stability Operations. In late August 2002 Collins's office began working on postwar reconstruction planning, often bypassing his nominal superior to work directly over the next few months for Elliott Abrams and Douglas Feith, then under secretary of defense for policy.[16] Because Collins's office was one of the few in the Pentagon to make contact with NGOs, it became the favored resource for the Pentagon's Defense Intelligence Agency (DIA), whose Operational Environmental Analysis Division was tasked, under international law, with developing a no-strike list of thousands of sensitive locations. This had been done successfully, with assistance from archaeologists, in both the 1991 Persian Gulf War and the war in Afghanistan, saving antiquities from destruction from bombing, as well as from berm building or other on-the-ground combat action.[17]

The military had other obligations under international law that it did not observe so meticulously, unfortunately. Under the 1949 Fourth Geneva Convention, for instance, it would be responsible for restoring public order and ensuring effective law enforcement as part of its obligations as an occupying power. That issue would be sidestepped by the simple expedient of not declaring an occupation to be in effect, even after President George W. Bush declared on May 1, 2003, that active combat operations were over.[18] The 1954 Hague Convention for the Protection of Cultural Property in the Event of Armed Conflict, with its requirement that parties to it "undertake to prohibit, prevent and, if necessary, put a stop to any form of theft, pillage or misappropriation of, and any act of vandalism directed against, cultural property," while observed by the United States generally, could be ignored, as America is one of a small number of countries to have never ratified it.

GETTING TO THE TABLE

Within the government, postwar planning efforts under way by the beginning of September 2002 were not simply uncoordinated, but in some cases deliberately so. Compounding the problem of coordination, planning was distributed across and within agencies in unexpected places, in an ad hoc manner. And postconflict protection of cultural sites was not to be found on anyone's priority list.[19] Little wonder, then, that as Houghton began to probe in earnest in September 2002, he had trouble locating anyone in government working on the issue of protecting cultural sites. More surprising, at this point, Houghton found that "there was no channel that was operative between anyone in the academic community: the Archaeological Institute of America, the American Association of Museums, you go right down the list of who should have been calling the Department of Defense, and not one took the responsibility in picking up the phone. Not one."[20]

Houghton began reaching out to the academic world, meeting at a dinner party one of the world's leading authorities on ancient Mesopotamia, McGuire Gibson of the University of Chicago's Oriental Institute, and contacting professors at Harvard and Duke. As Houghton recalls it, his focus was on

> the consequences of a post-Saddam Iraq, possibly in chaos, to Mesopotamian archaeological sites. In this context, and considering the apparent likelihood of a U.S. attack on Iraq, it seemed to me useful to review also what the U.S. does, or has done, to try to avoid damaging sites of cultural importance during hostilities, and what procedures it has set up to take these into consideration.

But he also expressed more general concern about "material culture, cultural property protection, etc., in a post-Saddam world," adding that "some thought should be given to what may emerge when it's over." To Gibson, who was well aware of Houghton's ties to the ACCP and that group's interest in liberalizing "retentionist" antiquities laws, this language set off alarm bells. Was the aim here really not protecting sites and museums, but changing Iraq's postwar laws to favor collectors? Houghton tried to reassure the archaeologist, professing that the ACCP "would have no interest in involving itself at this level of advice or intervention."

The ACCP did hope to raise awareness of the dangers facing Iraq's archaeological heritage, and at a meeting in early fall 2002 decided to pursue a three-pronged public strategy: op-ed pieces, public statements, and closed-channel communications with the government. Letters were sent to the secretaries of state and defense, and the national security advisor, as well as others in the concerned departments and the Joint Chiefs of Staff. These letters, the first known effort by cultural heritage interests to contact U.S. officials, asked that forces avoid damage to monuments or sites; that the military respect the integrity of sites and monuments; that the United States encourage any new administration in Iraq to quickly establish security for its own monuments, sites, and museums, especially through reconstituting the antiquities service; and that "an appropriate governmental planning mechanism be created" before the conflict to focus on these concerns. Missing from this list of concerns was any reference to the looting that had occurred in Iraq's regional museums and on archaeological sites in no-fly zones established after the 1991 war.

The ACCP followed up on its letter-writing campaign with an op-ed piece in the *Washington Post*, intended to get the attention of the White House and secure a meeting with high-level officials at the Department of Defense. Meanwhile, Gibson worked his own contacts. Just before Thanksgiving, he contacted Ryan C. Crocker, an old acquaintance then working as the deputy assistant secretary of state in the State Department's Bureau of Near Eastern Affairs.[21] Writing on behalf of the American Association for Research in Baghdad (AARB), Gibson told Crocker that there was deep concern on the part of U.S. scholars and academic institutions about the danger posed to archaeological sites by an invasion. Reminding the diplomat that the U.S. military had made a special effort to avoid such sites in the 1991 Persian Gulf War, Gibson urged paying special attention to the Iraq Museum: "Even if the museum survives bombing, in the chaos of war it will probably suffer major looting," Gibson said pointedly, in the clearest and earliest warning of what ultimately did transpire.

Gibson received no immediate response, perhaps because providing security in the aftermath of combat operations was not something the State Department would have seen as its responsibility. But a similar declaration sent to the Pentagon in January by the Archaeological Institute of America (AIA), noting that sites and museums were looted in 1991 and urging action "to prevent looting in the aftermath of the war," also went unanswered.[22]

It was bombing, however, not looting, that preoccupied the Pentagon. As 2002 drew to a close, an Internet news article on the Pentagon's efforts to protect culturally important sites detailed efforts to avoid targeting them, making no mention of the potential for postconflict looting. Over the next two months, cultural protection advocates and war planners would dance around this distinction between protection from destruction and protection from looting in a way that left advocates thinking mistakenly that their problem had been flagged.

In late December or early January, the ACCP's publicity barrage finally began to pay off. The DIA saw the op-ed piece and contacted Hawkins, requesting the ACCP's help in gathering information about cultural and archaeological sites. The ACCP had no expertise on this issue, and the AIA—which did—was already compiling a list of the top ten or fifteen most important sites at the behest of the State Department's Bureau of Educational and

Cultural Affairs (ECA).[23] But ECA and DIA were unaware of each other's activities, and the archaeological community lacked the lobbying expertise to get the attention of war planners or politicians. Neither the AIA nor the American Schools of Oriental Research, financially straitened organizations both, employed a lobbyist or even a policy professional on their staffs, which were located in Boston, not Washington.[24]

So it was that the ACCP managed to secure for itself what turned out to be the highest-level meeting to take place at the Department of Defense during the prewar period regarding protection of cultural heritage. Well aware that they had nothing concrete to provide to military targeters, but eager to press the general case for paying attention to the danger faced by Iraq's heritage, the ACCP turned to McGuire Gibson. At the meeting at Joseph Collins's office in the Pentagon, "there was only one archaeologist there—me," Gibson recalls. "The rest were artifact collectors and lawyers, the people from ACCP. I only went along to put my own point of view across, which was to plead for a minimizing of the bombing of known archaeological sites. But I wouldn't have stood a chance of getting a meeting with the Defense Department without the ACCP."[25]

After the meeting with Collins had been scheduled for January 24, Hawkins received a letter from Deputy Under Secretary of Defense William Luti, which did not mention the impending meeting with Collins but suggested that information on cultural sites to be avoided could be sent to his office. Luti is the highest-ranking U.S. official to respond to the prewar concerns raised by the cultural heritage community. His apparent ignorance about the impending meeting at the Department of Defense suggests that Collins's group was acting on its own mandate from Feith and Abrams to fulfill the military's duty to avoid destroying sites as required by the laws of war.

Once the meeting with Collins at the Defense Department was set, Houghton shot off a request to William Burns, assistant secretary for Near Eastern affairs, for a second meeting at the State Department. Noting pointedly that the Defense Department had asked to meet with ACCP to discuss their concerns, Houghton suggested that "it is also important to discuss related longer-range matters including the creation of an appropriate mechanism that could strengthen measures to protect and preserve Iraq's important villages and cultural monuments."[26] Unlike Gibson's earlier appeal to Crocker, this letter seems to have done the trick. Within days, a meeting at State, chaired by Crocker, was arranged for the afternoon of January 24, following the morning meeting at the Pentagon.

As he was preparing to head down to Washington, Gibson got a call from an entirely different quarter. Col. Gary Wager of Civil Affairs, which had been mobilized only a few weeks earlier and was just beginning to pull together information to disseminate to commanders operating on the ground, asked Gibson to send him a list of sites in need of protection.

Planners from three very different bureaucratic precincts, all with some mandate to attend to the problem of cultural sites in Iraq, were now engaging independently with the cultural heritage community (or at least with a tiny sliver of it). An effectively organized, unified effort to deal with the several threats that archaeologists had identified seemed possible. What transpired instead was a tragic series of missed opportunities, misdirected communications, and misstatements, culminating in the looting of the Iraq Museum and the depredation of Iraq's archaeological sites.

THE MEETINGS

On January 24, 2003, without having had a pre-meeting to clarify the topics they wanted to address, McGuire Gibson joined Ashton Hawkins, Arthur Houghton, and Maxwell Anderson, then president of the Association of Art Museum Directors, to meet at the Pentagon with Collins. They were joined by Caryn Hollis, principal director of Collins's office, and Maj. (now Lt. Col.) Chris Herndon. The Defense Department had requested the meeting because it was concerned about protecting sites, monuments, and museums from damage during active combat operations. It was not focused on protecting sites during the postconflict period—this despite Collins's being charged with attending to postcombat stabilization and reconstruction planning. Only Gibson saw looting as a second major threat that the Pentagon needed to be warned to take seriously. This mismatch of objectives between the ACCP and the Pentagon, on one hand, and Gibson on the other, together with Gibson being outnumbered, may explain why postcombat looting of museums and sites was treated as a secondary issue.

Gibson was left only a fraction of the meeting to broach the problem of looting; Houghton recollects that the issue was a very minor part of the meeting's agenda: "It must have occupied all of sixty seconds during the discussion."[27] Gibson says Houghton is wrong on this: "I talked about looting far more than two minutes," the archaeologist insists. "I told them that when Baghdad was taken, if they did not secure the bridges over the Army Canal, the poor people in what is now called Sadr City would come over and loot everything that could be moved. I made a special point of mentioning the museum and the sites."

Both Gibson and the ACCP came away from the meeting with the impression that the Pentagon had agreed to take steps to protect the museum and sites from looting by Iraqis. For its part, the Office of the Secretary of Defense got what it wanted from the meeting: access to good data on site coordinates that would enable the military to comply with the Geneva Convention and avoid destroying or damaging sites.

That afternoon, Gibson, Houghton, Hawkins, and Anderson, joined by Bonnie Burnham of the World Monuments Fund, made their way to the State Department for the meeting with Ryan Crocker, who brought along, among others, Assistant Secretary of State Patricia Harrison, the head of State's Bureau of Educational and Cultural Affairs. Crocker appeared surprised to learn that of the sixteen working groups in the Future of Iraq (FOI) Project, none dealt with culture, and he immediately ordered the State Department to create a new FOI Project working group on the cultural sector. Crocker's surprise is itself surprising, given that the FOI Project had realized late in 2002 that no working group had been established for culture, and the Bureau of Near Eastern Affairs had been asked at that point to take the lead in forming one.

Weeks more would go by before the working group on culture finally convened to hammer out a wish list of what ought to be done in the case of occupation. "Number one on that list," archaeologist Zainab Bahrani recalls, "was to put guards at all museums and as many archaeological sites as possible." But with the war weeks away, it was far, far too little, too late. The working group on culture produced no report.

It turned out not to matter anyway. As is now common knowledge, Pentagon postwar planners deliberately jettisoned as irrelevant the thousands of pages of analysis and recommendations that were developed by the other working groups. "This was a series of seminars, not a plan," scoffs Collins, a view shared by a RAND review of postwar reconstruction planning.[28]

Even if the Future of Iraq Project *had* included a working group on culture from the beginning, and if the Pentagon *had* actually adopted all of its recommendations for protecting museums and sites during the postwar reconstruction period, this would have made no difference to the fate of the museum and the shorter-term damage to archaeological sites. What was needed during combat and in its immediate aftermath was something much more basic: a plan to deploy security forces to prevent sites and museums from being looted. The Future of Iraq Project, a child of the State Department, had no way to make the Pentagon heed this need for security in the immediate aftermath of combat.

That such basic security considerations had been shortchanged by the Pentagon only began to emerge in mid-February. The administration admitted that the president had not made a final decision about how to proceed but expected the three-week-old Office of Reconstruction and Humanitarian Assistance (ORHA) to handle stabilization operations. Then, after a barrage of criticism, it was announced that postwar Iraq would be overseen by the military. But Franks wanted nothing to do with the messy, inglorious business of peace operations, and he scoffed openly at the Pentagon's independent program to train Iraqi exiles as a military police force. Originally envisaged as producing three thousand trained Iraqi civil affairs officers—among which, one must assume, at least some would have been detailed to cultural site protection—this program ultimately graduated only seventy-three men.[29]

In the absence of this force, the administration might have turned to coalition partners to provide military police. But the two major countries that had joined the United States' coalition of the willing, Great Britain and Australia, did not maintain constabulary forces.

It thus fell to ORHA to deal with the problem of postwar instability, an impossible task to accomplish in only six weeks. With more notice, ORHA might have developed the capability to field peacekeeping forces. It is quite unlikely, however, that a Carabinieri-like military police unit specializing in cultural protection would have been established, even with this extra time. Postwar planners are almost certain to see cultural protection as a low priority.

ORHA certainly did. Not until three weeks before the war did Army Lieutenant General Jay Garner, who was responsible for overseeing the initial phase of the occupation, even appoint someone to deal with the cultural sector. Ambassador John Limbert, an old State Department Middle East hand (and former Iranian hostage) who had never visited Iraq, was highly cultured, but he had no expertise in Iraq's archaeological holdings or in the hard-nosed practicalities of peacekeeping, not to mention the specialized requirements of museum and site protection. When he asked what he was expected to do with regard to culture, Limbert says he was told that he should work to help existing authorities in Iraq's Ministry of Culture operate for sixty days, at which point it was expected that the United States would be ready to turn full authority back over to the Iraqis. "Fine," Limbert replied, "give me the organizational chart for the ministry, and tell me where the ministry is located in Baghdad." "That's up to you to find out," he was told.

Had Limbert been in the loop—rather, had there *been* a loop—he might have been told about the Future of Iraq Project's newly established working group on culture, about the ACCP (which had met with Defense and State on January 24), or about the AIA (which wrote in January to Rumsfeld, and continued trying, unsuccessfully, to get its own meeting with Collins up until the onset of the war).[30] The AIA did finally manage to get a message through on March 18 to ORHA's Larry Hanauer, special assistant to Gen. Garner.[31] Hanauer, already in Kuwait, never responded, and Limbert was never informed.

As war loomed, AIA sent a "Declaration on the Protection of Iraq's Cultural Heritage" to the Pentagon, publishing a version of this in *Science* in mid-March. Other cultural preservation groups were belatedly raising their voices, including the International Council on Monuments and Sites (ICOMOS), the International Committee of the Blue Shield, and the Society for American Archaeology (SAA). The latter group wrote directly to Rumsfeld, explicitly warning of the threat of postcombat looting. "After the 1991 Gulf War," the president of the SAA noted, "there was widespread looting of museums and archaeological sites." An occupation would require "that the military establish units tasked with protection of Iraq's cultural heritage, including museums, libraries, archaeological sites, and other cultural institutions" to "ensure that looting does not occur," an obligation set out in Article 9, Section 1 of the 1999 Second Protocol to the 1954 Hague Convention.[32]

Perhaps because it couched its appeal in legal arguments, the letter was shunted to the Defense Department's General Counsel's Office, which finally responded on March 18, three days before the start of the war, with bland legal reassurances:

> Department of Defense recognizes the unique cultural history within Iraq and shares your concerns that this history be protected. As you are aware, the United States is not a party to the 1954 Hague Convention for the Protection of Cultural Property in the Event of Armed Conflict or the 1999 Second Hague Protocol. U.S. armed forces, however, conduct all their operations in accordance with the law of armed conflict, including those provisions of the 1954 Convention and 1999 Protocol that reflect customary international law.
>
> Contingency plans for Iraq (in the event Coalition action is necessary) specifically address providing assistance to any future government of Iraq to establish protections for Iraq's cultural property. Likewise, during military operations, Coalition forces will operate in accordance with the law of armed conflict and will take the requisite measures to protect Iraq's cultural and historical sites.

The absence in the last sentence of the words "from looting" is chilling, as is the deliberate vagueness about what "requisite measures" means, considering the SAA's emphasis on these two matters.

Did the cautions from archaeologists have any effect? Yes, but if the military is to be believed, not much. Questioned after the looting of the museum, Gen. Richard B. Myers, chairman of the Joint Chiefs of Staff during the Iraq war, recalled a warning, but indicated that he believed it had been about bombing alone. "And we did get advice on archaeological sites around Baghdad and in fact I think it was the Archaeological—American Archaeological Association [*sic*]—I believe that's the correct title—wrote the Secretary of some concerns," Myers said. "Those were passed to Central Command, and those sites around Baghdad were obviously—we tried to avoid hitting those."[33]

Back in Baghdad, the museum staff, well aware that looting might break out, could do little until early March, when the government authorized five museum employees—the Iraq Museum's director of antiquities and research, Dr. Donny George Youkhanna, not among them—to take down everything they could carry. Much was protected as a result, but in the rush several important pieces were left either sitting out or in desk drawers. No resources were available from the international community, which had no fund in place to provide support for governments seeking to protect their cultural property from the ravages of war. The 1999 Second Protocol called for setting up such a fund, but it had not yet come into effect, and even if it had, UN sanctions would have prevented any direct financial assistance to the Iraq regime.

As war loomed just days away, a few civilians, not trusting either the museum itself or U.S. forces to provide adequate protection, took direct action. Middle East scholar William R. Polk made his way to Baghdad in a quixotic quest to convince museum officials to ship the museum's priceless holdings to a safer location.[34] Wathiq Hindo, a Chicago-based Iraqi businessman and archaeology buff who ran a company in Iraq providing security for Gibson's sites, had a better idea: arm the local guards directly and proactively. Traveling to Iraq just weeks before the invasion, he struck a deal with a local tribal leader to provide eight guards to protect the Mesopotamian city of Kish, in exchange for $300 and a Kalashnikov assault rifle.[35]

On the day the war began, guards from Umma reported that dozens of men had arrived at the site, driven off the thirteen guards there, and begun looting it. Six days later, on March 26, ORHA sent to CENTCOM a list of sixteen institutions that "merit securing as soon as possible to prevent further damage, destruction and/or pilferage of records and assets." The national bank, which Gibson had warned might contain some of the museum's treasures, was first on the list, the museum second. The Oil Ministry (which ultimately *was* guarded) was sixteenth. ORHA would be told later that this memo had never been read.[36]

By April 4, with U.S. forces poised to take Baghdad, it seemed clear that the military had successfully avoided destroying cultural sites, and that the war would be over very soon. Gibson felt secure enough about the denouement to start jockeying for position against the ACCP over the shape of cultural heritage laws in an Americanized Iraq. He wrote to Joe Collins warning that "to let the ACCP have influence in the reconstruction of Iraq is to allow the fox into the henhouse."[37] But Gibson also sought in this e-mail to warn Collins, in the most graphic terms yet between the two, about the likely looting of sites after the shooting stopped. "If the guards run from their duties," he wrote, apparently unaware this had already happened at Umma, "especially on isolated sites in the desert between the rivers in the south, the looters will go right in and resume their work with front-end loaders." To prevent this, Gibson urged Collins to establish helicopter flyovers guided by antiquities department members.

Once again, the buck was passed. Collins, who considered looting a problem for reconstruction rather than stabilization, took no action beyond having

Gibson's message forwarded to the Civil Affairs staff at CENTCOM. And there the matter rested.

THE DISASTER

As a "small but lethal" force of twelve thousand soldiers—including not a single civil affairs officer—swarmed into Baghdad between April 5 and April 9, the local population quickly realized that the Americans were unwilling—or unable—to impose order. Mobs began looting businesses, sacking government buildings, and attacking the homes of regime officials. As radio reported that the looting had spread to Basra's banks on April 8, the archaeologists grew more and more anxious. The AIA and AARB shot off a letter to Secretary of State Colin Powell, Secretary of Defense Rumsfeld, and British Prime Minister Tony Blair, copying others involved more directly in operations.

On April 10, Gibson received an e-mail from Limbert. The hapless ORHA ambassador for cultural affairs had finally found his way to the archaeologist who had been dealing for months with the Pentagon, the DIA, Civil Affairs, and CENTCOM. Limbert was seeking "advice on the question of maintaining the integrity of Iraq's cultural heritage in the aftermath of the current fighting." He asked Gibson how to find qualified Iraqi specialists, but added, "I would also like to find someone knowledgeable in the international trade in antiquities, who could help the new Iraqis recover stolen and looted works of art." This was a red flag for Gibson, who wrote back immediately. "If looters get in," he remarked bluntly, "it is going to be a disaster."

In fact, the looters had probably already gotten in. According to the chronology developed by Matthew Bogdanos (see the third chapter in this volume), the museum had been left undefended when Drs. Jabber and George left on the afternoon of April 8, while an eyewitness reported that looters entered the compound on the evening of April 10, Baghdad time.[38]

As word of the museum's pillaging hit the world media, Rumsfeld had trouble taking what had happened seriously. "The images you are seeing on television you are seeing over and over and over," he fumed, "and it's the same picture of some person walking out of some building with a vase, and you see it twenty times, and you think, 'My goodness, were there that many vases? Is it possible that there were that many vases in the whole country?'"[39] Pressed again a few days later about whether the Pentagon bore any responsibility for what had gone wrong, the secretary continued to demur:

Q: [W]eren't you urged specifically by scholars and others about the danger to that museum? And weren't you urged to provide a greater level of protection and security in the initial phases of the operation?

SEC. RUMSFELD: Not to my knowledge. It may very well have been, but certainly the targeting people were well aware of where it was, and they certainly avoided targeting it, and it was not hit by any U.S.—this was—whatever damage was done was done from the ground.

Rumsfeld was perilously close to contradicting his own "Who could have known?" defense with the admission that the military had been in touch with archaeologists. Myers sprang to the secretary's aid at this point:

Some have suggested, "Well, gee, you should have delayed combat operations to protect against looting, or you should have had more forces, should have waited 'til more forces arrived." To that I would say this: The best way to ensure fewer casualties on [the] coalition side and fewer civilian casualties is to have combat operations proceed as quickly as possible and not prolong them. And so it gets back to the—a matter of priorities . . . the first thing you have to deal with is loss of life, and that's what we dealt with.

Powell was compelled to do damage control, issuing a written statement declaring looted items stolen property, based in part on a draft sent by legal scholar Patty Gerstenblith to Limbert. Powell, however, also took the highly unusual step of speaking on behalf of the Defense Department: "In addition to the well-reported efforts made to protect cultural, religious, and historic sites in Iraq" (a phrase that is hard to read as anything other than sarcastic), he announced, CENTCOM had instructed troops to protect museums and antiquities throughout the nation, U.S. radio broadcasts were encouraging Iraqis to return items, and ORHA would spearhead the effort to restore the artifacts and catalogs. To make clear that a new, multilateral day had dawned, Powell added that the United States would work with UNESCO and Interpol to these ends. The FBI and Interpol announced the following morning that they were dispatching teams to Iraq.

Despite Powell's pronouncements, it was five more days before the Iraq Museum was finally secured by U.S. troops, weeks before searches of antiquities dealers' stalls in Baghdad began, and several months before generators, air conditioners, furniture, and computers ordered on an emergency basis by the State Department arrived at the museum. State did succeed in getting the United States to push in late May 2003 for a UN resolution to prohibit trade in or transfer of items illegally removed from the museum, the National Library and Archives, or other locations in Iraq. Since the United States already prohibited trade in such objects, this was a cost-free gesture, and one much less effective than Britain's closing of the loophole that still allows unprovenanced artifacts to be purchased in the United States.

To find emergency money, the Office of Science and Technology Policy took on the role of coordinating a government-wide task force, including representatives from the Defense Department, USAID, the NEA, the National Endowment for the Humanities, the Library of Congress, the National Security Council, and the White House. At the end of April, the State Department announced that the United States would contribute $2 million—a sum roughly equivalent to the amount spent every fifteen minutes on the overall Iraq war effort, and one-tenth of the funding given to the Metropolitan Museum of Art by the City of New York in 2005. The list of programs for which the funds would be earmarked had one glaring omission: no money was allocated to address the now-rampant looting of Iraq's archaeological sites.

Those sites were under increasing and daily attack. As the support of state power evaporated, guards found themselves facing not casual looters but teams of determined men, often from their own village. In some instances, local guards were forbidden by U.S. soldiers to carry guns.[40] Fear of reprisals against family meant that even guards at Hatra, who were armed with automatic weapons, could not be relied upon.[41]

Just how bad things were on the sites did not become clear until a team toured Iraq in the second half of May 2003, sponsored by National Geographic.[42] The trip was sobering. The most famous locations—Hatra, Nimrud, Ur, and Babylon—were now under U.S. military protection, but otherwise, reported archaeologist Elizabeth Stone, "I don't think we saw any other site outside Baghdad that didn't have at least one looting hole."[43] Gibson peppered his contacts in the government and the military with pleas for helicopter flyovers, for site guards to be authorized, for the deployment of a civil affairs task force. Japan had offered to deploy troops that had successfully guarded sites in Cambodia, and the Dutch were willing to send their civil-military affairs units to sites, if only they received invitations. Nothing was done, and in July Gibson learned from a UNESCO assessment team that until the last week of June, digging had still been going on at his own site of Nippur, the premier U.S. archaeological site in Iraq.

As of winter 2006–2007, looting of Iraq's archaeological sites was proceeding at a rate of destruction estimated at 10 percent per year. Over the years, looting operations have become regularized, with convoys of backhoes pulling up at dusk and families staking out areas. The sites themselves are now almost impossible for foreigners to reach, and are extremely dangerous, as evidenced by the kidnapping of photojournalist Micah Garen and archaeologist Susanne Osthoff. Because of the danger, there is no foreign digging going on now in Iraq. Instead, the English Heritage team, in partnership with the Getty Conservation Institute and the World Monuments Fund, is training Iraqis in the latest surveying techniques, such as the use of global positioning system mapping equipment and satellite imaging. As an Assyrian commentator pointed out, however, "if the looting does not stop little will be left to survey or record."[44]

The museum itself has now walled off its collections to protect its holdings from looters. In October 2003, during riots by soldiers from the disbanded Iraq army, a number of rioters scaled the museum wall and tried to attack it, and in June 2006, fifty people were kidnapped near the building.

To cope with this increasingly desperate situation at both the museum and the sites, Donny George Youkhanna, who had become president of the State Board of Antiquities and Heritage, worked assiduously with Iraq's Ministry of Culture to develop a 1,400-man cultural heritage police force. Unfortunately, the funding for this patrol scheme ran out in September 2006, and is unlikely to be renewed, according to George. The Ministry of Culture has been taken over by Shiite fundamentalists who are at best indifferent to Iraq's pre-Islamic heritage. Under pressure from these officials to resign, whom he claims "have no knowledge of archaeology, no knowledge of antiquities, nothing," George fled the country with his family in August 2006 after his son received a death threat accusing his father of cooperating with foreign elements.[45]

Meanwhile, Iraqi artifacts have appeared on eBay and BaghdadMarketplace.com. Karl-Heinz Kind, one of only two Interpol officers assigned to deal with the global traffic in illicit art, believes the low prices being asked reflect an oversupply from the looting in Iraq.[46] The number of artifacts on the market can only be guessed at, but the magnitude must be enormous if, as Donny George Youkhanna reports, "some 17,000 items stolen from unregistered archeological sites were returned," and yet prices remain low.

Recently, the military contacted the Archaeological Institute of America and other archaeologists requesting information for archaeological sites in Iran. Among them was archaeologist Zainab Bahrani, who went to Iraq independently in July 2003 to try to help and eventually served as senior consultant for culture for the Coalition Provisional Authority: "When that news reached me, I said, 'Leave me out. I'm not giving you a single site.'"

NOTES

1. Roger Atwood, "In the North of Iraq," *Archaeology*, June 4, 2003, http://www.archaeology.org/online/features/iraq/mosul.html.
2. Andrew Lawler, "Mayhem in Mesopotamia," *Science* 301, no. 582 (August 1, 2003): 582–87.
3. Robert Perito, *Where Is the Lone Ranger When We Need Him?: America's Search for a Postconflict Stability Force* (Washington, DC: United States Institute of Peace Press, 2004), 298.
4. Robert Perito, private conversation with author.
5. On the story of the difficulties involved in deploying European cultural affairs units, see Kila's chapter in this volume.
6. Arthur Houghton, interview with author, March 3, 2005.

7. As late as 2004 the Afghan National Museum had still not gotten the help needed even to do an inventory of its objects. "A lot of people in Afghanistan are asking why the Americans are absent in cultural heritage," according to Omar Sultan, Afghanistan's deputy minister of information and culture. See John W. Betlyon, "Afghan Archaeology on the Road to Recovery," *The Daily Star*, October 12, 2004; and Andrew Maykuth, "A Plea to Save Afghan Antiquities," *Philadelphia Inquirer*, May 3, 2006, http://www.philly.com/mld/philly/entertainment/14485199.htm.

8. See Christina Lamb, "Looted Afghan Art Smuggled into UK," *Sunday Times*, March 12, 2006, http://www.timesonline.co.uk/article/02089-2081457_1,00.html.

9. Unwillingness to put one's one life at risk was of course not limited to cultural heritage NGOs; according to Bernard Trainor, "The State Department disaster relief team did not want to venture into areas of Iraq that were still contested by Saddam's supporters." See Michael Gordon and Bernard Trainor, *Cobra II* (New York: Pantheon Press, 2006) 154.

10. Gordon and Trainor, *Cobra II*, 106.

11. Gordon and Trainor, *Cobra II*, 107.

12. Gordon and Trainor, *Cobra II*, 205.

13. Maj. Christopher Varhola, interview with author, April 15, 2005.

14. The humanitarian group was one of four set up by Rice following a contentious Senate Foreign Relations Committee hearing in August, where the lack of post-conflict planning came in for heavy criticism. What is striking is the lack of a sense of urgency, even after this hearing, with the meeting being put off weeks until after summer vacation (an echo of what happened in August of 2001).

15. Elliott Abrams, quoted in Office of the Press Secretary of the President of the United States, "Briefing on Humanitarian Reconstruction Issues," February 24, 2003, http://www.whitehouse.gov/news/releases/2003/02/20030224-11.html. Like some archaeologists, some humanitarian NGOs were unwilling to associate themselves with the military. See William Bole, "Relief Groups, Bush Administration at Odds on Iraq Aid," Religion News Service, April 22, 2003, http://www.pcusa.org/pcnews/oldnews/2003/03203.htm.

16. Joseph Collins, Col., U.S. Army, Ret., e-mail to author, July 27, 2006.

17. A few sites, however, did sustain damage due to U.S. military action—bulldozers creating rocket positions scarred Tel al-Lahm, and a thirteenth-century mosque in Basra was badly damaged.

18. The U.S. and Britain did not formally accept the status of occupying powers until May 27, 2003, when the UN Security Council passed Resolution 1483. On arguments about the status of the United States in Iraq, see Jordan J. Paust, "The U.S. as Occupying Power over Portions of Iraq and Relevant Responsibilities Under the Laws of War," *American Society of International Law Insights*, April 2003, http://www.asil.org/insights/insigh102.htm.

19. As Collins says, "The whole stability operation, the post-conflict operation, if you will . . . there were a number of different planning sites for. The Abrams-Cleveland crew had only humanitarian assistance and the initial swipe of reconstruction estimates under our control. And as it turns out, the things that we spent most of our time working on, like refugees, turned out to be rather minor problems. Issues like

de-Baathification, governance in the province, law and order, what to do about the Iraqi military and police or whatever, that was handled by a completely different group. They made their battle plans in a very coordinated sort of way. Their other plans for postconflict issues were made seriatim and in a very ad hoc fashion. I don't know that there was ever sort of a plan, an organizational plan, to say, OK, you know, these are the twelve issues. There was no matrix." Collins, e-mail to author, July 27, 2006.

20. Arthur Houghton, interview with author, March 3, 2005.

21. Crocker eventually would be named ambassador to Pakistan, and then, in late 2006, as ambassador to Iraq.

22. "AIA Urges Protection of Iraq's Archaeological Heritage," *AIA News*, Archaeological Institute of America website, http://www.archaeological.org/webinfo.php?page= 10174.

23. Maria Kouroupas, Crouch et al., Bureau of Educational and Cultural Affairs, State Department, interview with author, April 15, 2005. It seems likely that both the ECA and the NEA were goaded into action by Ryan Crocker at the NEA after Gibson alerted Crocker in late November 2002.

24. One reason for the AIA's relative poverty despite its eight thousand-strong membership is that it does not allow active collectors or dealers to serve on its board, pursuant to its general ethics policy.

25. McGuire Gibson, interview with author, February 19, 2006.

26. Quoted by Houghton in interview with author, March 3, 2005.

27. Houghton interview.

28. Andrew Rathmell, "Planning Post-Conflict Reconstruction in Iraq: What Can We Learn?" *International Affairs* 81, no. 5 (October 2005): 1021. See also, and more definitively, Donald L. Dreschler, "Reconstructing the Interagency Process after Iraq," *Journal of Strategic Studies* 28, no. 1 (February 2005): 3–30; and Gordon and Trainor, *Cobra II*, 159.

29. Gordon and Trainor, *Cobra II*, 73.

30. One reason the AIA's early messages to the Pentagon might not have gotten through to Limbert is that they were intended to warn the U.S. government that while the ACCP and AIA both urged the United States to avoid or minimize damage to archaeological sites during military action, the two groups had very different interests and might well diverge in their concept of postwar planning for the preservation of the archaeological and cultural heritage of Iraq.

31. The list mentions Gibson and other archaeologists' provision of location information on sites, and bluntly states: "The National Museum in Baghdad and the regional museum in Mosul, as well as well-known sites such as Ur, Babylon, Nineveh, Nimrud and Ashur, need immediate security provided by U.S. military personnel to protect them from looting and other destruction."

32. Robert L. Kelly, President of the Society for American Archaeology, letter to Donald Rumsfeld, Secretary of State, February 27, 2003, http://www.saa.org/goverment/ Iraq.html.

33. U.S. Department of Defense, Office of the Assistant Secretary of Defense for Public Affairs, transcript of news briefing by Sec. Donald Rumsfeld and Gen. Richard

Myers, April 15, 2003, http://www.defenselink.mil/transcripts/transcript.aspx ?transcriptid=2413.

34. See William R. Polk, "Introduction," in Milbry Polk and Angela Schuster, eds., *The Looting of the Iraq Museum, Baghdad: The Lost Legacy of Ancient Mesopotamia* (New York: Harry Abrams, 2005), 5–9.
35. B. Glauber, "$300 and a Prewar Promise Save Famed Archaeological Sites," in *Zawya.com*, May 1, 2003, redacted at http://iwa.univie.ac.at/iraqarchive3.html (accessed June 13, 2007).
36. Paul Martin, Ed Vulliamy, and Gaby Hinsliff, "US Army Was Told to Protect Looted Museum," *The Observer*, April 20, 2003.
37. The rumor, which remains unsubstantiated, was published a few days later in an article that Gibson forwarded to Collins. The rumor may have originated in the exchange between Hawkins and Luti in early January 2003, discussed above on p. 13. Both Houghton and Hawkins vigorously deny having met with Luti.
38. See Matthew Bogdanos, "The Casualties of War: the Truth about the Baghdad Museum," *American Journal of Archaeology*, 109, no. 3 (July 2005): esp. 501–506.
39. U.S. Department of Defense, Office of the Assistant Secretary of Defense for Public Affairs, transcript of news briefing by Sec. Donald Rumsfeld and Gen. Richard Myers, April 11, 2003. http://www.defenselink.mil/transcripts/2003/tr20030411-secdef0090.html.
40. Elizabeth C. Stone, "Cultural Assessment of Iraq: The State of Sites and Museums in Southern Iraq," *National Geographic*, May 2003, http://news.nationalgeographic .com/news/2003/06/0611_030611_iraqlootingreport3.html.
41. On the problem at Hatra, see Atwood, "In the North of Iraq."
42. UNESCO had also arrived at almost the same time, but was restricted from traveling around the country.
43. Quoted in Mary Wiltenburg, "A Fertile Crescent for Looting," *Christian Science Monitor*, June 12, 2003, http://www.csmonitor.com/2003/0612/p03s01-woiq.html.
44. "The Massacre of Mesopotamia," *AssyriaTimes.com*, July 17, 2005, http://assyriatimes .com/engine/modules/news/article.php?storyid=156.
45. Lucian Harris, "Iraq's Top Cultural Official Resigns," *Art Newspaper*, August 26, 2006.
46. Christoph Plate, "Sumerischer Terracotta-Löwenkopf im Angebot. Interpol und die irakischen Behörden arbeiten gegen den Handel mit Artefakten im Internet," *Neue Zürcher Zeitung*, July 3, 2005.

CHAPTER 2

Preparations at the Iraq Museum in the Lead-Up to War

DONNY GEORGE YOUKHANNA AND MCGUIRE GIBSON

THE PROTECTION OF A MUSEUM'S HOLDINGS IN TIMES OF WARFARE OR CIVIL UNREST is a multifaceted and complicated issue. Because museums present themselves and are routinely projected by the media as storehouses and venues for the display of treasure, they become targets of looting for organized gangs and even ordinary citizens. Because invading armies see all armed personnel as potential enemies, guards at museums and other cultural establishments tend to be attacked or to slip away as fighting nears. If the invading army does not take responsibility for guarding cultural institutions that have lost their guards, looters quickly take advantage of the vacuum in civil order. This was the case in the looting at the Iraq Museum from April 10–12, 2003. It was also the case at universities in Baghdad and elsewhere, as well as dozens of other cultural institutions (the National Library and Archives, the National Academy of Arts, and institutes of music, dance, and art, among others). Likewise, the organized looting of archaeological sites, which began in the mid-1990s in southern Iraq, resumed at a greatly increased rate as the invasion was taking place. As of this writing, it continues unabated.

The Iraq Museum was a prominent potential target of looting, and in the United States before the war, several attempts were made in meetings with Pentagon and State Department officials to call attention to its significance and the threat to its holdings. Officials were warned that in the uprisings that occurred in the aftermath of the 1991 Persian Gulf War, nine of the thirteen regional museums in the south and north of the country had been damaged and looted, resulting in the loss of about five thousand artifacts, of which less than 10 percent have been recovered. As a result of those losses, the antiquities service no longer put on display at the regional museums (except for the Mosul Museum) any genuine objects, but instead used casts and photographic displays. Some of the museums at prominent archaeological sites, such as Babylon and Hatra, did still have some real objects, but these were well-guarded sites and were thought not to be as vulnerable as small museums in the centers of provincial towns.

In the months leading up to the 2003 war, interviews with U.S. and European academics and Iraqi officials drew media attention to the Iraq Museum. The first author of this chapter, who was then Iraq's director general for research but who was not yet in a position of responsibility for the museum, was quoted in one news report as saying that the objects from Hatra and the Mosul Museum were being transferred to the Iraq Museum, where it was thought that they would be safer. He was aware that, as in the Persian Gulf War of 1991, the museum itself would be put on a no-strike list.

William R. Polk, a Middle East expert, visited Baghdad before the invasion and tried to convince Iraqi authorities to send the museum's collections out of the country for safekeeping. Given the fact that just the dismantling of the museum's public galleries and the storing of most of the displayed items in a secret storeroom took more than two weeks to complete, it is highly unlikely that museum staff could have emptied the galleries and the storerooms in time to send the collections abroad. How anyone would have kept the hundreds of thousands of items intact and accounted for during the move was not addressed. It is unlikely that any museum anywhere is capable of dismantling its collections and shipping them off with any hope of maintaining the integrity of the artifacts and their identifications. Given the reduced staff numbers and the loss of trained museum professionals as a result of thirteen years of UN sanctions, it would have been unthinkable to consider such a course of action in Baghdad.

One of the major problems with the Iraq Museum, as with most museums, was the lack of a complete catalog with photographs of each item. Although a very fine master catalog in large ledgers recorded in English and Arabic has existed since the museum was founded in the early 1920s, and although this record could be correlated with excavators' find catalogs so that it was possible to determine the present location of an item from notations on this record and in museum display case and shelf logs, the maintenance of such records was seriously compromised due to layoffs of personnel during the sanctions regime in the 1990s. Adding to the difficulty was the massive influx of newly excavated objects derived from salvage digs carried out from the late 1990s until 2003 by the State Board of Antiquities and Heritage (SBAH), the parent body of the museum. These salvage operations were mounted to stop the looting of major sites in the south of the country. Prior to 1991, stretching back more than forty years, antiquities looting had been almost nonexistent in Iraq, but the lack of government control of the southern countryside under UN sanctions allowed industrial-scale pillaging of many sites. The salvage operations, carried out by the already overworked personnel of the SBAH and the museum, including the director general of museums, did impede looting to a certain degree and resulted in the exposure of important buildings and the recovery of thousands of artifacts. However, these finds represented a major problem for museum staff who had to process them in the normal system. Some of the more significant objects were given full recording, while others were set aside for later work. Steel trunks holding these finds from the field were pilfered during the looting of the aboveground storerooms in April 2003.

The necessity to dismantle the public galleries several times since 1980 led to an acceleration of problems. At the beginning of the Iran-Iraq War, when rockets often rained down on Baghdad, including a particularly deadly one that fell within 200 meters of the museum, the public galleries were dismantled, except for very large, permanently fixed objects, such as Assyrian reliefs, Islamic building facades, and massive wooden doors. Movable objects were put into storage, both above and below ground, with subsequent damage to some artifacts due to humidity. At the end of the Iran-Iraq War in 1988, the exhibits were remounted, but by then three halls were devoted to astonishing finds from the Neo-Assyrian Queens' Tombs, which Iraqis had found at Nimrud in 1988–1989. In late 1990, with the Persian Gulf War about to begin, displays were once again dismantled and put into storage. Many iconic and valuable objects, such as the Ur Cemetery gold and most of the finds from the Neo-Assyrian Queens' Tombs, were then transferred to a deep vault at the Central Bank. During the 1990s, because of sanctions and the possible renewal of warfare, the museum remained closed, except for occasional short-lived and small exhibitions. The objects in the Central Bank stayed there, and even when the museum was reopened in 2000 and most of the exhibits were arranged as they had been, there was no longer a display of the Queens' Tombs, with the exception of photos of some objects. The same was the case for some of the most famous items from the Ur tombs, shown in photographs in the cases that used to hold the objects.

In anticipation of the 2003 war, the SBAH, led by its chairman Dr. Jabber Khalil, after consultation with the Ministry of Culture, made several decisions that were meant to safeguard objects:

- All portable objects in Mosul, Babylon, and Hatra, including some life-size statues from Hatra and some objects from other provincial museums, were transferred to the Iraq Museum.

- A small group of five persons was given the responsibility of dismantling and hiding in a secret storage location, known only to those five, the portable objects from the museum's public galleries—they even swore on the Qur'an not to reveal the secret.
- Sandbags and foam were placed in front of or upon some of the large immovable objects, such as the Assyrian reliefs.
- The basic object records and many of the most important reference books from the Antiquities Library were hidden off-site in a bomb shelter, along with almost forty thousand manuscripts from the Manuscript House.
- The movable shelving of the Antiquities Library was put in the closed position and welded to make the remaining books and journals less accessible to looters.
- Windows and doors were blocked with concrete blocks, and the steel doors of storerooms and doors, meant to segregate specific areas, were closed and locked.

Dr. Donny George Youkhanna wanted to seal all outer doors to the museum and the administrative offices of the SBAH, but the chairman of SBAH did not want to go that far. As such, only a partial barrier was erected at the front entrance to the museum.

The ultimate protection for any museum is its guards, but as the war approached the museum, the staff of more than forty guards disappeared. Had they stayed in position, especially in their uniforms, they would most probably have been fired upon. Wisely, as they left, they discarded their uniforms and left some weapons in their quarters at the rear of the museum. Their discarded uniforms, which were very similar to Iraqi army issue, might have been mistaken later for Republican Guard uniforms. We have no evidence of any Republican Guard troops in the museum grounds. The only fighters museum staff reported seeing were a few Fedayeen irregulars, whose black clothing did not look like Republican Guard uniforms.

On April 8, as U.S. forces were arriving in the vicinity, Fedayeen came over the front fence and into the museum yard. By this time, there were only five persons left in the museum: Dr. Jabber Khalil, the president of SBAH; Dr. Donny George Youkhanna, the director of research; Muhsin, an employee who lived in a small house at the rear of the museum grounds; his son; and one guard. Dr. Jabber decided that rather than going into the basements and waiting for the fighting to end, as they had intended, everyone should leave the museum because there was a great likelihood that there would be great danger in remaining. They thought they could come back in a few hours, after the fighting had subsided. The group left by the back gate, except for Muhsin and his son, who locked themselves in their house behind the museum. There was no one of authority and no one with fluent English left to surrender the museum/SBAH complex, even if U.S. troops had been willing to take responsibility.

The lack of bullet holes in the walls around the museum garden attests to the fact that the fight between Fedayeen and U.S. troops was a minor one, and must have been very brief. Where major fighting took place, such as in the street behind the museum, the hundreds of bullet holes and extensive damage done to the colonnade fronting the shops opposite the museum/SBAH complex show what would have happened to the front of the museum had there been extensive shooting there. As it was, there were no more than two or three bullet holes in the walls, and the only notable damage was from one tank round that left a large hole in the front of the reconstructed Assyrian Gate that now houses a small children's museum (see image P1). According to Muhsin and his son, nothing happened to the antiquities complex for more than twenty-four hours after this skirmish. When the looting began on April 10, Muhsin, who never left the museum grounds, went out to the nearby intersection and asked U.S. troops, who were in a tank guarding the intersection just outside the main entry to the museum, to come drive off the looters. The tank crew, after conferring with commanders, said they could not do so. On April 12, reporters finally arrived at the museum and the looters took this as a sign to leave. Staff members who lived in the neighborhood came in and began to secure the building by chaining the doors and putting up a large sign indicating in Arabic that the premises were under the control of U.S. troops, which was not true. The bluff kept more looters from entering the grounds, although the mob continued milling around the main gate. Drs. Jabber Khalil and Donny George Youkhanna, who had been trying to return to the museum since April 8, but who were prevented from doing so because the bridges were all blocked, finally arrived on April 13. They had met with U.S. commanders at the Palestine Hotel and had gotten a promise that troops would be sent to secure the museum. Those troops finally arrived on April 16.

The actions of the staff of the Iraq Museum and the SBAH, in trying to secure the museum by removing the vast majority of items on public display into a secret storage place known only to a few staff, was to a great extent successful. Because the Ministry of Culture did not give them permission to remove the artifacts from display until about three weeks before the war began, the very limited number of staff involved in the transfer—just five people—were unable to remove all of the objects that were firmly affixed to the walls or that were extremely heavy, and thus the looters were able to take some of them, including the Warka Vase and the Bassetki Statue. With more time, staff would have been able to remove even those, leaving in the public galleries only the massive Assyrian bulls and slab reliefs, plus Islamic building facades and giant doors. More than eight thousand artifacts were removed from display and survived intact. The major losses, however, were from the storerooms, whose entry doors were blocked and locked (in one case, left unlocked by mistake).

With almost three full days of unhindered activity in the antiquities complex, the looters could have taken much more, had the great majority of them not been more interested in the contents of SBAH offices, from which they took furniture, computers, and other equipment, as well as the electrical fixtures and the wiring.

In retrospect, it might seem to have been a bad decision to remove much of the holdings of the Mosul Museum and the Hatra site to Baghdad, just before the war. But since the Mosul Museum was also looted, with some losses of important artifacts, on balance it would appear that it was better to consolidate the collections in one complex, which was presumed by its staff to be on a no-strike list. The staff had the experience of the 1991 Persian Gulf War, when the museum was not targeted, and they assumed that the complex would be secured. They were wise, however, not to trust in that assumption, but to take precautions and hide what they could of the major artifacts that were located in the public galleries.

CHAPTER 3

Thieves of Baghdad

The Looting of the Iraq Museum

MATTHEW BOGDANOS

AS WORD OF THE [IRAQ] MUSEUM'S FATE SPREAD LIKE WILDFIRE THROUGHOUT THE world, U.S. forces took a lot of heat. The "Why didn't you prevent the looting?" question had emerged right from the start, during the period that British columnist David Aaronovitch had summed up with "You cannot say anything too bad about the Yanks and not be believed."[1]

So why had the United States not "done more" to protect the museum? [After hundreds of interviews, and countless hours of forensic examinations of the entire museum compound—inside and out—here's what I knew in May 2003 about what actually occurred at the museum, and what U.S. forces could be expected to have done, faced with the situation on the ground].

Two months before the war began, in January 2003 . . . a group of scholars, museum directors, and antiquities dealers met with Pentagon officials to discuss their fears about the threat to the museum's collection. McGuire Gibson of the University of Chicago's Oriental Institute went back twice more, and he and his colleagues continued to barrage defense department officials with e-mail reminders. They could not have done more.

. . . Gibson and his colleagues were heard. But only partly. The Pentagon ordered the Iraq Museum placed on the coalition's no-strike list, and U.S. Central Command obliged, listing it as #3 [on the list]. But the planners had no idea of the extent to which the average Iraqi viewed the museum [not as housing the priceless cultural heritage of their country, but as Saddam Hussein's gift shop.[2] As a result, planners did not understand that many Iraqis would equate stealing from the museum with stealing from Saddam and not from themselves.] Even museum officials, who brought in sandbags and foam-rubber padding against possible bomb damage, were caught by surprise. The extraordinary Dr. Donny George Youkhanna [at the time, the museum's Director of Antiquities and Research] told the *Wall Street Journal*, "We thought there would be some sort of bombing at the museum. We never thought it could be looted."[3]

[Turning to the museum's protection by coalition forces, it is clear that] the law of armed conflict holds that cultural property should be protected against any act of hostility.[4] But the same international agreements that protect cultural property . . . *absolutely prohibit* the military use of cultural sites, specifying that such sites lose their protections when so used.

In clear violation of those provisions, the Iraqi Army had turned the museum [and the surrounding eleven-acre compound] into a fortress. [Please see images P2 and P3, which provide a photo and sketch of the museum compound.] Hussein's elite Special Republican Guard was stationed across the street. [A firing] position at the Children's Museum was aimed toward a traffic circle, offering an unobstructed field of fire on the high-speed avenue of approach that ran in front of the compound. That street, running between the museum and the Special Republican Guard facility, led to the strategically important al-Ahrar Bridge across the Tigris, nine hundred meters away. A sniper's position in the aboveground storage room provided a perfect flanking shot on any U.S. forces moving through the marketplace to reinforce any battle in front of the museum. The sniper's window also overlooked the ten-foot wall that protected soldiers running from the battle position in the back to the battle positions in the front courtyard. Each of those fighting holes, equipped with dirt ramparts and aiming sticks, provided interlocking fire. [For a close-up image of a firing range position in the compound, please see image P4.]

All of this was run from the makeshift command post that had been set up in the back of the [eleven-acre] museum compound.

. . . On the morning of April 8, armed Iraqi soldiers took up their previously prepared firing positions in the museum compound. The museum staff, including all museum guards, had already left, decamping when U.S. forces hit the outskirts of the city on April 5. The only exceptions were Dr. Jaber [Ibrahim al-Tikriti, the Chairman of Iraq's State Board of Antiquities] and Donny George, along with a driver and an elderly archaeologist who lived in the rear of the museum compound. Bravely, they had planned to stay throughout the invasion, but decided to leave when they realized the level of violence that was imminent.

The violence in question was, in fact, part of a campaign to attack Baghdad from the inside out. With all the Iraqi defenses facing the perimeter, General Tommy Franks [at the time, Commander of U.S. Central Command] had opted for "thunder runs" into the center of the city with tanks and mechanized infantry . . . . Crumbling from the inside out, Baghdad fell in days instead of months. One of these "thunder runs" ran directly in front of the museum. And the intensity of the fighting in the vicinity of the museum and the Special Republican Guard compound opposite it was directly proportional to this area's strategic importance.

At approximately eleven a.m. on April 8, after ensuring that all of the doors to the museum and the storage rooms were locked, the four museum staffers left through the rear exit, locking it behind them. They then crossed the Tigris into eastern Baghdad, hoping to return later the same day. As they left, the nearest U.S. forces were about fifteen hundred meters west of the museum, receiving heavy mortar fire as they proceeded in the direction of the museum. When Donny and his colleagues from the museum tried to come back several hours later, heavy fighting pinned them down on the other side of the river.

On April 9, a tank company from Task Force 1-64, the only U.S. unit in that part of Baghdad, moved to an intersection about five hundred meters west and slightly south of the museum. Their orders were to keep that crossroads open as a lifeline to support U.S. forces engaged in combat in the northern part of the city. Throughout that day, they took fire from the Children's Museum, the main building, the library, and the building to the rear of the museum that had previously been used as a police station. The tank company commander on the scene, U.S. Army captain Jason Conroy, reported that approximately one hundred to one hundred fifty enemy fighters were within the museum compound firing on U.S. forces. Some of these fighters were dressed in Special Republican Guard uniforms and some in civilian clothes. They were carrying RPGs [Soviet-designed, Iraqi-Army-issued rocket-propelled grenades[5]] or AK-47s.[6]

Later, many neighborhood residents told [renowned combat journalist] Roger Atwood . . . that "the Americans had come under attack from inside the museum grounds and that fighting in the area was heavy."[7] The neighborhood residents told me the same story, but they were merely confirming what the museum grounds and its countless spent shell casings and dozens of RPGs had already told me: This was a fiercely contested battleground. Indeed, the fighting was so heavy that for forty-eight hours, between April 8 and 10, some U.S. soldiers in Task Force 1-64's C Company never left the inside of their tanks. [Please see image P5.]

According to several accounts from nearby residents, it was during this time—on the ninth—that two Iraqi Army vehicles drove up to the back of the museum (near where the impromptu command post had been) and spent several hours loading boxes from the museum onto the vehicles before they left.[8] On the following day, April 10, Second Lieutenant Erik Balascik's platoon received word of looting "in the area of the museum and the hospital." They passed this information up to the Task Force 1-64 commander, Lieutenant Colonel Eric Schwartz, who ordered them to move closer to investigate. As soon as they did so, they began receiving intense fire from the compound. This forced one of the tanks to fire a single round in return from its 120 mm main gun, which took out the RPG position, put a hole in the Children's Museum, captured the world's attention, and inflamed critics [throughout the world].[9] [Please see image P1.]

Because the Iraqi army had fortified this cultural site and people were firing at them from it, Balascik . . . would have been entirely justified in taking any steps necessary to eliminate the threat. Even if they had simply stood their ground and fought back with ground-based supporting fire, there would have been nothing left of the museum either to save or to loot. Instead of conducting such an assault to "save" the museum, the moment that Schwartz—a former high school teacher—was informed of the situation, he made the militarily wrong but culturally brilliant decision to pull back those tanks from the museum. This was the only way to avoid the Hobson's choice between endangering his men and destroying the institution. It took real courage to pull back.

Because of that fire, and because, from their position to the west, the Children's Museum blocked their view into the main compound, they never advanced close enough to determine what was actually going on within the compound, let alone within the galleries and the storage areas of the museum itself.

One of the residents we interviewed said that the looters—estimated by some witnesses to number between three or four hundred at their height— first appeared at the museum on the evening of April 10, entering through the back of the compound. If this single source was accurate, his account strongly suggests that the original fighters had left the museum by that date—April 10. There was, however, still intense fighting around the museum on the morning of the eleventh. It was on that day, at the intersection directly in front of the museum compound, that [a U.S.] tank company destroyed an Iraqi Army truck and a Soviet-built armored fighting vehicle. This fighting in the front of the compound on the eleventh prevented U.S. forces from either approaching the museum or determining that enemy forces no longer occupied the museum itself. The eleventh was, however, the last day that fighting was reported near the museum.

On the afternoon of the twelfth, the museum staff came back, courageously chasing looters from the museum, a moment famously captured by a German film crew. The soldiers had already left. But when? It is entirely possible, especially considering all the uniforms we found lying around the compound, that some of the looters carrying out antiquities had been in uniform and carrying AK-47s only hours—or even minutes—earlier. We simply don't know. Regardless of when this retreat took place, however, it cannot be overstated how difficult it was for U.S. forces on the ground to have known when the last fighter left, and whether it was safe to enter without a battle that would destroy the museum. I rarely knew what was happening one hundred meters away— let alone on the other side of an eleven-acre compound.

Some critics have contended that if journalists were able to get into the museum on the twelfth, military forces should have been able to do the same on that day or even on the eleventh. With rare exceptions, however, journalists are not shot at simply because of who they are. Putting on a military uniform makes anyone a lawful target. Journalists, protected—officially at least—by their "noncombatant" status, are generally able to move more freely on the battlefield in order to report on the conflict. This is not to suggest that journalists aren't vulnerable to random fire, or that being a combat journalist doesn't take guts, or that journalists are never targeted illegally. Rather, it is to point out that neither journalists nor uniformed combatants should be judged by the distinct restrictions placed on, or the distinct freedoms enjoyed by, the other.

The only way uniformed military could have entered a compound the size of the museum's [was as part of a properly planned assault complete with supporting arms—tanks, mortars, and crew-served weapons—or by a "reconnaissance in force." This means having troops advance without supporting arms in the hope that they don't get shot. If no one shoots at them, it suggests that the buildings are clear. Either that or it's an ambush—with the risk that the football-field-sized open area between the compound wall and the buildings would become a killing ground.]

By April 12, the fighting in Baghdad had subsided, and the damage to the museum and its holdings was done. Once the staff was back on-site to guard the museum, there was no more looting.

On the afternoon of the twelfth and then again on the thirteenth, with the compound no longer a battlefield, Donny George and others approached Task Force 1-64, the Army tank unit, and asked for help. So why didn't U.S. forces just do what Donny and others asked and move a tank closer to the museum at that point? All it would have required, the Monday morning field marshals said, was a single tank.[10]

First, you can't just go hail a tank the way you hail a taxi. Unless you're requesting a suicide mission, you need a tank platoon. What those who have never been in combat do not understand is that a stationary tank is a death trap. While intimidating to look at, tanks are far from invulnerable—one well-placed round from an antitank weapon and you would need to use dog tags to identify the charred remains of the four men inside. The only way a tank can survive in combat, especially urban combat, is by virtue of speed and maneuverability, and by the firepower provided by other tanks. You have to have, at the least, tanks in pairs. You also need a squad of infantry alongside them, because tanks have blind spots. But mostly, once you draw fire, you have to return fire until you have eliminated the threat—right down to the plumbing in the basement—if that's what it takes to save the lives of those in your charge.

Okay, so it's not as simple as sending in a tank. Then why not send in some ground troops instead? Committing "just" ground troops would have been criminally irresponsible on the part of the commander, whose obligation is to protect the lives of the men under his command. A proper military assault would have required supporting arms. And this once again brings us back to the specter of the museum reduced to rubble.[11]

Moreover, if the mere presence of uniformed military had not dispersed the crowd, what would these ground troops have done, anyway—shoot the looters? Perhaps the critics would like to have been there with an M16, mowing down the local residents swarming through the museum. But people who know the law of war know that deadly force can only be used in response to a hostile act or a demonstration of hostile intent. Shooting unarmed looters in civilian clothes who were not presenting a risk to human life would have been a violation of the law of armed conflict and prosecutable for murder under Article 118 of the Uniform Code of Military Justice.[12]

Well, couldn't they have just fired some itsy-bitsy warning shots? Here we see the influence of movies on assumptions about what is possible in a law enforcement or military engagement. A warning shot only works if you are a member of the Screen Actors Guild. In real life, firing a weapon merely escalates the situation, usually causing unarmed participants to arm themselves, which once again means drawing return fire. Moreover, the bullets fired from the muzzle of a weapon—be they "warning shots" or shots aimed at center mass—do not just disappear into the ether. Eventually, they come back to earth and hit something—often with fatal effect—which happens all the time when revelers fire celebratory shots into the air during holidays and weddings.[13] [For this reason, among others, the rules of engagement in effect in 2003 specifically instructed soldiers that if they must fire, they must "[f]ire only aimed shots. NO WARNING SHOTS" (caps in original). Doubtless in recognition of the deteriorating security situation, by 2005, the rules had changed to permit warning shots to be fired as a last resort.]

The bottom line here is that any suggestion that U.S. forces could have done more than they did to secure the museum before the twelfth is based on wishful thinking or political ideology rather than on any rational appreciation of military tactics, the reality of the conflict on the ground, the law of war, or the laws of physics. "If I'd raced up from south Baghdad to the museum, I'd have had a lot of dead soldiers outside the museum," the tank commander for this sector, Lieutenant Colonel Eric Schwartz, told the BBC. "It wasn't the museum anymore—it was a fighting position."[14]

The blame for the looting must lie squarely on the looters. But the blame for creating chaos at the museum from the eighth through the eleventh that allowed the looting to occur must lie with the Iraqi Army. It was they who chose to take up fighting positions within the museum, they who chose to fire on the American tanks, and they who kept American forces from investigating the reports they had received of looting "in the area of the museum." After the eleventh, however, the blame clearly shifts to the U.S.

The U.S. Army showed up to secure the compound at ten a.m. on the morning of the sixteenth. If critics want to question U.S. reaction, the delay between the twelfth to the sixteenth is fair game. I will go one step further: this delay was inexcusable. Although nothing was taken during this period, that does not make the indictment any less valid—because our forces had no way of knowing that looters wouldn't come back. You can thank the museum staff for guarding the compound for those four days and not the U.S. military.

This leaves us with the more pointed question—the one that is never asked: Before the battle, why was no unit assigned the specific mission of moving in to protect the museum the moment Baghdad was secure?

There are two basic kinds of orders in the military. The first is the standard type that directs a unit to achieve a specific objective at a specific time. "At 0800 tomorrow, you will seize the beachhead and advance to the cliff wall." Then there are the kinds of orders that warn a unit that they will be expected to achieve a specific objective at a time yet to be determined. [This is a be-prepared-to order, telling that unit to get ready to execute that mission, thereby enabling] the commander on the ground to conduct proper reconnaissance, develop a tactical plan, and identify personnel and resources needed for the mission when it *is* ordered.

No such be-prepared-to-execute order was issued for the museum, and therefore no unit was either assigned or prepared to be assigned to secure it until the tank platoon showed up on the morning of the sixteenth. Why wasn't such an order issued? Why was there such a delay in responding to repeated requests for assistance on April 12 and 13? The answer is the same for both questions—and it is neither complicated nor entirely satisfactory.

Ultimately, the same "catastrophic success" on the battlefield that outstripped the ability of the Iraqi forces to react also outstripped the ability of coalition planners to anticipate security needs once Baghdad fell [months sooner than originally expected]. In the case of the museum, this was coupled with a lack of a sense of urgency on the part of military planners—which, in turn, was grounded in a failure to recognize the extent to which Iraqis identified the museum with the former regime. Thus, despite the prior warnings, planners simply did not believe that the museum—unlike the presidential palaces and governmental buildings that were more overt manifestations of the regime—would be looted. To put it another way, planners naively thought that the recognition of the Iraqi people in their extraordinary heritage would deter them from looting the museum. Even if coalition forces had properly planned for the museum, however, given the lack of sufficient forces in country, there would have been no spare units to assign anyway. As I said, not entirely satisfactory. But not sinister or callous either—just human error exacerbated by the speed of the fall of Baghdad and not enough boots on the ground.

Once I had the timeline for the fighting worked out, I began to use it as a template to sort through the rest of what had happened. I needed this structure to help explain the unfolding of the three distinctly different crimes: the thefts in the public galleries and restoration area, in the aboveground storage area, and in the basement storage area.

In Baghdad, we did not have access to the kind of judicial and governmental apparatus that would have allowed us to determine precisely how many missing antiquities had been stolen in the years or even decades before the war—though sources told us the number was high. Because the museum had been open to the public only once since 1991—on April 28, 2000, Saddam's birthday—and closed again shortly thereafter, we could not even turn to museum visitors for independent verification as to what was in the museum just prior to the arrival of coalition forces. So even when we were able to determine what was missing, we were not always able to determine—independent of what the staff told us—when it was *first* missing. This didn't affect our day-to-day operations, however, because our primary job was simply to get the stuff back.

In order to do *that*, though, we had to come up with three different investigative approaches to begin tracking down three different types of thieves—professionals, people off the street, and insiders. These three different categories of crooks had taken three different kinds of loot—marquee items from the galleries, random artifacts from the storage area, and high-value smaller pieces from the basement.

From the twenty-eight galleries and landings on two floors, and from the nearby restoration room, thieves stole forty of the museum's most treasured pieces. All evidence suggests that these marquee items were carefully chosen, implying that the thefts were professional. Whether or not these thieves were assisted by museum staff, the selection and removal of these items showed the mark of a professional. Likewise, the underworld connections necessary to move and sell these items required a level of professionalism beyond that of a low-level staff member or neighborhood looter. Indeed, we had been told that professionals had come in just before the war—possibly through Jordan—waiting for the fog of war and the opportunity of a lifetime.

One of the most telling clues to the professional eye of these thieves was that they passed right by the unmarked copies and lesser pieces and went straight for the highest-ticket items. There was one exhibit in particular that had twenty-seven cuneiform bricks running from Sumerian through Akkadian and Old Babylonian to New Babylonian.[15] The nine most exquisite bricks were taken—selected from each time period—and all the others were left behind. That kind of selectivity happened repeatedly, also implying some measure of organization. [Please see image P8.]

Of course, some observers have given credit where it wasn't due, citing, for instance, the fact that the stela containing Hammurabi's code was untouched. But it would not have required a master thief to read the large sign next to the display telling anyone in Arabic and English that this is a copy, and that the original is in the Louvre.

Others used the discovery of a pair of glass cutters as further evidence of professionalism and the advance planning that goes with it. But this tool was a rusty relic that should have been junked long ago, and it was never used on any of the glass inside the museum.[16] Moreover, why would a pro bother bringing along such a tool to a museum with neither a security system nor guards on the scene?

To me, the rusty glass cutters argued just the opposite—that while the professionals went about their business, they no doubt had to put up with any number of bumbling amateurs getting in their way. Would-be looters in off the street knocked over statues and, unsuccessfully, tried to drag them away on their foam-rubber padding. We could trace every single heavy piece that did leave the museum by following the trail of skid marks left in the floor. It's safe to say that these guys had never done this sort of thing before and had no idea what they were getting into. This is not to say that some random bumblers in the gallery area didn't get lucky. The guys who walked off with the Sacred Vase [of Warka, for example], were average joes, not an experienced gang of thieves imported for the occasion.

Altogether, in the galleries, corridors, and nearby restoration room, twenty-five pieces or exhibits were damaged by this sort of activity, including eight clay pots, four statues, three sarcophagi, three ivory reliefs, two rosettes, and what remained of the Golden Harp of Ur. (Fortunately, the golden bull's head that was stolen from the harp while it lay in the restoration room was a modern replica. Unbeknownst to most of the staff, the original had been removed to the Central Bank of Iraq before the 1991 Gulf War.) Sadly, one of the damaged statues was a two-foot-high terra-cotta lion from Tell Harmal dating from the Old Babylonian period of approximately 1800 B.C. [Please see image P9.]

It is also safe to say that some of the thievery in the galleries had been carried out by a third category of persons. That so many pieces originally missing from the galleries "miraculously" showed up on the restoration-room floor [during the weeks and months we lived in the museum] strongly suggests that they had been lifted by sticky-fingered staff who later chose to take advantage of our amnesty program [by returning many dozens of antiquities to the room we had repeatedly announced we would search last]. Moreover, seven of the most precious items from the museum had been collected and left in the restoration room: the Golden Harp of Ur, the Mask of Warka, the Lioness Attacking a Nubian, two plates inlaid with shell depicting ritual scenes from the royal tombs of Ur (2600–2500 B.C.), a large ninth-century B.C. Assyrian ivory-relief headboard, and a ninth-century B.C. wheeled wooden firebox from Nimrud. Although the room itself had two small safes that could have housed the Mask, the Lioness, and the plates, none of the objects were secured. Instead, everything was left on a table and stolen, except for the wooden body of the harp, a reproduction that was severely damaged, the fragments of its intricate ivory inlay left scattered across the room.

. . . From the two aboveground storage rooms, 3,138 excavation-site pieces (jars, vessels, pottery shards, etc.) were stolen—though I knew that number would surely grow by another one to two thousand when inventories were finally completed.[17] Valuable in their own right, they were of significantly less value than the signature pieces that had been in the public galleries. This was largely the work of random looters—indiscriminate, or at least undiscerning. This is where we saw traces in the dust where an arm had swept across an entire shelf, dragging anything and everything into a sack—and then dumping out the contents of the sack a few aisles away [as if they had found something they liked better]. Somebody took an entire shelf of fakes, leaving untouched an adjacent shelf containing pieces of infinitely greater value.

But these rookie mistakes do not rule out the possibility that our other bad actors made the amateur heist a lot easier. Neither of the two storage rooms that were looted showed any signs of forced entry on their exterior steel doors. [Please see image P6.] One of the looted rooms was on the first floor, and the other was on the second, and both were connected by an interior stairwell—meaning that entry to one automatically enabled entry to the other. The second-floor room was where the sniper team was located. So our best judgment was that the looters gained access [to both rooms] when the sniper team decamped, leaving the door open behind them. But it was also possible that either the professionals who stole the high-end artifacts or the insider(s) with the keys to the basement may have left the doors open—intentionally. Crowds destroy evidence and help cover tracks.

[As for the underground storage area, individuals with an intimate insider's knowledge of the museum and its storage practices breached a wall blocking entrance to the basement and walked past room upon room of tens of thousands of priceless antiquities until they got to the farthest corner of the farthest room of the most remote recesses of the sealed basement to steal—our best count to date—5,144 cylinder seals, as well as 5,542 pins, glass bottles, beads, amulets, and other small items of jewelry.] They knew how to get in, they knew where to find the keys, and they knew what they were looking for.

Given this level of preparation, the loot they took was more likely to have a middleman buyer and make its way into the hands of organized smugglers able to move it out of Iraq and into the international market. My plan to recover those big-ticket items once they had left the country, then, would depend on monitoring a rarefied group of known buyers and on developing confidential sources within the art community, most of whom would be museum employees and university professors. But because potential whistle-blowers risked losing their jobs, the challenge was, first, to find them, and, second, to protect their identities. [The plan also including persuading] coalition forces to tighten borders in the hopes of interdicting the loot before it got to the collector.

[Similarly,] the most likely way of recovering loot from more sophisticated thieves, especially when the items in question were small and easily hidden, was . . . at border crossings, where law and custom allow inspection of baggage on less than probable cause. As a result of Iraq's neighbors increasing the effectiveness of their border security and inspection programs to thwart terrorists, they were also intercepting many antiquities that would otherwise have slipped through. While relevant borders were far from airtight, and antiquities smuggling had become a quasi–cottage industry in many regions, the increased effectiveness of border inspections had probably discouraged many less experienced smugglers from even making the attempt. Old hands, of course, would simply increase their patience and resourcefulness.

[But increasing inspection rates is never enough to stop the traffic.] A law enforcement official must be able to articulate a rationale in order to seize an item in transit, and at a glance these smaller artifacts were not necessarily recognizable as contraband. The key strategy, going forward then, would be to educate law enforcement authorities so that they could immediately recognize illicit antiquities and therefore be justified in seizing what they found.

[As a result, the plan I developed] was to treat recoveries inside Iraq and interdiction at the borders not as separate approaches, but as two prongs of the same pincer designed to work together to put the squeeze on the bad guys. Increased border inspections increase the risk of trying to move stolen goods out of the country, which keeps them in Iraq, which makes them more likely to be seized through raids based on good intelligence inside the country. But the pressure of seizures inside Iraq pushes smugglers to risk export, which makes them more susceptible to interdiction at a border with improved inspection programs and better-educated guards. These actions would be further enhanced by the increased scrutiny and investigative resources that would result from heightened public interest and improved public awareness.

In summing up our investigation, I can offer some—albeit tentative—answers to the most basic questions: Of the forty objects stolen from the public galleries and restoration rooms, sixteen have been recovered, including six of the finest pieces the museum possessed: the Sacred Vase of Warka, the Mask of Warka, the Bassetki Statue, one of two Ninhursag Bulls, a ninth-century B.C. Assyrian ivory headboard from Nimrud, and a headless inscribed limestone statue from Lagash. The amnesty program [we had established throughout Iraq with the assistance of sheikhs, imams, and local officials] netted two pieces (the Ninhursag bull was returned as a walk-in, and the vase after [New York City Police Captain] John Durkin's skilled negotiation), while seizures accounted for the other four—two inside Iraq (the Warka mask and the Bassetki Statue) and two outside Iraq by Jordanian customs (the ivory headboard) and U.S. Customs (the headless statue).[18]

... We know that at least 3,138 pieces were stolen from the aboveground storage rooms—though this number is [still] likely to go up by as much as one to two thousand as excavation catalogues are checked and inventories completed. Of these, 3,037 have been recovered. Roughly 1,924 of the recoveries were via the amnesty program, and 1,113 through seizures. Since I compiled these numbers in December 2003, there have been other recoveries (through both amnesty and seizures) of excavation-site objects, but I have not personally confirmed those more recent recoveries and do not list them here.

Our efforts to recover antiquities stolen from the basement have not proven so successful. Slightly more than ten thousand cylinder seals remained safe in the museum, but of the 10,686 objects stolen from underground ... only 2,307 have been recovered.[19] Part of the problem ... is that the entire haul from the basement could fit in one backpack. Looking at the recoveries of items stolen from the basement another way, 911 were recovered inside Iraq, and 1,396 internationally.[20]

[As of December 2003], then, approximately 5,400 objects have been recovered—roughly 1,950 via amnesty and 3,450 via seizures.[21] Moreover, another 62,000 pieces were "found" in other locations in Baghdad. These include 8,366 display-case items found in [a top-secret vault within the museum that a select group of museum staff had referred to as "the secret place," 39,453 ancient manuscripts found in a bomb shelter in Western Baghdad], the collection of Iraq's royal family in the Central Bank's old building (6,744), and the burial goods from the royal tombs of Ur and Nimrud in the Central Bank's new building (the last two totaling approximately 7,360 pieces altogether). Sadly, though, at least 8,500 pieces—many of them truly priceless—were still missing. These include nine Sumerian, Akkadian, and Babylonian cuneiform bricks, a Babylonian boundary stone, and five heads from Hatra: a copper head of winged victory, a stone head of a female deity, and marble heads of Apollo, Poseidon, and Eros[22] . . . The list of missing pieces also includes the one that breaks my heart. It is the piece that is on the cover of [*Thieves of Baghdad*]: the Lioness attacking a Nubian Boy, an extraordinary eighth century B.C. chryselephantine ivory plaque inlaid with lapis and carnelian and overlaid with gold. [Please see image P10.] It is, in my view, the single most exquisite and historically significant piece that is still missing. Which is why it is on the cover—a painful reminder to me that my journey has only just begun . . .

NOTES

For a more exhaustive treatment and a more complete list of notes and works cited, see M. Bogdanos, *Thieves of Baghdad: One Marine's Passion to Recover the World's Greatest Stolen Treasures* (Bloomsbury 2005) and M. Bogdanos, "The Casualties of War: The Truth About the Iraq Museum," in the *American Journal of Archaeology* 109 (2005), pp. 477–526 (also available from ajaonline.org).

1. His full quote was more colorful: "And the only problem with [reports that the museum was 'looted under the very noses of the Yanks, or by the Yanks themselves'] is that it's nonsense. It isn't true. It's made up. It's bollocks" (D. Aaronovitch, "Lost from the Baghdad Museum: Truth," *Guardian* [London], June 10, 2003).
2. The museum had, for example, been closed for 20 of the previous 24 years—open only once (on Saddam Hussein's birthday in 2000) and then closed again shortly thereafter.
3. "Iraqis Say Museum Looting Wasn't as Bad as Feared," *Wall Street Journal*, April 17, 2003. Dr. Ahmed Kamel, the museum's deputy director, shared his surprise, remarking that "[w]e didn't think anybody would come here and steal things because it has never happened before" ("Iraq Museum Still Counting the Cost of Invasion," *Peninsula* [Qatar], July 1, 2004).
4. See the Protocol Additional to the Geneva Conventions of August 12, 1949 (Protocol I), June 8, 1977; Protocol Additional to the Geneva Conventions of August 12, 1949 (Protocol II), June 8, 1977; Convention for the Protection of Cultural Property in the Event of Armed Conflict, The Hague, May 14, 1954; Protocol for the Protection of Cultural Property in the Event of Armed Conflict (Protocol I), The Hague, May 14, 1954; Second Protocol to the Hague Convention of 1954 for the Protection of Cultural Property in the Event of Armed Conflict (Protocol II), The Hague, March 26, 1999.

5. An RPG, or Raketniy Protivotankoviy Granatomet, is an extremely effective shoulder-fired weapon, using an 85-mm armor-piercing shaped warhead that is capable of penetrating up to 35 cm of armor. The ubiquitous Soviet-introduced RPG-7 weighs 8.5 kg with its warhead and is devastatingly effective up to 500 m against a stationary target and 300 m against a moving target. An RPG-7 can penetrate a Bradley armored personnel carrier, and although it cannot penetrate the heavily armored portions of the U.S. Army's main battle tank, the M1A1 Abrams, there are areas of the tank that are vulnerable as well.

6. An AK-47, or Automat Kalashnikova Model 1947, is an assault rifle capable of firing up to six hundred rounds per minute at the cyclic rate in its automatic fire mode. Its 7.62-by-39-mm bullet can penetrate U.S. body armor and is lethal to 300 m.

7. "Inside Iraq's National Museum," *Wall Street Journal*, July 17, 2003. For this well-researched account, Roger Atwood interviewed approximately thirty neighborhood residents in addition to the museum staff.

8. See Al-Radi, S. 2003, October. "War and Cultural Heritage: Lessons from Lebanon, Kuwait, and Iraq." *The Power of Culture*, in which she states that she also received information that on April 9 two Iraqi army vehicles drove up to the back of the museum.

9. When we'd arrived two weeks earlier, and I'd seen the infamous hole in the façade of the Children's Museum—the result of a single round fired from the 120 mm main gun of a U.S. M1A1 Abrams tank—I was furious and began to understand the world-wide condemnation. Then I saw the evidence. The tank gunner said that he fired only after someone had fired an RPG, rocket-propelled grenade, at him from that building. On the roof, we found a stash of RPGs and, inside, blood splatter whose pattern suggested that at least two shooters had been on the third floor when the round hit its mark(s).

10. "All it would have taken was a tank parked at the gate," said Jane Waldbaum, president of the American Institute of Archaeology. *USA Today*, April 14, 2003.

11. In a similar vein, some critics complained about how coalition forces protected the oil ministry, but not the museum. What those critics failed to take into account is that to "secure" a building in combat, you usually have to physically occupy it, at least temporarily. If the building is fortified, that means a battle. In this comparison, there are three facts that such critics blithely ignored. First, the "securing" of the oil ministry began with U.S. air strikes on April 9. It was a lawful target, and we dropped a bomb on it. We were not going to bomb the museum. Second, the oil ministry did not contain soldiers—it had not been turned into a fortress that housed people who were trying to kill us. The museum was filled with Republican Guards shooting at Americans with automatic weapons and tank-killer rocket-propelled grenades. Finally, the oil ministry is just one building—the coalition "secured" it in less than an hour. The museum was an eleven-acre complex of interconnecting and overlapping buildings and courtyards. Securing it would have required a serious firefight that would likely have reduced the place to expensive rubble. Comparing the museum with the oil ministry, then, is more politics-based than fact-based.

12. Although the use of nonlethal measures such as tear gas might have satisfied legal standards, several factors would have argued against their employment. First, even "nonlethal" measures sometimes result in death, particularly among the elderly and children. Second, there is the question of effectiveness. Nonlethal measures would have dispersed the looters (and have caused them to drop larger items). But most of the looted items were the smaller excavation-site pieces, and the use of tear gas, for example, would not necessarily have caused the looters to empty their pockets or drop their bags as they ran away. Finally, while it is easy to judge these events with the benefit of hindsight, any argument that U.S. military should have used force, nonlethal or otherwise, to disperse a crowd at the museum, must first consider the extraordinarily negative reaction it would have been expected to ·cause among a people that in April 2003 believed that such governmental sponsored violence had ended with the fall of the Hussein regime.

13. Both of the standard-issue rifles for U.S. forces, the full-size M16A2 as well as the smaller M4 carbine, fire a NATO bullet that measures 5.56mm in diameter and 45mm in length, weighs 3.95 g, and leaves the muzzle at a velocity of 905.5 (M4) or 974.1 (M16A2) meters per second. The bullets return to the ground at lethal terminal velocity.

14. Cruickshank, D., and D. Vincent. 2003. *People, Places, and Treasures Under Fire in Afghanistan, Iraq and Israel*. London: BBC Books.

15. On one of the second-floor landings was a group of twenty-seven bricks with royal inscriptions placed in chronological order from the cuneiform tablets of Eanna-tum I (ruler of Lagash, c.2470 B.C.), Naram-Sin (king of Akkad, c.2250 B.C.), and Hammurabi (king of Babylonia, 1792–1750 B.C.) to Assurnasirpal (ruler of Assyria, 885–858 B.C.), Nebuchadnezzar (king of Babylon, 605–562 B.C.), and—the most recent—a Latin-inscribed brick from a Roman barracks of the first century B.C. The nine that were stolen were carefully selected.

16. "Glass cutters left behind at the scene are viewed as another indication of professionals at work alongside the mob" (Rose, M. 2003, April 15–July 11. "Taking Stock in Baghdad." *Archaeology*). Another popular claim is that these professionals "even brought equipment to lift some of the heavier pieces" (F. Deblauwe, quoted in Elich, G. 2004, January 3. "Spoils of War: The Antiquities Trade and the Looting of Iraq." *Center for Research on Globalisation*). No one brought any such equipment to the museum. At least, no one used any such equipment. In the case of the Bassetki Statue, we followed the cracks in the floor made by thieves who dropped it several times, and who certainly had no equipment at hand to assist them.

17. In the absence of any master inventory, the numbers of missing items are based on the museum's staff's hand counting—shelf by shelf, aisle by aisle, room by room—those items still present and comparing those objects with the excavation catalog for the particular site represented by that shelf and then writing out in longhand a list of the missing items by designation. Thus, the numbers will change as each shelf and box in each aisle in each room is inventoried [and is] likely to take many years.

18. These numbers are accurate as of the summer of 2006, with the revealing recovery of the headless inscribed limestone statue from Lagash, from approximately 2450

B.C. "Revealing," because before it was seized by U.S. customs in New York, it had gone from Baghdad to Damascus to Beirut to Geneva.

19. As with the storage rooms, the numbers for the basement are accurate as of the last time I personally verified the losses and recoveries in December 2003. Altogether, the museum had approximately 15,000 cylinder seals in its collection in four different locations. One-third, then, was stolen by the insiders.

20. Neighboring countries report having recovered a total of approximately 1,866 Iraqi antiquities altogether (Jordan 1,450 items; Syria 360; Kuwait 38; and Saudi Arabia 18). Donny George believes that approximately 700 came from the museum and the rest from archaeological sites. No antiquities have been seized (or, to be more precise, acknowledged to have been seized) by the other two border nations, Turkey and Iran.

21. Although Italian authorities have seized another 300 artifacts that they believe came from the museum, they are not included this number because neither Donny nor I have yet verified that the items are from the museum.

22. The female deity was the only statue whose head the thieves cut off. Discovered in a Hatrene temple dedicated to the worship of Hercules, it may, therefore, represent his wife (Basmachi, F. 1975–76. *Treasures of Iraq Museum*. Baghdad: al-Jamahiriya Press, 309). The three heads of Poseidon, Apollo, and Eros were exquisite Roman copies of c. A.D. 160 after Greek originals of the fourth century B.C.

CHAPTER 4

Who Are the Looters at Archaeological Sites in Iraq?

JOANNE FARCHAKH-BAJJALY

SITTING IN THE BACKSEAT OF THE JEEP, I WAS LOOKING OUT INTO THE DESERT, searching for Umma. I did not understand what the landscape in front of my eyes meant. I saw craters and mounds of sand but could not identify what they were. As we arrived, I saw young men sleeping under the trees. They got up and waved politely as they would when greeting people from the front door of their home. Then they turned and disappeared. When we stopped, I jumped out of the car to catch them and talk to them, but I fell. I was standing in what I refused to realize: I was surrounded by broken pottery, and I had fallen into a looter's dig. Umma was destroyed. Umma was looted. And I wanted to know who did that, and why.

That was in May 2003. The invasion had just ended. I returned to the same sites a year later, only to find out that extensive looting of archaeological sites in Iraq hadn't stopped. As of this writing in 2007, nothing has changed. Sumerian cities have been destroyed. The cradle of civilization is being emptied of humanity's history and treasures.

So who is to blame for this disaster? If the driving force behind the destruction of civilizations is the antiquities market, blame shouldn't fall on the people who are excavating the sites. But since the antiquities collectors are often seen as untouchable, the blame is likely to fall on the suppliers. Simple, isn't it? They are the looters, the "tomb raiders and temple thieves,"[1] the "vandals ransacking the sites,"[2] or "thieves that have done their work."[3] And as is always mentioned, "The Iraqis did it. They did it to their own history, physically destroying the evidence of their own nation's thousands of years of civilization."[4]

The looters are accused of erasing their own history in their tireless search for artifacts. But this brings up a set of questions: Who are these looters whom we accuse of doing damage? Do they consider these monuments as their own heritage at all? My purpose here is not to defend or judge them, but to try to understand their motives. To do so, it is vital to understand their social and cultural background. Talking to a few of them while in southern Iraq gave me insight into their way of thinking. By discussing their responses with guards at archaeological sites, Iraqi journalists and intellectuals, and archaeologists working in Dhi Qar province—people such as Abdel Amir Hamadani and his team; Dr. Donny George Youkhanna, formerly of the Iraq Museum; Professor Jean-Louis Huot;[5] and Professor McGuire Gibson of the Oriental Institute at the University of Chicago—and by reading the works of Pierre-Jean Luizard,[6] I developed a better understanding of the situation.

It is common knowledge to say that living in the same age doesn't necessarily imply sharing the same values. In a way, rural society in southern Iraq is a different world than the one we live in—we perceive history and heritage differently. We look at southern Iraq as the cradle of civilization. Looters in the Sumerian desert do not know much about these ancient peoples. They see themselves as the "lords of this desert and owners of all its possessions."

We see in archaeological sites the heritage of mankind. Many Iraqi peasants see in them "fields full of pottery that you can dig up whenever you're broke," as Ahmad, one of the looters, said when asked about what he was doing. "We come here and dig. Sometimes we find a plate or a bowl that is broken, and then we cannot sell them. But perhaps, if you are lucky, you will find something with some writings on it."

The looters know, as they are told by the traders, that if an object is worth anything at all, it must have an inscription on it. A cylinder seal, a sculpture, or a cuneiform tablet can bring in hard cash. For this, they work all day, hoping to find an artifact that they can sell to the dealer for a mere few dollars. We consider looting dangerous work that is poorly paid. They consider their looting to be part of a normal working day. To them, there isn't much difference between working in the field or digging a site—it's all work. With some luck, the site is much more rewarding than the field. A cylinder seal or a cuneiform tablet earns $50, and that's half the monthly salary of a regular government employee.

So who are these looters? Are they the declared culprits, driven by the greed of making a small fortune from the selling of the archaeological remains? There may be another side to consider. Most of them are simple peasants living in the villages close to the sites. In their fields they grow wheat, barley, and lentils. A few years ago, under the Baathist regime, they used to sell all their agricultural products to the government and get the cash needed for their families.

If the World Bank definition for the poverty line is anything to go by, all these people live well below it. However, in the social context of Iraq, they survive economically. Most of them are not starving. Agriculture provides for bare necessities, but they do not possess any sort of items that they may consider a luxury, not even running water. They live in mud-brick houses built around a central courtyard. Their houses are divided into rooms, one for each family.

In this society, individualism is an unexciting notion. The father is the leader of the group; his sons help him achieve the goals he sets for the entire family. When a son is married, if he has the financial ability, he can move to a house nearby. But this separation is superficial since he still blindly follows his father's decisions. This patriarchal scheme is a small prototype of the tribal system that today controls large parts of Iraq, especially in the south.

The house, or *bayt*, actually represents the first basic cell of the tribe, or the *qabîla*. Eventually the sons will marry, enlarge the house, and form what is known as *al-fakhdh*, which is the union of all these families under the authority of one *shaykh*, whom they choose. The union of all the *fakhdh* creates the *ashira*, or the clan. It is led by one *shaykh*, the *shaykh al mashyakha* or the overall *shaykh*, who in consensus with the *shaykhs* of the *fakhdh* make the major decisions that involve all members of the clan. Decisions like going to war, establishing peace, banning habits, or following a religious leader are all made here.

The power of the *shaykh al mashyakha* must not be underestimated. Saddam Hussein, in a message addressed to them on March 25, 2003, asked them to use their weapons "because the enemy did not violate only Iraq but also their clans and tribes."[7] Saddam knew what he was doing. When a *shaykh* refers to the power of his tribe, he would say (as one of them told me in April 2003 in Nasiriyah) "we represent one hundred thousand guns in this district. No one would dare touch a hair of one of our sons, because they know we will revenge them." And since dignity, honor, and loyalty are the rules of life in this part of the world, no one would dare to defy such a statement.

So, with the blessings of one of the *shaykhs* in the region, who ordered members of his clan to protect us, I went out to witness the looting of archaeological sites in 2003. We drove in a convoy of three cars. Each was equipped with machine guns and men who knew how to use them. We were told that the sites were guarded by armed looters who would fire on any "unfriendly" vehicle. But when the looters saw us coming with members of powerful tribes, they rapidly abandoned the site. Shapes of men carrying their shovels blended into the desert in the distance. In their silent language of power, they understood each other. And that's what makes the tribal system simultaneously so strong and dangerous. At times they are even more powerful than governmental institutions.

In 2004, when we returned to southern Iraq, we went again to Umma. This time we were escorted by a police unit. Sitting in the back of a truck, they sported their guns. When we arrived on the site they started firing over the heads of looters, who quickly fled. Yet they refused to go to visit the home of the *shaykh* of the local tribe. They were afraid of his reaction. In response, he came to them. With one car, he blocked the way. Then he gently stepped out of his vehicle and asked the lieutenant to do the same. Calm and composed and in a barely audible voice, the *shaykh* asked the police lieutenant to release his relatives who had been taken into custody a few days earlier when they were caught digging at Fara (ancient Shuruppak), an archaeological site near Umma. The lieutenant tried to tell him that he could not do so because they were looting an archaeological site and therefore they had to be imprisoned. That's when the *shaykh* put his hand gently on the lieutenant's shoulder and asked him to change the report and write that they were just working in their field growing barley. Then he left. When I asked the policeman what he intended to do, he replied that he will try to keep the *shaykh*'s relatives imprisoned for a few more days, but he then had to release them. Otherwise, he would risk a direct confrontation between this tribe and his own. He had to compromise, and archaeology had to pay the price.

What is important to understand is that the *shaykh* did not ask him to release his relatives because he wanted them to loot the archaeological site. He knew that their work was illegal, and in normal circumstances he would have been helping the government assert law and order.

It is this kind of tribal support that the tribes gave archaeologists from 1998–2002, during archaeological site rescue operations in southern Iraq. At the time, archaeologists working for Iraq's State Board of Antiquities and Heritage were trying to stop looting by excavating archaeological sites and hiring the local peasants as workers. Tribal leaders gave them full support because they saw in this an economic benefit for their communities. But in the current situation and since coalition forces are not buying the farmer's agricultural products, forbidding people from looting archaeological sites would mean condemning them to starvation.

In the eyes of the looters, excavating an archaeological site is not a crime. Even in local police records looters are not written up as thieves, but as people digging for artifacts. This is because within a tribal society, to be called a thief is a tremendous insult. Everyone responds according to the rankings of his or her own values, and the looters' cultural backgrounds come from the tribes to which they belong.

Dignity and righteousness are essential ingredients for an honorable tribesman. Their cultural heritage is the legacy of Arab poetry. At night, religious stories are often told, as well as the stories of heroes and wars between clans. They all know the legendary stories of their greatest hero, Antar Ibn Chaddad, but they have never heard of Gilgamesh. They are the descendants of the Arab tribes that settled in this land after the huge bedouin immigration of the late eighteenth century.[8]

People in southern Iraq feel that their allegiances go first to their own tribes, and therefore abide by the decisions of their *shaykhs*. In the rules of a tribe "members are equal no matter what their relationship is to the *shaykh* and the priority of decisions is for the benefit of the all the members of the clan."[9] Primarily for these reasons, people may not want to leave the tribal system completely and put their faith in a nation where they may become just another number and an ordinary, equal citizen with no real power or support. Besides, a nation may not satisfy their basic needs.

No individual can survive alone in the desert. Families sharing a common ancestry and centuries of knowledge can deal with the challenges of life. For them, there is no real kinship other than blood relation. A common saying—blood never becomes water—depicts exactly this. And this blood relation unites not only families, but also tribes and clans. Somehow they are all cousins; their origins can be traced back to one forefather. This is what binds them. Members of different tribes communicate almost nonverbally; they all know each other, and they know each other's strengths and weaknesses.

Members of the tribe follow their *shaykh* more than anyone else, even when it comes to the choice of religious leaders. In the Shiite Muslim faith, any religious *shaykh* or *sayed*—a *shaykh* descended directly from the family of the prophet Muhammad—can make so-called fatwas, or religious edicts, that forbid or allow certain activities of followers. Since each group can choose its religious *shaykh*, people within that group become independent of leaders and decision-makers in the cities. So there's a difference in the sense of belonging between Iraq's urban and rural societies that stretches back to the eighteenth century and the migration of the bedouins. Urban societies in Iraq were never interested in the changes taking place in the desert or in the battles that tribes were launching against one another. The only link that existed between the two societies was an economic one, mainly to provide the necessary agricultural products.

The separation between the two worlds ended with the 1920 revolution, when both societies allied against British forces. However, this did not last long enough to give birth to social changes. The gap remained until the 1958 coup d'état and the birth of the Republic of Iraq. With Abdel-Karim Qassem, the prime minister of Iraq from 1958–1963, came the first "socialization" of the tribes through social reforms, and the maintenance of that system continued to form part of the plans of any government taking control in Baghdad until the Iraq war in 2003.

From 1958 to 1990, Iraq's understanding of its past changed. After centuries of decline, Baghdad was again the capital of culture in the Arab world. Its status was so great that people used to say that Cairo writes, Beirut publishes, and Baghdad reads. On the one hand, books were written about Iraq's history and the civilizations that lived in this land, and on the other, people showed real interest in knowing and preserving archaeological sites and visiting museums. The rise of this intellectual society was the beginning of the death of the tribal societies and their search for their history. The rich Baathist government was offering job opportunities for every Iraqi. The sense of Iraqi citizenship—and pride that Iraq was an emerging power in the region and a rich country that could provide its inhabitants with many forms of security and development—slowly deadened the need to be part of a tribe and to be dependent on the *shaykh*'s authority, especially when people had paid allegiance to the *Rais* (Saddam Hussein) themselves. Life in the cities fascinated the peasants who were getting needed education in their schools where the history of Mesopotamia was taught.

Rural Iraq did not know any real law enforcement until after the revolution of 1958, and effectively only after the Baath Party took power. The Baathist government introduced measures to revive Iraq's rural areas, hoping to induce within the population a stronger notion of belonging to a wider group than the tribe and the clan. At the time, the Baath Party stressed the concept of citizenship and the importance of governmental laws.

The history of Mesopotamia had been taught in schools since the 1930s, and education was made obligatory for both boys and girls. However, before the Baathists this was not strictly enforced. Under Saddam, unfortunately, history lessons were greatly politicized. Saddam Hussein was represented as the modern-day version of Hammurabi, Sennacherib, Nebuchadnezzar, and Saladin. Past civilizations were not only part of history; they now had an extension into modern, everyday life: one was made to feel Sumerian or Babylonian.

Since the 1958 revolution, looting of archaeological sites was a crime punishable by fine or imprisonment. This brought an end to the looting of antiquities. However, after the 1991 Persian Gulf War, following the looting of thirteen regional museums in the country, the antiquities trade was revived and looting began again in desert areas of southern Iraq.

Two factors influenced the rapid resumption of looting. One was Saddam's bloody suppression of the 1991 Shia uprising, which lead to the complete alienation of the population and the UN's subsequent imposition on Iraq of a no-fly zone from the 33rd parallel southward. This no-fly zone deprived Saddam of control of the countryside and allowed for the revival of tribal power. The other was the impoverishment of the population by UN sanctions. The renewed plundering of archaeological sites became a sort of revenge against the system. Peasants sought to destroy something dear to Saddam's heart, and at the same time they were making money. The antiquities market, as always, was there to take full advantage of people's ignorance, hatred, and suffering.

The sanctions regime created demand for black markets; it also created tribes that specialized in illicit trade. These tribes would deal in anything that could bring in cash, gradually targeting the attractive antiquities market. But Saddam, as a reaction to the revival of the looting and trade, introduced the death penalty in the 1990s as a revision of Iraqi antiquities laws. The penalty was carried out in some cases, but the government lacked the ability to halt the looting of sites in the southern countryside. Only occasionally could smugglers be apprehended along the unfenced borders of Iraq. So the digging and selling of antiquities became a relatively safe way to support cash-strapped families. Slowly but surely, looting archaeological sites transformed itself from a hobby into a profession. People started developing techniques for looting and began using heavy equipment. For those not involved with the smuggling of black market Iraqi oil, antiquities represented a good alternative. Whole tribes were living off of this illicit trade.

At the end of the 1990s, Saddam tried to regain the support of the tribes and clan leaders by giving them full control over the areas where their members lived. This resulted in a powerful resurrection of the tribal system. Saddam's government supported and funded programs to stop the looting of archaeological sites. It offered peasants regular jobs as workers for Iraqi archaeologists. The strategy worked, and the looting stopped. But with the beginning of the war in March 2003, the workers turned into professional diggers: they were able to be paid extra money for digging the sites because they knew how to excavate without breaking the objects. It is important to mention that since no "training" on the value of archaeological sites and antiquities were given to these workers, they did not see a problem in their "new job." They did not see the difference between an archaeological mission and the looting of a site. For them, in both cases it concerns objects that are looked for and are taken away, and whether these antiquities end up in a Baghdad museum located very far away from their homes or another one in the West, the equation is still the same. With time, the tribes of southern Iraq were becoming the "organized killers of civilization": a principle that the West had led them to decades before.

During the late nineteenth century, local tribesmen were aware of pottery and other artifacts in the mounds near their fields. Western explorers in the region at the time were discovering Sumerian civilization and showed interest in learning more about it by buying cuneiform tablets. Spurred by the foreign interest, the peasants began looting the site of Umma, which yielded thousands of cuneiform tablets that were sold in Baghdad. Until the government brought a halt to the practice in the 1950s, the farmers would, from time to time, go to this and other mounds to dig for objects to sell. Looting could be compared to playing the lottery in our modern civilization: a little effort that might bring fortune. But with the recent expansion of the art and antiquities market and with the increasing demand for Sumerian artifacts, the scale of looting has changed, especially after in the aftermath of the Iraq war. What had started more than a century ago as the "tradition" to make extra money is developing today into the eradication of history.

As long as there is no other economic alternative, people will keep digging at archaeological sites. The objects found represent real revenues as long as the buyers are there, and those are constantly increasing since the trend of owning an archaeological object is growing by the day. Well-established antiquities shops and auction houses in the West are testimony to this.

As in the West, there is also a proverb in the Arab world that history always repeats itself, and one tends to refuse to see the difference in context between events. For anyone who believes this proverb, digging at an archaeological site under the Ottoman Empire and selling objects to European travelers or to the Turks is equivalent to an Iraqi living under American occupation selling objects to a dealer who will eventually sell it to a foreigner. So the questions that remain are why the world did not learn the lessons of history and to what extent are we all responsible for the industrial-scale looting of the archaeological sites and the loss of Mesopotamia.

NOTES

1. Luke Baker, "Archaeologists Mourn Plunder of Iraq's Treasures," Reuters, April 5, 2004.
2. Deborah K. Dietsch, "Robbing the Cradle of Civilization," *Washington Post,* January 29, 2005.
3. Robert Fisk, "Raiders of the Lost Iraq," *Independent* [UK], June 3, 2003.
4. Fisk, "Raiders of the Lost Iraq."
5. Professor emeritus at the Sorbonne University and previous director of the IFAPO (Institut Francais de l'archéologie au Proche Orient), he was the head of the French mission excavating at Larsa in Iraq from the 1970s to 1990.
6. Middle East specialist and researcher at the French National Research Center (CNRS). His books on Iraq are considered a reference: *La formation de l'Irak contemporain* (Paris: CNRS Éditions, 2002); *La question irakienne* (Paris: Fayard, 2002).
7. The full text of this appeal may be found at http://www.albasrah.net/maqalat_mukhtara/khetab_sdm_250303.htm.
8. Luizard, *La formation de l'Irak contemporain,* 65.
9. Luizard, *La formation de l'Irak contemporain,* 67.

CHAPTER 5

See No Evil

Museums, Art Collectors, and the Black Markets They Adore

MATTHEW BOGDANOS

IN THE YEARS SINCE THE LOOTING OF THE IRAQ MUSEUM, MUCH HAS HAPPENED TO reinforce the core lesson we learned in the back alleys of Baghdad: that the genteel patina covering the world of antiquities rests atop a solid base of criminal activity. Witness the events taking place in the United States from 2003 to the date of this article. In New York, the Metropolitan Museum accepted what amounted to a plea bargain with Italian authorities—agreeing to (eventually) return twenty-one separate antiquities the Italian government says were stolen, including one of the Met's most prized items: the Euphronios krater, a sixth century B.C. Greek vase. In Missouri, the St. Louis Art Museum broke off negotiations with Egypt over the museum's possession of a thirteenth century B.C. pharaonic mask that Egyptian authorities claim was stolen and smuggled illegally out of their country. In California, the director of the J. Paul Getty Museum agreed to recommend to its trustees that the Getty return antiquities the Greek government says were stolen—while the Getty's longtime curator for ancient art resigned and is currently on trial in Rome on charges of conspiracy to receive a completely different set of stolen artifacts. More trials are sure to follow.

I am delighted that nations are moving to reclaim their patrimony. I am also delighted to see media attention beginning to illuminate certain well-appointed shadows where money changes hands and legitimate—but inconvenient— questions of the provenance (origin) of the object are too frequently considered outré.

But shadows remain. In March 2006, for example, private collector Shelby White donated $200 million to New York University to establish an ancient studies institute, prompting one of the university's professors to resign in protest over what he considered the questionable acquisition practices of the donor. Ms. White and her late husband Leon Levy have generated considerable debate since at least 1990, when the Met (of which Ms. White is a Trustee) presented a major exhibition of 200 of their artifacts from Greece, Rome, and the Near East. The Met did so despite the fact that a study later published in the *American Journal of Archaeology* determined that more than 90 percent of those artifacts had no known provenance whatsoever.[1] As with the Euphronios krater, Italian authorities have consistently maintained that they can prove many of the antiquities in the Levy-White collection were illegally excavated (a.k.a., stolen) and smuggled out of their country.

Not only did the Met proudly display that collection, dubious provenance notwithstanding, but it also (coincidentally?) celebrated the opening of its new Leon Levy and Shelby White Court for Hellenistic and Roman antiquities on April 15, 2007. Other institutions continue to hold out one hand while covering their eyes with the other. In 2000, Cornell University accepted a gift from well-known collector Jonathan Rosen of 1,679 cuneiform tablets from Ur. They said, "Thank you very much," despite reports of widespread looting at Ur after the 1991 Persian Gulf War, and despite the fact that the provenance of 10 percent of the tablets consisted of the phrase "uncertain sites." Harvard University has done equally well in neglecting to ask awkward questions—witness its Shelby White-Leon Levy Program for Archaeological Publications.

But this is nothing new.

In 1994, a decade before its current imbroglio, the Getty displayed a major exhibition of classical antiquities owned by Lawrence and Barbara Fleischman. Like the Met, the Getty proudly held this exhibit despite the fact that 92 percent of the objects in the Fleischman collection had no provenance whatsoever, and the remaining eight percent had questionable provenance at best.[2] To put it in starker terms, of 295 catalogued entries, not a single object had a declared archaeological find spot and only three (one percent) were even described as coming from a specific location.

Sometimes, however, the questionable practices extend beyond merely willful ignorance. Consider the following. Prior to the exhibition in 1994, the Fleischman collection had never been published. Thus, the first catalogue for, and hence first publication of, the Fleischman exhibit was the Getty's—of which Ms. Fleischman was a trustee. Fewer than two years later, the Getty purchased part of that collection for $20 million. But the Getty had a stated policy of not purchasing objects unless they have been previously displayed in published collections. How, then, could they possibly have justified the acquisition? Easy: the Getty was quick to point out that the collection had been published just two years earlier . . . by themselves.

Further sweetening the deal, while the collection had been purchased originally at a much lower price, it was valued at $80 million at the time of the sale to the museum. Tax laws use the fair market value at the time of the sale rather than the original purchase price in determining the value of a bequest. As a result, the difference between the 1996 valuation of $80 million and the $20 million sale price to the Getty would be deemed a gift of $60 million—affording a $60 million tax deduction for the Fleischmans. Under these terms, the gift to the Getty, therefore, was actually financed by U.S. taxpayers. Enron's accounting team could not have done a better job.

In many respects, then, we have advanced very little since the imperial nineteenth century, when Lord Elgin could haul away the Parthenon Marbles (now in the British Museum and commonly referred to as the "Elgin Marbles") and Henry Layard could haul away the Nineveh reliefs (now in the Met). Despite the hue and cry of the last several years, the Met's current policy is to require documentation covering only the last ten years of an object's history. This, even though most institutions view 1970—the year of the landmark United Nations Educational, Scientific and Cultural Organization (UNESCO) Convention to regulate the transfer of antiquities—as the cut-off date for requiring proof that an antiquity was not illegally looted.

The imposition of a firm date (here, 1970) is crucial in stopping the trade in illegal antiquities. As each year passes, it becomes less and less likely that a previously unpublished (and hence unknown) antiquity can appear on the market and be legal—either in the sense of having come from a properly sanctioned excavation or from some ancient collection that was assembled before the imposition of any requirement of documentation. To put it another way, as each year passes, it becomes increasingly certain that previously unpublished items are stolen.

Thus, the Met's policy of requiring documentation covering only the last ten years of an object's history becomes more unsupportable as each year passes. For example, in May of 2013, the Met could begin to buy items stolen from the Iraq Museum in April 2003 without violating its stated policy. All it need do is not ask where it comes from before the ten-year window.

As if to flaunt the Met's policy of 'see no evil,' Philippe de Montebello, the museum's director, told the *New York Times* in February 2006 that the context in which an artifact is found is virtually meaningless; in his opinion, it accounts for less than two percent of what we can learn from antiquity. His position is as absurd as the equally unreasonable view of some purists that context is everything.

But far from this world of museum receptions and limos waiting at the curb, however, there has been an even more troubling development. In June 2005, U.S. Marines in northwest Iraq arrested five insurgents holed up in underground bunkers filled with automatic weapons, ammunition stockpiles, black uniforms, ski masks, and night-vision goggles. Along with these tools of their trade, were thirty vases, cylinder seals, and statuettes that had been stolen from the Iraq Museum. Since then, the scenario has been repeated many times. It does not take a counterterrorism expert to detect the sinister adjustment that has taken place. In 2003, when pursuing leads to recover antiquities, we usually came across weapons and links to violent groups. Now, as security forces pursue leads for weapons and insurgents, they find antiquities. In a modern-day version of the old "molasses to rum to slaves" triangle trade of pious New England ship captains and owners who sang hymns and offered prayers while getting rich off human misery, the cozy cabal of academics, dealers, and collectors who turn a blind eye to the illicit side of the trade is, in effect, supporting the insurgents who are killing our troops in Iraq.

This is not surprising. As the National Commission on Terrorist Attacks Upon the United States (9-11 Commission) noted, international law enforcement has aggressively attacked traditional means of terrorist financing by freezing assets and neutralizing charities that had previously served as fronts for jihadists. But terrorists are nothing if not adaptive. In late 2005, the German newspaper *Der Spiegel* reported that 9/11 conspirator Mohammed Atta had approached a professor at the University of Goettingen trying to sell Afghan antiquities to raise money to buy an airplane. While nothing came of that inquiry, times have changed. Like the Taliban in Afghanistan who have learned to finance their activities through opium, insurgents in Iraq have discovered a new source of income in Iraq's cash crop: antiquities.

We do not have hard numbers—the traffic in art for arms is still too recent a phenomenon, and some of the investigations remain classified because of the connection to terrorists. But this illicit trade has become a growing source of revenue for the insurgents; ranking just below kidnappings for ransom and "protection" money from local residents and merchants. Iraq is a war zone, but it is also the cradle of civilization, with 10,000 poorly guarded archaeological sites. Among the most prized items from those sites are cylinder seals, intricately carved pieces of stone about the size of a piece of chalk, that can sell for $250,000, enabling an insurgent to smuggle millions of dollars in his pocket. Given this almost limitless supply of antiquities, the insurgency appears to have found an income stream sufficiently secure to make any chief financial officer sleep well at night.

NOTES

1. Christopher Chippindale and David W.J. Gill. "Material consequences of contemporary classical collecting," *American Journal of Archaeology* 104, no. 3 (July 2000): 463–511. In this ground-breaking study, the authors analyzed seven celebrated collections and exhibitions in terms of their provenance (as defined in terms of an object's origins, or find spot, and its history since unearthing) and concluded that the overwhelming majority had no declared or credible find spots and simply surfaced as orphans without history.
2. Two-thirds of the collection had been shown at the Getty and at the Cleveland Museum of Art. Chippindale and Gill.

CHAPTER 6

The Western Market in Iraqi Antiquities

NEIL BRODIE

SINCE THE LOOTING OF THE IRAQ MUSEUM IN APRIL 2003 AND THE SUBSEQUENT widespread illegal digging of Iraqi archaeological sites, there has been discussion and recrimination about what—if any—plans were in place to protect cultural sites during the invasion by coalition forces, and why those plans failed. The perspective offered in this volume is that the military planners, through either inadequate expert consultation, poor communication, or even simple lack of interest, failed to predict that during an invasion museums and sites would be targeted by thieves, and thus neglected to ensure that troops on the ground would be ready and able to offer them physical protection. I would suggest, however, that this analysis is incomplete. Because Iraq's cultural sites are being plundered for artifacts to feed an international trade, without concomitant strategies of market reduction, policies of site protection on the ground are likely to be expensive, ineffective, and even costly in terms of human life.

Furthermore, if political action had been taken to constrain the market in Iraqi antiquities during the late 1990s, when there was good evidence to show that a large part of it was illegal, then the looting of the Iraq Museum might not have happened, nor would archaeological sites have been looted, as there would have been no demand for their contents.

I have previously written at some length about the market in Iraqi antiquities in the 1990s, showing how artifacts were being openly traded in the United Kingdom and the United States without any apparent enforcement of the trade embargo placed on Iraq by United Nations Security Council Resolution

(UNSCR) 661, or for that matter of any of the other regulatory laws that were available.[1] However, the open market in Iraqi antiquities appears to have diminished since April 2003. In this chapter, I want to revisit and enlarge upon these observations and also consider in more depth the failure of law enforcement and the reasons for that failure.

THE MARKET IN IRAQI ANTIQUITIES (AUGUST 1990 TO APRIL 2003)

The state of the reported London antiquities market over the period from August 1990—when UNSCR 661 was adopted—to April 2003—when the Iraq Museum was looted—can be gauged from statistics describing antiquities sales held at Christie's auction house. Christie's is used for this analysis because of the three major London auction houses that sell antiquities—Sotheby's, Christie's, and Bonhams—only Christie's maintained sales through the period in question, holding major antiquities-only sales two or three times per year. Figure 6.1 shows the combined number of unprovenanced Mesopotamian cylinder seals and cuneiform tablets consigned for sale each year.[2] Both types of artifact are found mainly in Iraq, and so can be taken as indicators of the larger market in Iraqi antiquities. Clearly, during the period in question and despite UNSCR 661 the quantities of unprovenanced artifacts being offered for sale did not diminish; in fact if anything they increased over the years running up to 2003.

The issue of provenance is crucial here. Provenance is known ownership history, and so if an artifact is offered for sale with provenance, it is easy to ascertain whether the piece is legally on the market. For an unprovenanced artifact, however, it is hard if not impossible to know whether it is on the market legally or not. Thus the unprovenanced Iraqi material being sold at auction between 1990 and 2003 might have been moved out of Iraq in part or in total be-

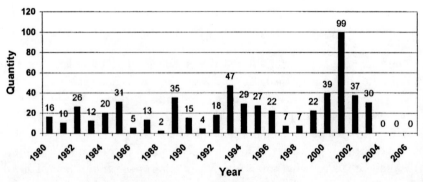

Figure 6.1. Annual Sales of Unprovenanced Mesopotamian Cylinder Seals and Cuneiform Tablets at Christie's London

fore 1990, or it might equally have been exported after that date. As I will make clear below, subsequent events showed that the second possibility is the most likely, and suggest that a large part of the unprovenanced material on the market in the 1990s was in fact there unlawfully.

For New York, the largest data run available is for Sotheby's auction house, and the number of unprovenanced Mesopotamian cylinder seals and cuneiform tablets offered annually at Sotheby's are shown in figure 6.2. On average, fewer artifacts were sold at Sotheby's than at Christie's London. Auction statistics are not a straightforward reflection of the total antiquities market, but the ones presented here do suggest that the New York market in unprovenanced Iraqi artifacts was smaller in volume than that in London. This observation is fully in accord with other evidence suggesting that much of the trade out of Iraq during the 1990s was passing through London.[3]

Outside the auction market, and away from the public eye, some large private collections were also built up during the 1990s, including the ones accumulated by Jonathan Rosen, who donated 1,500 cuneiform tablets to Cornell University in return for a substantial tax deduction,[4] and Martin Schøyen, whose 650 Aramaic-inscribed incantation bowls lent for study to University College London became the subject of an internal university enquiry.[5] Some demonstrably looted pieces were offered for sale privately, thus confirming the existence of a large "invisible" market operating outside the confines of the auction rooms, with dealers selling directly to clients.[6] It was widely reported, for example, that pieces of relief sculpture removed from the Assyrian palaces of Nineveh and Nimrud were available for purchase,[7] and one was bought in good faith in 1995 by collector Shlomo Moussaieff for about $15,000, which he subsequently sold back to the Iraqi government.[8]

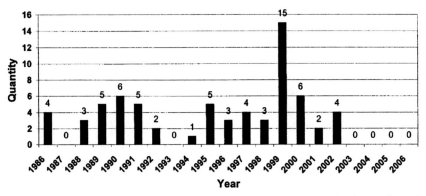

Figure 6.2. Annual Sales of Unprovenanced Mesopotamian Cylinder Seals and Cuneiform Tablets at Sotheby's New York

In response to international concern about the damaging consequences of the antiquities trade, UNESCO adopted in 1970 the Convention on the Means of Prohibiting and Preventing the Illicit Import, Export and Transfer of Ownership of Cultural Property, which offers a legal framework for international regulation of the trade through diplomatic cooperation. Unfortunately, for Iraqi artifacts from 1990 to 2003 this convention was impotent. Although Iraq had become party to the convention in 1974, and the United States had done likewise in 1983, no collaborative action was possible as diplomatic relations between the two countries had been suspended at the time of the 1991 Persian Gulf War. The United Kingdom did not ratify the 1970 Convention until 2002. However, the trade did carry on in spite of the sanctions placed on Iraq in 1990 by UNSCR 661. Article 3(a) of UNSCR 661 stated specifically that states should prevent "[t]he import into their territories of all commodities and products originating in Iraq or Kuwait exported therefrom after the date of the present resolution." By 1994, notice of the UN trade embargo had been provided by the major London and New York auction houses in their relevant sale catalogs, though there was no explicit mention of a prohibition on consignments originating in Iraq. As the auction statistics in figures 6.1 and 6.2 show, the trade embargo made no impact whatsoever on the volume of their trade. Presumably, the same was true of the antiquities market more generally. On April 17, 2003, for example, in the immediate aftermath of the break-in at the Iraq Museum, I identified eight websites that among them were offering forty-seven unprovenanced cuneiform tablets for sale, with a further five tablets available on eBay.

In the United Kingdom, the licensing system in place to control the export of cultural objects offered another opportunity to regulate the trade in Iraqi antiquities; however, it was not utilized. The operation of this licensing system is complicated in that it must satisfy two separate laws, one domestic and one European. In brief, the relevant European legislation is the 1992 European Council Regulation No. 3911/92 on the export of cultural goods, which came into effect in the UK in April 1993. Article 2.1 of this regulation demands that "The export of cultural goods outside the customs territory of the Community shall be subject to the presentation of an export licence." As defined in that legislation, the term *cultural goods* includes "archaeological objects more than 100 years old." Individual member states of the European Union can choose to exclude archaeological objects from licensing requirements "where they are of limited archaeological or scientific interest, and provided that they are not the direct product of excavations, finds and archaeological sites within a Member State, and that their presence on the market is lawful."

The text describing these exclusions is unfortunately ambiguous, and it is not clear whether the proviso about material being lawfully on the market applies to archaeological artifacts from all countries, or only from member states of the European Union. The UK government has chosen the latter interpretation, so that while a license might be required for for the export of an artifact of non-EU origin on the grounds of archaeological significance, no check will be made on whether or not it is legally on the market.[9]

I have counted the license requests made by the UK government for unprovenanced cuneiform tablets offered at four auction sales held over the period November 1998 to April 2000.[10] Licenses were required for the export of eighteen out of thirty-eight lots offered for sale. These licenses were required for pieces that had been judged to be of "archaeological interest," and thus not excluded from licensing requirements on the grounds of "limited archaeological interest." This statistic probably provides a biased estimate of licensing requirements, as inscribed objects such as the cuneiform tablets are more likely to be judged of archaeological interest than uninscribed objects. What is clear though is that many Iraqi objects were able to be exported without a license. In practice, it probably didn't matter very much. As I have already described, even when a license is required, for artifacts of non-EU origin it is issued without any check being made on the legality of export from its country of origin.

In Britain, parliamentary and government-sponsored enquiries into the illicit trade have both recommended that the checks on legal export that are presently made on artifacts of EU origin should be extended to artifacts from all countries, but the government has proved reluctant to change its licensing procedures, arguing that it will require a change in European law.[11] If the government is right, then perhaps this change should have been initiated back in the 1990s, when it first became clear that there might be a large illegal trade in Iraqi artifacts. If export licensing requirements had been applied more rigorously in the 1990s, it is arguable that any illegal trade through London would have been severely disrupted and perhaps even stopped altogether.

To be fair to the government department concerned—the Department for Culture, Media and Sport—I am not aware that the archaeological community made any systematic, concerted, or determined representation about the possibility of using the licensing system to regulate the trade in Iraqi artifacts, probably because no archaeologist was aware of the system's existence or familiar with its legal and operational complexities. On the other hand, it could be argued that it was the department's responsibility to have been monitoring the market and to have initiated an appropriate response. Nevertheless, there appears to have been a breakdown in communication between archaeologists and civil servants and it is still not apparent today what the appropriate forum for such communication would be.

From 1990 to 2003, neither the UK nor U.S. government considered the trade in illegally acquired Iraqi antiquities problematic. No political incentive to interfere with the trade existed, and no extra resources were allocated or hypothecated to police agencies to enable the effective enforcement of regulatory legislation already in force to stop the trade. One reason why the trade was not perceived to be a political priority was that the archaeological community had not carried through the research necessary to demonstrate the damage the trade was causing, nor did it promote with sufficient vigor its belief that this damage was serious. Certain individuals within academia were certainly outspoken, but overall they constituted a small minority. There was probably much hand-wringing in private, but not much in terms of primary research or political lobbying. This weak archaeological engagement with the illicit trade is not confined to Iraq, and it doesn't show much sign of improving. When in 2000 the UK government held an inquiry into the nature and extent of the illicit trade internationally, it gathered information from a range of private and public sources. Yet at the time only two pieces of academic research were available for consultation. Only a few more studies would be available today.

One reason for the apparent reluctance of academic archaeologists to research the trade is that such research does not attract any kudos in the university system, where the subject is considered to fall outside the intellectual purview of archaeology and be more properly the domain of criminologists or lawyers. Another reason is that, even in 2006, not all academics regarded the trade of unprovenanced artifacts as something that is inherently wrong or that should be stopped. They make the arguments that the trade "rescues" material that would otherwise be lost from view or destroyed, and that any attempts either within the profession or by legislators to regulate access to traded material are attacks on academic freedom. In May 2006, for example, the Biblical Archaeology Society posted on its website a "Statement of Concern" about attempts by the Archaeological Institute of America and the American Schools of Oriental Research to stop members from making initial publication of unprovenanced artifacts in the academic literature. By September 2006 this statement had attracted 158 signatures.

Those academics who vigorously defend their right to study unprovenanced (and probably illegally traded) material in the name of academic freedom often know more than they are prepared to admit publicly about its provenance, in terms of where it came from and who has handled it. By not publishing this provenance information they are themselves obstructing academic research. In fact, they can be quite virulently dismissive of the rights of their fellow academics to study the trade, proving that in this area at least academic freedom is a very limited concept. The ongoing debate within academia about whether scholars should publish unprovenanced material is an important one, but its frame of reference should be expanded to include whether scholars should publish what they know about the trade itself. To put it another away, the criminal trade is in as much need of research and publication as the products of that trade.

THE MARKET IN IRAQI ANTIQUITIES SINCE APRIL 2003

In May 2003, United Nations Security Council Resolution (UNSCR) 1483 lifted trade sanctions on Iraq, except for those on weapons and cultural objects. Article 7 of UNSCR 1483 specifically states that the trade in Iraqi cultural objects is prohibited when "reasonable suspicion exists that they have been illegally removed" from Iraq since the adoption of UNSCR 661, and that the return of any cultural objects stolen from cultural institutions or other locations in Iraq since that time should be facilitated. In June 2003, UNSCR 1483 was implemented in the United Kingdom as Statutory Instrument 2003 No. 1519, the Iraq (United Nations Sanctions) Order 2003. Article 8 of Statutory Instrument (SI) 1519 makes it a criminal offense to hold or to deal in any cultural object that has been removed illegally from Iraq since August 6, 1990 (the date of UNSCR 661), unless there is no knowledge or reasonable suspicion of its illegal export.

Since April 2003, as figures 6.1 and 6.2 show, the sale of unprovenanced Iraqi antiquities at public auction in New York and London has stopped entirely, perhaps because of the widespread negative publicity that followed the break-in at the Iraq Museum, or in the United Kingdom because of the enactment of SI 1519.

The fact that unprovenanced Iraqi antiquities suddenly disappeared from the auction market after the entry into force of this law is an important one. It suggests that before 2003, a large part of the unprovenanced material on the market had been illegally exported; if the material had in fact possessed a legal though unadvertised provenance it could have continued to be sold quite openly after that date without breaking the law.

In 2004, I thought the deterrent effect of SI 1519 might have extended throughout the market, but I am no longer so sure that this is the case. There is evidence to suggest instead that large numbers of artifacts are being openly traded on the Internet. On one day, December 5, 2006, I identified fifty-five websites that were offering antiquities for sale and that might be expected to sell Iraqi objects.[12] In fact, twenty-three of these sites were offering for sale or had recently sold cylinder seals and/or cuneiform tablets. In total there were 78 cylinder seals and 147 cuneiform tablets listed. These data can be compared with the April 2003 data referred to earlier.

The comparison is not exact because the April 2003 search was conducted simply to show that Iraqi antiquities were available for sale on the Internet, and was therefore less thorough than the later December 2006 search. Nevertheless, the comparison of the two data sets does suggest that the sale of Iraqi material on the Internet has not markedly diminished since 2003.

Table 6.1. Physical Locations of Dealers Offering Cuneiform Tablets for Sale on the Internet (December 5, 2006)

Country	Number of Dealers	Number of Tablets
USA	9	29
UK	3	11
UK/USA	1	56
Australia	3	51

In reality, the situation might be worse than these data suggest. There is no guarantee that what is openly offered for sale on a website represents the entire stock available for sale, and some sites specifically state that this is in fact the case. Thus, there might be more material available for sale than is advertised—potentially much more. When interviewed on radio in September 2006, the head of the Metropolitan Police's Art and Antiques Unit said that he believed the London market to be "flooded" with Iraqi material.[13]

Where information is available, most dealers offering Iraqi antiquities for sale on the Internet are physically located in the United States, the United Kingdom, or Australia, including all sites offering cuneiform tablets (table 6.1). Hardly any of these tablets are advertised with a verifiable provenance, so it seems likely that at least some dealers are acting in breach of UNSCR 1483. This suggests that existing laws are still not being properly enforced, despite the lessons that should have been learned since 1990.

As already discussed, one reason for poor law enforcement is political inaction. However, there are probably two further related reasons.

The first is that within police agencies, antiquities and—more generally—art crime specialists cannot successfully compete for resources and personnel with what are perceived to be more serious crimes. In the United Kingdom, for example, the Metropolitan Police's Art and Antiques Unit has a police complement of only four people, and though it can draw upon greater operational support when the situation demands it, the number of prosecutions brought to court must surely be limited by the number of available personnel.

The second reason concerns the evidential burden of proving that an object was actually found in Iraq. Because some objects are found outside Iraq, without proof of an Iraqi origin it is hard for the police to proceed with a criminal prosecution under UNSCR 1483 or appropriate national stolen property laws. It is instructive in this context to note the named findspots of the cuneiform tablets discovered during my Internet search (table 6.2). It is suspicious that although the modern nation-states of Iran, Israel, and Syria are identified as findspots, Iraq is not named once. Presumably the term *Mesopotamia* is used instead. There is no evidence provided on any website to allow any of the findspots to be verified,

Table 6.2. Provenance and Findspot
Information Provided for Cuneiform Tablets
Available for Sale on the Internet (December
5, 2006)

Provenance or Findspot	Number of Tablets
Named previous owner	3
Mesopotamia	71
Mediterranean	12
Israel	8
Syria	8
Iran	1
Elam	1
Isin	1
Lagash	1

and some of them seem unnecessarily vague. For example, what does *Mediterranean* mean? The reluctance of dealers to list Iraq as a geographical identifier suggests that even if they have no specific knowledge of illegal provenance they are well aware that many Iraqi objects are illegally on the market, and have also realized that specifying a findspot other than Iraq helps to confound police action. In fact, so long as care is taken to not attribute the findspot to Iraq, it would appear possible to sell illegally exported Iraqi material with relative impunity.

One answer to poor law enforcement is for the archaeological community to put pressure on politicians through research and lobbying. But in view of the evidential burden of proving findspot, and the inhibitory effect that it has upon law enforcement, a useful policy initiative would be to bring together archaeologists, lawyers, and police to discuss what might constitute acceptable evidence of origin for use in criminal trials. If some firm guidelines could be produced, they would enable archaeologists to sponsor or conduct the type of research that could be used as evidence in court, and so improve police effectiveness with no extra input of resources.

Auction houses may be more reluctant than many of the Internet-based dealers to sell unprovenanced Iraqi material, because they probably have more to lose if they are caught selling illicit material. Auction houses are high-profile institutions of long standing and their sales are easily monitored by means of their fully illustrated catalogs. In other words, they are easy targets for police action, and the damage caused to their reputation by a successful prosecution might have a significant negative impact upon their business. Websites, by contrast, are harder to police because there is no complete or permanent record of their sales activities and, for some Internet dealers at least, any damage to reputation caused by a successful prosecution could easily be overcome by inventing a new identity.

CONCLUSION

In this chapter I have tried to show how the Western market in Iraqi antiquities has thrived since 1990, despite legislation aimed at its control. The existence of this market has stimulated the widespread plunder of archaeological sites and museums in Iraq, including the looting of the Iraq Museum in April 2003. I have argued that the reluctance of governments to ensure that regulatory laws are enforced is partly the fault of archaeologists for not pursuing the research necessary to establish the scale and nature of the problem, and that within academia there needs to be a more progressive archaeological engagement with the issues involved. There is no reason why this research should not have a practical utility, and I have suggested that an interdisciplinary investigation into what might constitute legally acceptable proof of origin might improve standards of law enforcement.

In chapter 1 of this book, Lawrence Rothfield states that the U.S. military has contacted the Archaeological Institute of America requesting information about archaeological sites in Iran. In this context, it is probably worth mentioning that during my December 2006 Internet search for Iraqi artifacts I discovered for sale a large amount of material from Iran (and a similar amount from Afghanistan). If the relevant U.S. authorities are concerned about protecting Iranian archaeological sites, they might do well to start by tackling this market. Decisive action now would reduce the need for prophylactic military intervention and ultimately lessen the risks posed to people's lives, both soldiers and civilians, through unnecessary fighting over archaeology. Hopefully, this eventuality will not come to pass. It would be one of the more tragic and insane ironies of the early twenty-first century if effective protection of archaeological heritage came to depend upon the direct and indirect threats of destruction posed to it by military action.

NOTES

1. Neil J. Brodie, "Iraq 1990–2004 and the London Antiquities Market," in *Archaeology, Cultural Heritage, and the Antiquities Trade*, ed. Neil J. Brodie, Morag M. Kersel, Christina Luke, and Kathryn W. Tubb (Gainesville: University Press of Florida, 2006), 206–26.
2. *Provenance* is defined here as ownership history. Verifiable provenance in a catalog entry is considered to be a named previous owner, publication, or sale, thus providing a means to establish at what date an object was outside Iraq. *Unprovenanced* means that there was no verifiable provenance included in the catalog entry. It is important to note that when defined in this way provenance does not necessarily equate to legality: for example, it would be possible for the provenance of an artifact to date back only to the mid-1990s.
3. Brodie, "Iraq 1990–2004," 214–22; McGuire Gibson, "The Loss of Archaeological Context and the Illegal Trade in Mesopotamian Antiquities," *Culture Without Context* 1 (Autumn 1997): 6–8.

4. David D'Arcy, "Collector Gets Tax Break for Donating Cylinder Seals to University," *Art Newspaper* 139 (2003): 5.

5. University College London, "UCL Establishes Committee of Enquiry into Provenance of Incantation Bowls," press release, May 16, 2005, http://www.ucl.ac.uk/media/library/bowls.

6. This market is called "invisible" because, unlike the auction market, there is no public record of sales.

7. John Russell, "The Modern Sack of Nineveh and Nimrud," *Culture Without Context* 1 (Autumn 1997): 8–20.

8. Martin Gottlieb and Barry Meier, "Of 2,000 Treasures Stolen in Gulf War of 1991, Only 12 Have Been Recovered," *New York Times*, April 30, 2003.

9. Department for Culture, Media and Sport, *Guidance to Exporters of Cultural Goods* (London: Department for Culture, Media and Sport, 2003).

10. The auctions were Bonhams November 1998, Bonhams April 1999, Bonhams April 2000, and Christie's April 2000.

11. David Gaimster, "Measures against the Illicit Trade in Cultural Objects," *Antiquity* 78 (2004): 703.

12. I included in the search websites selling ancient Mediterranean or "Classical" antiquities, either solely or in part, but excluded websites that specialize in, for example, pre-Colombian or African artifacts. The websites offering cuneiform tablets or cylinder seals, or both, were the following:

> http://www.trocadero.com/stores/comminges (France)
> http://www.antiquities.co.uk (UK)
> http://www.vcoins.com/ancient/ancientbyways/store/dynamicIndex.asp (USA)
> http://www.artemission.com (UK)
> http://www.bcgalleries.com.au (Australia)
> http://www.collector-antiquities.com (UK)
> http://www.ancient-art.com (USA)
> http://www.harlanjberk.com/antiquities/antqmain.asp (USA)
> http://www.heliosgallery.com (UK)
> http://www.hixenbaugh.net (USA)
> http://www.vcoins.com/ancient/jencek/store/dynamicIndex.asp (USA)
> http://www.trocadero.com/janus (USA)
> http://www.medusa-art.com (Canada/USA)
> http://www.oldmoney.com.au (Australia)
> http://www.vcoins.com/ancient/pegasi/store/dynamicIndex.asp (USA)
> http://www.dcancientart.com (USA)
> http://www.vcoins.com/ancient/windsorantiquities/store/pricelist.asp (USA)
> http://www.xanthos.com.au (Australia)
> http://www.barakatgallery.com (USA/UK)

There were also four U.S.-based sellers on eBay.

13. BBC, "The Search for Iraq's Treasure," BBC Radio 4, September 2006.

Part II

PREVENTING FUTURE LOOTING AFTER ARMED COMBAT

THE CASE OF IRAQ MAKES CLEAR THAT NATIONAL AND INTERNATIONAL INSTITUTIONS responsible in some degree for protecting cultural heritage are responding inadequately to the peculiar challenge posed by war-related looting. The reasons for this vary from institution to institution. In some instances, there may be a mismatch between an organization's orientation and what is demanded: NGOs whose mission and focus is on peacetime site management are unlikely to be able to effectively deal with the more brutal and basic requirements of securing sites from armed looters; militaries designed to destroy the enemy are unlikely to be very good at guarding museums against mobs. In other instances, the focus may be the right one, but the job does not get done because capacity is inadequate or leadership is lacking. Lastly, failure may stem from a structural lacuna in the cultural heritage protection safety net, with no agency or organization accepting responsibility for coordinating with other agencies to address their piece of the problem.

The lessons to be learned from Iraq, then, depend on whether one is a war planner, a legislator, a cultural minister in a country at risk, and so forth. For each, there is a distinct set of policy steps that should be taken now, or in the run-up to any future war, to prepare for the worst. To help each stakeholder understand what is to be done, we turn in this section to a series of articles designed specifically for them.

THE WAY FORWARD

For Legislative Bodies with Respect to International Law

OVER THE LAST CENTURY, AN INTERNATIONAL LEGAL FRAMEWORK HAS BEEN gradually built up to prevent the pillaging and looting of cultural property in times of war. International law today encompasses several conventions and protocols intended to ensure protection of cultural heritage during armed conflict and occupation. (The relevant documents are collated in appendices A and B of this volume.) The war with Iraq that began in 2003, however, exposed serious shortcomings in this framework, not least of which was its failure to be fully adopted, through ratification and implementing legislation, by the United States. In this section, scholars describe the obligations laid out in the relevant international legal instruments, discuss the barriers to their ratification, and warn of the pitfalls involved in translating the general language of these conventions and protocols into positive domestic law.

CHAPTER 7

The 1954 Hague Convention on the Protection of Cultural Property in the Event of Armed Conflict

Its Background and Prospects for Ratification in the United States

PATTY GERSTENBLITH

THE 1954 HAGUE CONVENTION ON THE PROTECTION OF CULTURAL PROPERTY IN the Event of Armed Conflict was based on earlier international conventions regulating the conduct of warfare, including the 1899 and 1907 Hague Conventions, and on a draft started before the outbreak of World War II. The 1954 Convention was completed in the wake of the large-scale intentional looting and destruction of cultural property perpetrated by Nazi Germany during World War II, and it was the first international convention to address exclusively the subject of cultural property.[1] There are currently 116 States Parties to the main convention, 93 to the First Protocol, and 44 to the Second Protocol, which entered into force only in March 2004. Neither the United States nor the United Kingdom has ratified the main convention and its protocols. However, virtually all other states involved in the war in Iraq in 2003 were party to at least the main convention, including Iraq, which became a party to the main convention and the First Protocol on December 21, 1967.

THE 1954 HAGUE CONVENTION AND ITS PROTOCOLS

The convention lays out the basic principles for protecting cultural property. It begins with a preamble, which sets out the reasons for the adoption of the convention. It is worth noting two of the introductory paragraphs in particular:

> Being convinced that damage to cultural property belonging to any people whatsoever means damage to the cultural heritage of all mankind, since each people makes its contribution to the culture of the world;

> Considering that the preservation of the cultural heritage is of great importance
> for all peoples of the world and that it is important that this heritage should re-
> ceive international protection . . .

These phrases are part of a tradition of imposing obligations on nations to care for the cultural property located within their borders and to safeguard both their own and their adversaries' cultural property during warfare.

Article 1 of the Hague Convention offers a broad definition of cultural property as "movable or immovable property of great importance to the cultural heritage of every people." There follows a list of examples of cultural property, which is clearly intended not to be exhaustive, but includes "monuments of architecture, art or history, whether religious or secular; archaeological sites; groups of buildings which, as a whole, are of historical or artistic interest; works of art; manuscripts, books and other objects of artistic, historical or archaeological interest; as well as scientific collections and important collections of books." In addition to movable and immovable property, cultural property also includes repositories of cultural objects, such as museums, libraries, and archives, as well as refuges created specifically to shelter cultural property during hostilities.

Article 2 defines the "protection of cultural property" as consisting of two components: "the safeguarding of and respect for such property." Safeguarding refers to the actions a nation is expected to take during peacetime to protect its own cultural property. This is embodied in Article 3, which elaborates that nations are obligated to safeguard cultural property located within their territory during peacetime from "the foreseeable effects of an armed conflict." Respect refers to the actions that a nation must take during hostilities to protect both its own cultural property and the cultural property of another nation. This obligation is embodied in the two main substantive provisions of the convention: Article 4, which regulates conduct of parties during hostilities, and Article 5, which regulates the conduct of occupation.

The central premise of these articles is that parties to the convention are to show respect for cultural property by avoiding exposing cultural property situated in their own territory to danger and by avoiding causing harm to cultural property situated within the territory of another State Party to the convention. Under Article 4(1), nations are to avoid jeopardizing cultural property located in their territory by refraining from using such property in a way that might expose it to harm during hostilities. This means that nations should not use cultural property as the location of strategic or military equipment nor should such equipment be housed in proximity to cultural property. Also under Article 4(1), a belligerent nation should not target the cultural property of another nation. In what is perhaps the most controversial aspect of the Hague Convention, Article 4(2) provides that the obligations of the first paragraph "may be waived only in cases where military necessity imperatively requires such a waiver."

Article 4(3) sets out the obligation "to prohibit, prevent and, if necessary, put a stop to any form of theft, pillage or misappropriation of, and any acts of vandalism directed against, cultural property."[2] Paragraph 3 also prohibits the requisitioning of movable cultural property located in the territory of another party to the convention. Paragraph 4 of this article prohibits carrying out acts of reprisal against cultural property. Paragraph 5 states that if one State Party has failed to comply with Article 3 by not preparing to safeguard its cultural property during peacetime, this failure does not mean that another State Party can evade its obligations under Article 4.

Article 5 sets out the obligations of a State Party during occupation, emphasizing that the primary responsibility for securing cultural property lies with the competent national authority of the state that is being occupied. Thus the first obligation imposed on the occupying power is to support these national authorities as far as possible. The obligation of the occupying power to care for and preserve the cultural property of the occupied territory is very limited and applies only when the national authorities of the occupied territory are unable to do so, only when the cultural property has been "damaged by military operations" and only "as far as possible." The fact that the obligation to preserve cultural property is limited to circumstances where the property was damaged during hostilities may be viewed as an attempt to protect such cultural property from undue interference by the occupying power. This is bolstered by the other provisions of this article, which emphasize the primacy of the role of the competent national authorities.

Article 6, permitting the distinctive marking of cultural property by a special emblem, and Article 7, requiring that States Parties undertake to educate their military and introduce regulations concerning observance of the convention, complete the general substantive provisions of the convention. Articles 8 to 14 are concerned with the conditions of special protection, which may be accorded to certain categories of cultural property under specific conditions. These provisions, however, have rarely been used. The remaining articles address such topics as personnel (Article 15), the distinctive emblem (the Blue Shield, Articles 16–17), the scope of the convention's applicability (Article 18–19), and procedural matters (Articles 20–40). One of the main criticisms of the Hague Convention is that it does not contain provisions for punishment of those who violate its terms. In order to prosecute violations, it is necessary for some other mechanism to be established, primarily through national domestic law.

The First Protocol, written at the same time as the main convention, prohibits in its first section the removal of cultural objects from occupied territory and requires the restitution of any objects that have been removed at the close of hostilities. This includes a requirement that a State Party return illegally removed cultural objects to a nation even though it was not the occupying power. In addition, an occupying power that failed to prevent export from occupied territory must pay an indemnity to a holder in good faith who must return cultural property to the competent authorities of previously occupied territory. The second section requires a State Party in whose territory cultural property was deposited for safekeeping from another State Party to return the cultural property at the end of hostilities to the competent authorities of the territory from which it came. The First Protocol also permits nations to opt out of either the first or second section at the time of ratification or accession.

Following the Balkan Wars of the 1990s, the convention was updated in its Second Protocol of 1999. Article 6 of the Second Protocol clarifies and narrows the circumstances in which the military necessity waiver, allowed in Article 4, Paragraph 2 of the main convention, applies to a situation in which the "cultural property has, by its function, been made into a military objective" and "there is no feasible alternative available to obtain a similar military advantage." Furthermore, the waiver provisions apply to excuse the use of cultural property for purposes that are likely to expose the cultural property to harm only when there is no other option that will give a similar military advantage. Article 7 requires the taking of precautions to ascertain whether a military objective includes cultural property, avoidance and minimization of incidental damage to cultural property, and refraining from undertaking an attack that will cause harm to cultural property that is disproportionately excessive in comparison to the expected military advantage.

Article 10 of the Second Protocol provides for the granting of "enhanced protection" to cultural property that meets the following three criteria:

a. it is cultural heritage of the greatest importance for humanity;
b. it is protected by adequate domestic legal and administrative measures recognising its exceptional cultural and historic value and ensuring the highest level of protection;
c. it is not used for military purposes or to shield military sites and a declaration has been made by the Party which has control over the cultural property, confirming that it will not be so used.

Cultural property that meets these criteria must be placed on a list managed by a committee established by the Second Protocol and is then entitled to enhanced protection. Any cultural property under enhanced protection is entitled to absolute immunity from attack except under narrow circumstances delineated in Article 13. The Second Protocol also clarifies the criminal responsibility of individuals who violate its provisions and requires nations that are party to the protocol to establish criminal offenses under their domestic law.

Article 9 of the Second Protocol strengthens the provisions for protection of cultural property during occupation by prohibiting the illegal export or transfer of ownership of cultural property. Furthermore, it forbids the carrying out of archaeological excavation, except "where this is strictly required to safeguard, record or preserve cultural property," and "any alteration to, or change of use of, cultural property which is intended to conceal or destroy cultural, historical or scientific evidence." Finally, Article 9 also states that "[a]ny archaeological excavation of, alteration to, or change of use of, cultural property in occupied territory shall, unless circumstances do not permit, be carried out in close co-operation with the competent national authorities of the occupied territory."

NEXT STEPS: STATUS OF U.S. RATIFICATION

Perhaps the most critical issue concerning the Hague Convention is the failure of the United States, the world's largest military power, to ratify the convention and at least the First Protocol. The United States signed the convention soon after its writing, but throughout the Cold War, the U.S. military objected to ratification. The military withdrew its objections with the collapse of the Soviet Union, and President Clinton transmitted the Hague Convention and its First Protocol to the Senate for ratification in 1999.[3] The Letter of Transmittal stated:

> United States military policy and the conduct of operations are entirely consistent with the Convention's provisions. In large measure, the practices required by the Convention to protect cultural property were based upon the practices of U.S. military forces during World War II. . . . I believe that ratification of the Convention and accession to the Protocol will underscore our long commitment, as well as our practice in combat, to protect the world's cultural resources.[4]

In February 2007, the State Department placed the Hague Convention and First Protocol on its treaty priority list for consideration by the Senate Foreign Relations Committee. However, it is uncertain whether consideration of the First Protocol will proceed at this time because of questions concerning the opt-out of the first section and the indemnity requirement.[5] If the Senate Foreign Relations Committee recommends ratification of the convention, it must then be ratified by two-thirds of the Senate for the United States to become a State Party. The Second Protocol has not yet been vetted by any administrative agencies and so the prospects for its ratification in the near term seem unlikely.

The U.S. military already follows numerous of the principles of the 1954 Hague Convention under the 1907 Hague Convention (IV) respecting the Laws and Customs of War on Land and its Annex (of which the United States is a party) and as a matter of customary international law.[6] Nonetheless, ratification of the convention would accomplish the following:

- clarify the obligations of the U.S. military
- encourage marking of cultural sites
- give added impetus to the training of U.S. military personnel in their obligations to protect cultural heritage
- require the U.S. military to ensure that an adequate number of properly trained cultural heritage professionals are part of the military
- encourage better preparation during war planning and gathering of information as to the locations of cultural sites in a potential war zone
- bring greater awareness of the provisions of the convention to war planners
- allow for concerns to be incorporated at an earlier stage of war planning
- prevent resorting to last-minute efforts to obtain the necessary information and minimize the risk that cultural sites might be accidentally targeted

As was noted in the Report of the American Bar Association endorsing ratification:

It should be the duty of the United States to encourage and to help other countries to protect their cultural property by creating appropriate domestic preparations in case of emergency/armed conflict. By ratifying the 1954 Hague Convention, the United States would demonstrate to cultural communities the importance the United States places on the protection of the cultural heritage of humanity. . . . [Ratification] would create an awareness among military commanders of the importance of cultural property and its need for protection from theft and "the avoidance of unintended damage incidental to attack of legitimate targets." It also would "make the general public and the political leadership of each community, and those dedicated to the safeguarding of cultural property, aware of their responsibilities." Ratification would ensure that cultural property is not used for military purposes and would require military forces to separate cultural property from possible wartime targets.[7]

In short, ratification of the 1954 Hague Convention would indicate to the world the seriousness with which the United States approaches the preservation of cultural sites, monuments, and objects and the willingness of the United States to play a leading role in this regard. This is particularly apt at a time when the United States is trying to reach out to different parts of the world, each with their own distinctive cultural past and heritage, and attempting to demonstrate our respect for these cultures. With the announcement in

May 2004 that the United Kingdom will ratify the convention and both protocols and with its progress toward that goal,[8] the United States will soon be the only major military power not to be a party to the convention.

The experiences of the 2003 Iraq war also demonstrate the urgency for ratification of the First Protocol. There may be a perception that because the United States is a party to the 1970 UNESCO Convention on the Means of Prohibiting and Preventing the Illicit Import, Export and Transfer of Ownership of Cultural Property[9] that there is no need for the United States to ratify the First Protocol. This perception is not correct, however, in large part because of the United States' minimalist implementation of the 1970 Convention, through the Convention on Cultural Property Implementation Act (CPIA), which implements only Articles 7(b) and 9 of the UNESCO Convention.[10] The first of these provisions, 19 U.S.C. § 2607, prohibits the import into the United States of stolen cultural property that was "documented as appertaining to the inventory of a museum or religious or secular public monument or similar institution." The other provisions create mechanisms by which the United States in response to a request from another State Party can impose import restrictions pursuant to either a bilateral agreement or an emergency action on designated categories of archaeological or ethnological materials that have been illegally removed from their country of origin after the effective date of the import restrictions, 19 U.S.C. §§ 2602–3.

While the looting of the Iraq Museum in Baghdad received extensive media coverage, the larger issue is the extensive looting and destruction of archaeological sites. This has far more detrimental consequences for our knowledge and understanding of the past because the sites, the objects, and their associated contexts have never been recorded. While it is difficult to quantify the extent of this looting, the World Monuments Fund took the unprecedented step of placing the entire country of Iraq on its 2006 list of 100 Most Endangered Sites. Under normal circumstances, there would be no legal mechanism to prohibit the import of such looted objects into the United States.[11] The sanctions that had been in place since August 1990 prohibiting the import of goods into the United States from Iraq provided a unique circumstance by which the import of illegally removed cultural materials happened to have been prohibited before the war began.[12] Furthermore, Congress recognized the emergency nature of the situation and the difficulty of the process mandated under the CPIA by enacting special legislation that allows the president to impose import restrictions under the CPIA in the case of Iraq under a significantly simplified process.[13] In so doing, Congress indicated its policy to prevent looted artifacts from entering the United States. In case of any future war, it is extremely unlikely that the unique circumstances of the pre-existing sanctions against Iraq will be in place. Ratification of the First Protocol would prevent the United

States, the largest market for antiquities in the world, from becoming a haven for antiquities looted during time of war and occupation.

Ratification of the Second Protocol is a distant likelihood because it must first be reviewed by the Defense and State Departments. However, the U.S. government should undertake this effort because the Second Protocol clarifies certain provisions, particularly those concerning the military exception waiver and criminal conduct. The Second Protocol also imposes clearer obligations to preserve cultural property that would be relevant to avoiding or minimizing the types of damage that were done to the cultural heritage of Iraq by the looting of the Iraq Museum and of the archaeological sites. The first of these, in Article 8, states that "[t]he Parties to the conflict shall, to the maximum extent feasible: (a) remove movable cultural property from the vicinity of military objectives or *provide for adequate in situ protection*" (emphasis added). The reference to "the Parties to the conflict" clarifies that this obligation falls on all parties, both the attacker and the party being attacked (unlike the provisions of Article 4 of the main convention where this is left unclear). Article 7 requires states to avoid incidental damage to cultural property and to "refrain from deciding to launch any attack which may be expected to cause incidental damage to cultural property . . . which would be excessive in relation to the concrete and direct military advantage anticipated."

These provisions seem to broaden the obligations of parties to a conflict beyond simply prohibiting direct harm to cultural property and, instead, requiring avoidance, when possible, of indirect harm. Even the Second Protocol could do more in terms of affirmatively requiring the protection of cultural property during conflict and occupation and incorporating modern cultural resource management principles into activities carried out during occupation. Nonetheless, ratification of the Second Protocol (along with ratification of the main convention and the full First Protocol) would likely help to avoid repetition in a future war of the disastrous consequences for cultural heritage that have occurred in Iraq.

NOTES

1. The text of the convention, its two protocols, and list of States Parties may be found at: http://portal.unesco.org/en/ev.php-URL_ID=13637&URL_DO=DO_TOPIC&URL_SECTION=201.html. Excerpts of the 1954 Convention and the First Protocol are reprinted in appendices A and B of this volume. This subject is treated in greater detail in my article, "From Bamiyan to Baghdad: The Conduct of Warfare and the Preservation of Cultural Heritage at the Beginning of the Twenty-First Century," *Georgetown Journal of International Law* 37 (2006): 245–349.

2. Until the 2003 Iraq war, this provision elicited little commentary or interpretation. For reasons explained at greater length in Gerstenblith, *supra* note 1, at 308–11, I

believe that this provision does not impose an obligation on an attacking force to protect cultural property from the actions of the local population. The invading military clearly has an obligation to prevent such actions by its own forces.

3. The United States never signed the First Protocol. The State Department memo that accompanied President Clinton's transmittal recommended that while the United States should accede to the First Protocol, it should exercise its option and declare that it would not be bound by the first section of the First Protocol, which contains most of the substantive provisions of the protocol, because of questions concerning the indemnity requirement. The memo also stated that the State Department would undertake further study of the indemnity requirement to determine whether it comports with current U.S. law, which generally does not require payment of compensation for good faith purchasers of stolen or otherwise illegal property that is returned to its owner.

4. Letter of Transmittal, 106th Cong., Senate Treaty Doc. 106-1 (January 6, 1999), iv, available at http://frwebgate.access.gpo.gov/cgi-bin/getdoc.cgi?dbname=106_cong_documents&docid=f:td001.106.

5. *See supra* note 3. The State Department never undertook the further study of the indemnity requirement recommended in the memo accompanying the transmittal letter. It is likely that this further study will be conducted in conjunction with a future review of the Second Protocol by the Department of Defense and the Department of State.

6. Department of Defense, January 1993 Report of Department of Defense, United States of America, to Congress on International Policies and Procedures Regarding the Protection of Natural and Cultural Resources during Times of War.

7. American Bar Association Section of International Law and Practice, Report to the House of Delegates (2001): 4–5 (quoting Hays Parks, "Protection of Cultural Property from the Effects of War," in *The Law of Cultural Property and Natural Heritage: Protection, Transfer, and Access*, ed. Marilyn Phelan (Evanston, IL: Kalos Kapp Press, 1998), 3–26).

8. See http://www.culture.gov.uk/global/consultations/2005+current+consultations/hague_convention.htm?properties=2005+current+consultations%2C%2Fglobal%2Fconsultations%2Fdefault%2C&month=. For the Consultation Paper released in September 2005, see Department of Culture, Media, and Sport, "Consultation Paper on: The 1954 Hague Convention on the Protection of Cultural Property in the Event of Armed Conflict and Its Two Protocols of 1954 and 1999 (September 2005)," available at http://www.culture.gov.uk/NR/rdonlyres/C234A6B1-3178-4350-8C72-C354F24D1CF9/0/HagueConvention.pdf.

9. The text of the 1970 UNESCO Convention and its States Parties may be found at http://portal.unesco.org/en/ev.php-URL_ID=13039&URL_DO=DO_TOPIC&URL_SECTION=201.html. The looting of cultural property is also prohibited under the earlier Hague Conventions of 1899 and 1907, but these provisions apply to looting by the military of an occupying power. Furthermore, these conventions do not adequately address the particular problems of trade in looted cultural materials from territory engaged in armed conflict or subject to military occupation.

10. The implementing legislation is the Convention on Cultural Property Implementation Act (CPIA), 19 U.S.C. §§ 2601–13. Article 7(b) of the convention is implemented in 19 U.S.C. § 2607 and Article 9 is implemented through 19 U.S.C. §§ 2602–3.
11. The Cultural Property Implementation Act (CPIA) requires that before import restrictions can be imposed under either a bilateral agreement or an emergency action, the other nation must submit a request to the United States with supporting documentation, the request must be reviewed by the Cultural Property Advisory Committee, and the delegated decision-maker must determine whether the statutory criteria are satisfied. This process, even under normal circumstances, can take from many months to several years to complete.
12. The president imposed sanctions under the International Emergency Economic Powers Act, 50 U.S.C. §§ 1701–7, pursuant to Executive Orders 12722 and 12744. These sanctions were continued following the 2003 war as applied to certain goods, including illegally removed cultural materials, 31 CFR 575.533 (b)(4). Unlike import restrictions imposed under the CPIA, the sanctions carry the potential for criminal punishment.
13. Miscellaneous Trade and Technical Corrections Act of 2004, 108 P.L. 429 (2004), §§ 3001–3. This legislation fulfills, at least in part, the United States' obligations under UN Security Council Resolution 1483.

CHAPTER 8

The Implementation of International Treaties at the National Level

Law and Practice

GUIDO CARDUCCI

THE WAR IN IRAQ WAS A REMINDER TO WHAT EXTENT ARMED CONFLICTS ARE FAR from being a remote legacy of the past. They are a reality, particularly in some areas of the world. They may break out nearly at any time with varied forms, manifestations, and degrees of aggressiveness.

The same war drew the attention of the public at large, among others, to the relevance of international law in situations of armed conflict with regard to issues such as military operations, occupation,[1] and "pre-emptive self-defense" (without prior international authorization).[2]

The focus of this article is, first and briefly, the international legal protection of cultural property in the war in Iraq and, thereafter, the multifaceted and crucial process that is the implementation of international treaties at the national level.

The following remarks on implementation are potentially relevant for any treaty. They certainly include the protection of cultural property under treaties, in particular the 1954 Hague Convention for the Protection of Cultural Property in the Event of Armed Conflict (hereafter, the 1954 Hague Convention) for its States Parties,[3] and the war in Iraq that began in 2003, and extend beyond to other treaties and other fields of law.

One caveat: addressed to a large public with diverse backgrounds, this brief article endeavors to be sufficiently accurate on implementation in law and practice of treaties, yet accessible and succinct.

THE IRAQ WAR AND THE PROTECTION OF
CULTURAL HERITAGE UNDER INTERNATIONAL LAW

Cultural heritage exists worldwide under a variety of forms and legal and conceptual definitions. As UNESCO is the UN agency with a specific mandate in the field of culture, the international community within UNESCO has negotiated and adopted several conventions dealing with tangible cultural heritage (whether movable or immovable, on land, or underwater), intangible cultural heritage, and national cultural policies (1954, 1970, 1972, 2001, 2003, 2005).[4] In spite of their different scopes of application, all of these conventions share the same philosophy and objectives: the protection or safeguarding of cultural heritage.[5] A similar common philosophy exists at the national level under most domestic legislations covering cultural heritage.

The 1954 Hague Convention

The 1954 Convention represents the first international multilateral treaty focusing exclusively on the protection of cultural heritage in the event of armed conflict. Under the convention, States Parties undertake primarily to do the following:

1. They must undertake to prepare in times of peace to "safeguard" cultural property situated within their own territory against the foreseeable effects of an armed conflict by taking such measures as they consider appropriate (Article 4).
2. They must "respect" cultural property situated within their own territory as well as within the territory of other States Parties by refraining from any use of the property and its immediate surroundings or of the appliances in use for its protection for purposes that are likely to expose it to destruction or damage in the event of armed conflict, and by refraining from any act of hostility directed against such property. This obligation may be waived only in cases in which military necessity imperatively requires such a waiver (Article 5).
3. They must support as far as possible the competent national authorities of the occupied country (another State Party) in safeguarding and preserving its cultural property (Article 5).

Turning to the war in Iraq, the standing of international legal protection of cultural property appears somehow double-faced.

The Applicability of the 1954 Convention

On the one hand, the most common information refers to the looting of the Iraq Museum and later of a number of archaeological sites. It is regrettable that, though exceptionally, reference has been made to these events in terms of alleged violations of the 1954 Convention, even though it was not applicable in this conflict. Although Iraq is a State Party to the 1954 Convention and its First Protocol, other states are not parties to it, such as the United States and the United Kingdom. The convention is not binding upon non–States Parties belligerents. In these circumstances, real or alleged noncompliance with it does not, as such, amount to a "breach" of the Hague Convention by a state that has not consented to be bound by it.[6] This is true also for the 1954 First Protocol and 1999 Second Protocol to the Hague Convention, which were also not applicable in this conflict.[7]

Obviously, if the Hague Convention was not applicable as treaty-law, a distinct issue is whether customary international law exists with regard to armed conflict[8] and the events experienced in the war in Iraq and, if so, whether it was applicable in the circumstances and whether belligerents acted in line with it.

Providing a reliable answer to this distinct issue would require extensive research on and analysis of state practice (*usus*) and *opinio iuris*. While we undertook an endeavor of this kind with regard to a narrower issue (whether or not a customary obligation to return cultural property in case of armed conflict exists),[9] this article does not allow an additional endeavor with regard to this broader issue, which is whether or not a customary obligation to generally protect (beyond restitution) cultural property (movable *and* immovable) in case of armed conflict exists, and if so under what content and effects.

The International Committee of the Red Cross undertook a study of what may be considered, at least from the authors' perspective, customary international humanitarian law, including the protection of cultural heritage in armed conflict.[10]

Measures Taken on an Ad Hoc Basis
On the other hand, rather rapidly after the beginning of the conflict, the international community took serious steps for the protection of Iraq's cultural property and, from a legal perspective, adopted regulations both at the levels of the United Nations (UNSC Resolution) and European Union (EU Regulation[11]) with a view to facilitating restitution of cultural property illegally removed from Iraq.

Paragraph 7 of Resolution 1483 (2003) adopted by the Security Council on May 22, 2003, deserves to be mentioned here:

> 7. *Decides* that all Member States shall take appropriate steps to facilitate the safe return to Iraqi institutions of Iraqi cultural property and other items of archaeological, historical, cultural, rare scientific, and religious importance illegally removed from the Iraq National Museum, the National Library, and other locations in Iraq since the adoption of Resolution 661 (1990) of 6 August 1990, including by establishing a prohibition on trade in or transfer of such items and items with respect to which reasonable suspicion exists that they have been illegally removed,

and *calls upon* the United Nations Educational, Scientific, and Cultural Organization, Interpol, and other international organizations, as appropriate, to assist in the implementation of this paragraph.

This paragraph is important. It reflects and contributes to put into practice an international coordinated effort to facilitate restitution of Iraqi cultural property. It cannot be overemphasized that it intervenes on the restitution of cultural property, a field that is politically and culturally sensitive as well as legally complex, in both private[12] and public[13] international law.

These UN and EU regulations are ad hoc regulations, specifically addressing a given situation. As such, they are different from that of treaties presented briefly in this article. Their implementation framework in national law is also distinct. It reflects the different status of, respectively, the resolution of the UN Security Council and the regulations of the European Union in its member states.[14]

The Distinctiveness of Treaties

It is not infrequent to hear an all-encompassing reference to "conventions" and "protocols" in a given field, as is the case with protecting cultural heritage. However, to prevent misunderstandings and false expectations, it is a safe precaution to start from the basic idea that each legal text, be it of an international nature (for example, a convention or recommendation) or a domestic one (for example, a law or decree), is specific to its subject matter, its nature, and its needs, and thus is distinct in its scope, content, and legal effects. This variety of scope, objectives, content, and effects reflects the specificity of each legal text. These variety and specificity are a reality also within conceptually delimited areas, such as "cultural heritage" and its "protection."

DEFINING TREATIES

Conventions are international agreements among states.[15] Only within their scope of application[16] and according to their content do States Parties mutually recognize the existence of rights and obligations and are thus entitled to expect compliance as a result of a legal obligation, beyond a mere voluntary act or conduct.

One of the difficulties, especially for nonlawyers, arises with regard to terminology. It is a fact that those drafting the text, usually representatives of states, use a variety of terms, such as pacts, international agreements, charters, or covenants. What is actually meant by each of these terms is a matter of interpretation of the drafters' intention and should be assessed on a case-by-case basis. Generally, all of these terms refer to the elaboration of a written text whereby participating states agree to be bound through consent, which is usually expressed separately and at a later stage.

This basically amounts to a treaty—a binding agreement regulated by international law. For the sake of clarity, the definition of "treaty," as adopted by the 1969 Vienna Convention on the Law of Treaties, includes an international agreement concluded between states in written form and governed by international law, whether embodied in a single instrument or in two or more related instruments and whatever its particular designation (Article 2 (1), a).

Beyond this broad definition, the subject matter of a treaty may be extremely diverse, from peace treaties to the extradition of criminals to uniform private law, among other matters, and thus may require diverse political considerations as well as legal expertise, tools, and solutions.

IMPLEMENTATION VERSUS
OTHER TYPES OF A TREATY'S "IMPACT"

A treaty may have a variety of impacts. For instance, it may raise public awareness of the need to take measures referred to in the treaty. It may enhance and further understanding. Or it may lead relevant national authorities to explore new methods for accomplishing policy goals.

These examples of the impact of a treaty are not necessarily tantamount to its implementation. To prevent misunderstanding on "who does what" in the presence of a treaty (assuming it is in force for the State Party concerned), the term *implementation* gains in clarity if it is *reserved for national measures taken by national authorities as a direct consequence of the treaty and its substantive provisions.*

Most of these provisions are generally binding upon the State Party, and implementation serves as fulfillment of the obligation to take measures at the national level. In this sense, implementation is generally understood to refer to what the relevant treaty requires the State Party to do.

However, some other provisions may merely offer an option to a State Party, without compelling it to act. When national authorities decide to follow such options and give them effect domestically, this is also a form of implementation of the treaty, although the treaty itself does not strictly require it.

As an instrument of international law, the treaty addresses the State Party, and only its authorities play a role in terms of its implementation. In exceptional cases, the treaty grants specific implementation roles to individuals or private law entities.

This clarification is probably not superfluous. Indeed, the distinction between "state" and social constituencies and "civil society," as well as the significance of this distinction, for the purposes of international law, are not always uniformly clear or understood worldwide.

For instance, in ordinary situations, if an NGO located on the territory of a State Party finds inspiration in the preamble of the treaty to launch a public campaign, this act is not tantamount to a legal implementation of the treaty by the national authorities. Nonetheless, this campaign may qualify, broadly speaking, as an indirect and unofficial contribution to the implementation of the treaty to the extent that it may generate positive input, primarily in terms of raising public awareness, and facilitate the implementation of the treaty by national authorities.

JOINING THE TREATY PRECEDES IMPLEMENTATION

Treaties are the result of interstate negotiations that are often politically sensitive, legally complex, and time-consuming. Even more so are the negotiations of crucial multilateral treaties through an open-ended negotiation process, as within the United Nations. Assuming it is adopted by the relevant body, the draft treaty becomes the official treaty or convention at the end of the process.

However, the treaty becomes binding vis-à-vis a given state, and implementation is expected only once the treaty has reached the minimum number of ratifications[17] and thus entered into force (also) with regard to this State Party.

Clearly joining the treaty precedes implementation. Joining first requires a decision to join by national authorities, which includes deliberations on "political" considerations in addition to the necessary more "technical" ones, such as legal or economic issues, due to the subject matter of the treaty.

STANDARDS OF IMPLEMENTATION

How should a state, which joins a treaty and thus becomes "party" to it, implement it? There is no easy answer. Actually, presenting exclusively uniform implementation standards would be inaccurate.

Reality is more complex. Standards for implementation are in part codified in international law, and in part relative and depending on the nation and jurisdiction concerned.

General Standards

General standards of implementation at the national level for States Parties are codified in the 1969 Vienna Convention on the Law of Treaties. Such codification is certainly beneficial, primarily from the perspective of legal predictability. However, the uniform framework this codification achieves and generates is real only within its scope of application.

The main standards codified in 1969, and in part preexisting in customary law, may be summarized as follows:

1. Every treaty in force is binding upon the parties to it and must be performed by them in good faith (Article 26).
2. A party may not invoke the provisions of its internal law as justification for its failure to perform a treaty (Article 27).[18] The principles that a state may

not invoke its internal law to set aside an international obligation, and that it has to bring its domestic law into conformity with such obligations, are widely recognized.[19]

3. Unless a different intention appears from the treaty or is otherwise established, its provisions do not bind a party in relation to any act or fact that took place or any situation that ceased to exist before the date of the entry into force of the treaty with respect to that party (Article 28).

4. Unless a different intention appears from the treaty or is otherwise established, a treaty is binding upon each party in respect of its entire territory (Article 29).

Indeed, the majority of treaties express no different drafters' intention, and thus apply to the whole territory of a State Party. For instance, this is also the case of the 1999 Second Protocol to the 1954 Hague Convention. However, the 1954 Hague Convention includes a provision that enables States Parties to limit the territorial extension of the convention's application. In this case the convention binds national authorities for implementation purposes only with regard to the part of the state's territory which has not been excluded (Article 35).

Relative Standards and National Variables of Implementation

While national law differs from state to state, international law is often understood as "universal" law. This view is excessively generous in the scope it grants to international law.

Actually, treaties apply only among their States Parties—those states that express their consent to be bound by them, primarily, but not exclusively, through ratification.

Customary international law, generally seen as evidence of a general practice accepted as law, requires particular care in handling it in order to prevent false statements regarding its existence, content, and applicability in a given situation. It is relevant only insofar as it is deemed to exist with regard to the relevant issue, and only insofar as the state concerned has not expressed an opposition from the start of that custom.

In addition to the specificity of each treaty and custom with regard to their existence, applicability, and scope, implementation of each treaty or custom is not universally uniform but is influenced by national variables and specificities. Depending on the state and jurisdiction concerned, these variables may include a number of key issues, such as the following:

1. Who interprets the international law provisions to be implemented and under what criteria? For instance, one issue is identifying the "right" balance between textuality and contextuality in interpretation of written provisions, which is the normal form for treaties but not necessarily for customary developments, until they reach some sort of formalization.

2. What impact do checks and balances and separation of powers doctrines have on constitutions and treaties?
3. What is the significance of various categories of international treaties or agreements? An example is the distinction between "treaty" and "executive agreement" in the United States.
4. What form of legalization in domestic law does a treaty require, considering that a treaty is generally seen as non-self-executing? Once this form is identified (generally as "implementing legislation") and used, distinct issues are the status of the treaty provision with regard to other sources of law at the domestic level, as well as with regard to subsequent law (*lex posterior*, among others).

How each of these issues is dealt with depends on each nation and its legal system. For instance, the impact of checks and balances and separation of powers doctrines on the U.S. Constitution and treaties is particularly important in the United States,[20] while it is less so in other nations.

Beyond implementation, another relevant variable is whether the state concerned wishes to use reservations.[21] If so, the reservation would exclude or modify the legal effect of certain provisions of the treaty.[22]

THE NEED FOR AN INTEGRATED AND MULTI-INSTITUTIONAL APPROACH TO IMPLEMENTATION

The specific subject matter of each treaty makes some entities within the government, and then some groups within the parliament, more concerned than others. Federal systems need additional care to ensure an integrated and multi-institutional approach to implement treaties at the national level.

Depending on the subject matter of a treaty and political sensitivity, one ministry or agency takes the lead in proposing a treaty for ratification and in the preparation of its implementation at the national level. As such, it may but does not necessarily cooperate with other ministries or agencies that may be concerned, although more incidentally, with at least some of the aspects and provisions of the treaty and its implementation.

In this case, the degree of integrated implementation is low and some provisions of the treaty may suffer from a weak implementation. It may occur more or less frequently depending on a number of factors, such as the following:

1. the government structures and legislature-government relationships in the state concerned
2. the technical and legal expertise available, which affect, among others, the degree of accuracy in the analysis of the treaty
3. the cooperation skills between different relevant ministries or agencies
4. the degree of commitment or interest of the various stakeholders

In the field of cultural heritage protection, generally the ministry of culture stands at the forefront. It does so at least in terms of initiative to request consideration of the treaty in view of its ratification and, if the decision to ratify is taken, to ensure its proper implementation. Practice shows that in some countries budgetary considerations may extend or limit further action of the ministry of culture within the government or vis-à-vis parliamentary bodies, or both.

This role in terms of initiative should not be confused with implementation responsibility. Generally speaking, it would be erroneous to expect that a ministry of culture is exclusively and automatically in charge of, and actually responsible for, the implementation at the national level of all the substantive provisions of the treaty[23] related to culture.

An example is provided by the 1954 Hague Convention, in its Article 7 on military measures, which reads as follows:

1. The High Contracting Parties undertake to introduce in time of peace into their military regulations or instructions such provisions as may ensure observance of the present Convention, and to foster in the members of their armed forces a spirit of respect for the culture and cultural property of all peoples.

2. The High Contracting Parties undertake to plan or establish in peace-time, within their armed forces, services or specialist personnel whose purpose will be to secure respect for cultural property and to co-operate with the civilian authorities responsible for safeguarding it.

These two crucial elements—introduction of relevant provisions into military regulations and planning or establishing specialist personnel within the armed forces—are not likely to be effectively implemented by the ministry of culture alone. Operationally, they generally belong to the competence of the ministry of defense.

Constructive and fruitful cooperation between the two ministries (or equivalent agencies) is necessary from the time draft-implementing legislation is being considered. This cooperation should be continued during the (numerous) years of the implementing legislation's operation, and should be strengthened in case a conflict becomes a potential threat. Obviously, this cooperation is a fact and common practice in some countries, but this optimism should not be generalized to any country, to any time, and to any treaty.

Similar needs of cooperation exist between the ministries of culture and justice (or equivalent agencies), in particular with regard to sanctions in case of violation of a treaty. This need appears ever-increasing as several treaties tend to strengthen sanctions and related mechanisms.

A useful example is provided by the 1954 Hague Convention and its 1999 Second Protocol. The former referred only to the steps to be taken to prosecute and impose penal or disciplinary sanctions upon those persons, of whatever nationality, who commit or order to be committed a breach of the convention (Article 28). Quite differently, forty-five years later and in light of remarkable developments in international humanitarian law, the drafters of the 1999 Protocol went as far as establishing a Chapter (IV) on criminal responsibility and jurisdiction. This set of provisions has ramifications on issues as important as universal jurisdiction, prosecution, extradition, and legal assistance among States Parties.[24]

It cannot be overemphasized to what extent the proper implementation of these provisions requires the involvement of all relevant stakeholders, primarily the ministries of culture and justice, at least from the time implementing legislation is considered.

In federal systems, the legislative power is distributed between a central legislature and a number of provincial legislatures, and both levels have spheres of competence. These systems need even more attention in devising suitable mechanisms to ensure such an integrated and multi-institutional approach of implementation of treaties at the national level.

Obviously, serious and integrated implementation is key to achieving the treaty's objectives. This holds true also for the protection of cultural property in the case of armed conflict under the 1954 Hague Convention.

While this convention is not applicable to the war in Iraq, other conflicts have benefited and it is hoped, for the sake of preservation of cultural heritage, many others will benefit from the applicability and proper implementation of this convention and its protocols.

Generally and also beyond situations of armed conflict, it cannot be overemphasized that prompt, serious, and integrated implementation is the best guarantee for any treaty to reach its aims at the national level.

NOTES

1. For instance, Adam Roberts, "Transformative Military Occupation: Applying the Laws of War and Human Rights," *American Journal of International Law* 100, no. 3 (2006): 580.
2. See recently, W. Michael Reisman and Andrea Armstrong, "The Past and Future of the Claim of Preemptive Self-Defense," *AJIL* 100, no. 3 (2006): 525.
3. See sections "The Iraq War and the Protection of Cultural Heritage under International Law" and "Joining the Treaty Precedes Implementation."
4. See http://portal.unesco.org/culture.
5. Safeguarding, in particular, with reference to intangible cultural heritage under the 2003 Convention.
6. Assuming that not only the consent to be bound, but also the signature of the treaty or the exchange of the instruments constituting the treaty have not taken place, there is no obligation for states not to defeat the object and purpose of a treaty prior to its entry into force (1969 Vienna Convention on the Law of Treaties, Art. 18).

7. On these instruments see Jiří Toman, *The Protection of Cultural Property in the Event of Armed Conflict: Commentary on the Convention for the Protection of Cultural Property in the Event of Armed Conflict and Its Protocol, signed on 14 May 1954 in The Hague, and on other Instruments of International Law Concerning such Protection* (Brookfield, VT: Dartmouth Publishing Company/UNESCO, 1996); Patrick K. O'Keefe, "The First Protocol to the Hague Convention Fifty Years On," *Art Antiquity and Law* IX, no. 2 (2004): 99. On the relationships between the 1954 Protocol, states' practice, (ad hoc and codification) treaties and customary law, see Guido Carducci, "L'obligation de restitution des biens culturels et des objets d'art en cas de conflit armé : droit coutumier et droit conventionnel avant et après la Convention de La Haye de 1954 (L'importance du facteur temporel dans les rapports entre les traités et la coutume)," *Revue Générale de Droit International Public* (2000): 289.

8. See Stanislaw E. Nahlik, "La protection internationale des biens culturels en cas de conflit armé," in *Recueil des Cours de l'Académie de Droit International (La Haye)* [Hague Academy of International Law Collected Courses], 120, no. II (1967): 61–163. More generally, Pietro Verri, "Le destin des biens culturels dans les conflits armés," *Revue internationale de la Croix-Rouge* 752 (1985): 67–85 and 753 (1985): 127–39.

9. See Carducci, "L'obligation."

10. Jean-Marie Henckaerts and Louise Doswald-Beck, eds., *Customary International Humanitarian Law* (Cambridge, UK: Cambridge University Press, 2005).

11. Council Regulation 1210/2003 of July 7, 2003, concerning certain specific restrictions on economic and financial relations with Iraq and repealing Regulation (EC) 2465/96.

12. See Guido Carducci, *La restitution internationale des biens culturels et des objets d'art. Droit commun, Directive CEE, Conventions de l'UNESCO et d'UNIDROIT* (Paris: LGDJ, 1997); Georges Droz, "La Convention d'Unidroit sur le retour international des biens culturels volés ou illicitement exportés (Rome, 24 juin 1995)," *Revue Critique de Droit International Privé* 86 (1997): 239; Lyndel V. Prott, "Problems of Private International Law for the Protection of the Cultural Heritage," *Hague Academy of International Law Collected Courses* 217, no. V (1989): 219; Kurt Siehr, "International Art Trade and the Law," *Hague Academy of International Law Collected Courses* 243, no. VI(1993): 9.

13. See Carducci, "L'obligation."

14. See Guido Carducci, "The Growing Complexity of International Art Law: Conflict of Laws, Uniform Law, Mandatory Rules, UNSC Resolutions and EU Regulations," in *Art and Cultural Heritage: Law, Policy and Practice*, ed. Barbara T. Hoffman (Cambridge, UK: Cambridge University Press, 2005), 68–86.

15. More exceptionally, international organizations.

16. For instance, for the purposes of the 1954 Hague Convention, the term *cultural property* covers, irrespective of origin or ownership,

   (a) movable or immovable property of great importance to the cultural heritage of every people, such as monuments of architecture, art or history, whether religious or secular; archaeological sites; groups of buildings which, as a whole, are of historical or artistic interest; works of art; manuscripts, books and other objects of artistic, historical, or archaeological interest; as well as scientific collections and important collections of books or archives or of reproductions of the property defined above;

(b) buildings whose main and effective purpose is to preserve or exhibit the movable cultural property defined in subparagraph (a) such as museums, large libraries, and depositories of archives, and refuges intended to shelter, in the event of armed conflict, the movable cultural property defined in subparagraph (a);

(c) centers containing a large amount of cultural property as defined in subparagraphs (a) and (b), to be known as "centers containing monuments."

17. This number varies depending on the instrument.

18. It should be added that this rule is without prejudice to Article 46 (Provisions of internal law regarding competence to conclude treaties) which reads as follows:

1. A State may not invoke the fact that its consent to be bound by a treaty has been expressed in violation of a provision of its internal law regarding competence to conclude treaties as invalidating its consent unless that violation was manifest and concerned a rule of its internal law of fundamental importance.

2. A violation is manifest if it would be objectively evident to any State conducting itself in the matter in accordance with normal practice and in good faith.

19. Generally, Ian Brownlie, *Principles of Public International Law*, 6th ed. (Oxford: Oxford University Press, 2003), 34.

20. See John Norton Moore, ed., *The National Law of Treaty Implementation* (Durham, NC: Carolina Academic Press, 2001).

21. When signing, ratifying, accepting, approving, or acceding to the treaty.

22. 1969 Vienna Convention, Art. 2, 1 (d).

23. Leaving aside primarily the final clauses and any other provision not to be implemented.

24. See Articles 15 (Serious violations of the Protocol), 16 (Jurisdiction), 17 (Prosecution), 18 (Extradition), 19 (Mutual legal assistance), 20 (Grounds for refusal), and 21 (Measures regarding other violations).

THE WAY FORWARD

For Legislative Bodies and Military Commanders: Beyond Implementing International Law

WHILE INTERNATIONAL LAW IS THE MOST EXPLICIT INSTRUMENTALITY FOR DEALING with cultural heritage protection in the event of armed conflict, legislative bodies also have the power to take a number of steps independent of the specific regimens prescribed by international law. International law in itself does not compel military compliance, even when national legislation is in place to implement it, because military commanders have powers of their own determined by the chain of command. In this section, contributors describe a variety of domestic measures, over and above the crafting of implementing legislation, that could be undertaken in support of a more robust policy of wartime heritage protection.

CHAPTER 9

Congressional Responses to the Looting of Iraq's Cultural Property

PATTY GERSTENBLITH AND KATHARYN HANSON

THE ROLE OF CONGRESS IN PREVENTING WAR-RELATED LOOTING GOES BEYOND ratifying international conventions concerning the laws of war. Congress can take a variety of other steps, including legislative measures, appropriations, and oversight of executive-branch operations. Congress's most powerful instrument for effectuating policy is, of course, the enactment of laws.

In the case of antiquities looted abroad, the U.S. legal regime addressing the international movement in stolen and illegally exported cultural objects deals with such objects, to a large extent, as a problem of trade and importation. This is hardly surprising, since regulation of interstate and international commerce is a power granted to Congress under the Constitution, providing the authority for federal legislation on the trading of antiquities. In principle, prohibiting the importation from war-ravaged countries of undocumented antiquities, which are likely to have been looted, should decrease demand in the United States for such artifacts, thereby reducing the economic incentive to loot sites.

Because trade laws already on the books are such a big part of the picture, we begin by reviewing existing U.S. legislation that addresses the trade in illicitly excavated archaeological artifacts, regardless of whether such artifacts are the spoils of war. As we shall see, the special conditions faced by countries at war, and the nature of the legislation itself, make it a relatively weak tool for deterring postcombat looting of antiquities. We then go on to analyze the U.S. legislative response to the looting of the Iraq Museum and the ongoing looting of archaeological sites in Iraq. Finally, we consider what other types of actions Congress can take to discourage the looting of archaeological sites.

PREVIOUSLY EXISTING TRADE LEGISLATION

The first international convention to address the trade in stolen and illegally exported cultural objects was the 1970 UNESCO Convention on the Means of Prohibiting and Preventing the Illicit Import, Export and Transfer of Ownership of Cultural Property (1970 UNESCO Convention).[1] One of the first market nations to ratify this convention, the United States enacted implementing legislation, the Convention on Cultural Property Implementation Act (CPIA), in 1983.[2] The United States adopted only two provisions of the UNESCO Convention, Article 7(b) and Article 9.

To implement Article 7, Section 2607 of the CPIA prohibits the import of stolen cultural property that had been documented as part of the inventory of a museum or similar public institution.[3] Objects stolen from museums in Iraq[4] fall under this provision of the CPIA so long as the documentation is available to establish that the object was part of the museum's inventory. However, the inventory records of the Iraq Museum were severely compromised in the ransacking of 2003, and some artifacts had not been inventoried. This lack of complete documentation complicates the effort to recover artifacts looted from the museum. Moreover, the CPIA carries no criminal penalties, as it is purely a civil statute, and the only remedy for a violation is forfeiture and restitution of the objects.

Article 9 of the 1970 UNESCO Convention is intended to provide a mechanism by which States Parties will provide assistance to each other in cases of pillage of archaeological and ethnological materials.[5] Under the CPIA, another State Party that wishes to avail itself of the protections of Article 9 must submit a request to the United States for a bilateral agreement for the imposition of U.S. import restrictions on looted archaeological and ethnological materials. The process by which such import restrictions may be imposed is lengthy, complex, and burdensome to the requesting nation. The nation must prepare a request and provide supporting evidence that addresses the four statutory requirements for a bilateral agreement.[6]

The request is then referred to the Cultural Property Advisory Committee,[7] which makes recommendations to the assistant secretary of state for educational and cultural affairs, to whom the president has delegated the authority to make the final decision as to whether to negotiate an agreement. If the statutory criteria are satisfied, the United States enters into negotiations to finalize a bilateral agreement. Once import restrictions are in place, objects that fall into the designated categories may only be imported into the United States if they are accompanied by an export certificate from the country of origin or if the importer can demonstrate that the artifacts left the country of origin before the effective date of the import restriction. These agreements last a maximum of five years, but they may be renewed an unlimited number of times.[8]

The second provision of the CPIA allows the United States to impose unilateral import restrictions, without the negotiation of an agreement, in case of an "emergency." The CPIA describes three circumstances that constitute an "emergency condition."[9] However, this provision is available *only* if the other State Party has already submitted a request for a bilateral agreement, something unlikely to be done by a state on the verge of war, or in a state of war—and especially unlikely if the war in view is with the United States! For a nation in the process of collapse during a war, moreover, the notion that a request on this issue would be forthcoming is entirely unrealistic. In short, despite its name, the emergency provisions are not at all suited to allowing the U.S. government to respond expeditiously in many cases of cultural heritage crises caused by war.

The case of Iraq illustrates this problem. Even though Iraq is a party to the 1970 UNESCO Convention, it was not able to bring a request for import restrictions once the looting of sites became a problem in the decade of the 1990s because such requests must be submitted through diplomatic channels. Because the United States and Iraq did not have diplomatic relations during this time period, it was not possible for Iraq to submit a request. Although diplomatic relations between the United States and Iraq were reestablished after the 2003 war, it has still not been possible for Iraq to bring such a request forward, at first because of a lack of clear governmental authority to do so, and now because of the continuing chaotic situation.

In addition to the CPIA, other statutory mechanisms exist to deter trade in and handling of looted archaeological objects. The most useful of these general laws is the National Stolen Property Act (NSPA), which prohibits the transport interstate or across international boundaries, as well as the receipt and possession, of stolen property.[10] Objects that are stolen from institutions are clearly categorized as stolen property, and anyone who knowingly handles such objects is violating the NSPA.

The NSPA also applies to archaeological artifacts whose ownership is vested in the nation. If an object is excavated and removed from that nation without consent of the government, then the object is stolen property and retains that characterization after it is brought to the United States. This legal principle was first formulated in the decision *United States v. McClain*[11] and was reaffirmed in the conviction of prominent New York antiquities dealer Frederick Schultz for conspiring to deal in antiquities stolen from Egypt.[12] For illegally exported antiquities to be considered stolen property under U.S. law, the *Schultz* decision establishes two criteria: the nation where the artifacts are discovered must have a statute that clearly vests ownership of such artifacts in the nation, and the national ownership law must be enforced within the country claiming ownership, not just after export. Iraq has had a strong national ownership law since 1936,[13] which clearly vests ownership of antiquities in the nation of Iraq.

Given the clear statement of national ownership in the Iraqi antiquities law and what is known of internal enforcement of this law, at least prior to the war in Iraq in 2003, archaeological artifacts removed from Iraqi sites are stolen property and anyone who knowingly deals in, possesses, or transfers such objects (if they are worth more than $5,000) would be violating the National Stolen Property Act. The import of such objects would also be barred under the customs statute, which prohibits the import of goods "contrary to law."[14] Objects that are imported into the United States by means of false statements are also subject to seizure and forfeiture.[15]

Despite the availability of prosecution and forfeiture under the NSPA, it did not provide the clear deterrent effect necessary to discourage trade in looted artifacts from Iraq, because the criteria set out in the *Schultz* decision had not been applied in court to Iraq. U.S. courts would need to analyze the Iraqi ownership law, and the testimony of Iraqi officials as to how the law was internally enforced would be required. This left open the possibility of some uncertainty as to how the NSPA might apply.

EMERGENCY LEGISLATIVE MEASURES IN RESPONSE TO THE IRAQ CRISIS

A month after the news of the looting of the Iraq Museum and other cultural repositories in Iraq, Representative Phil English (R-PA) introduced a bill, the Iraq Cultural Heritage Protection Act, H.R. 2009, on May 7, 2003.[16] In light of the looting of Iraq's cultural repositories, the destruction of the Iraq Museum's inventory documentation, the incipient looting of archaeological sites, and Iraq's inability to bring a request for import restrictions under the CPIA,[17] this legislation was intended to provide a quick method of imposing import restrictions on looted archaeological materials from Iraq.

In addition to imposing import restrictions directly on Iraqi cultural materials, H.R. 2009 also sought to amend the CPIA in various ways so that the U.S. government would be in a position to respond quickly and efficiently to future similar emergency situations without the need to enact new, special legislation. To this end, H.R. 2009 proposed to eliminate the need for a country to request a bilateral agreement in order for the United States to impose import restrictions under the emergency provisions of the CPIA; it expanded the definition of archaeological materials to include artifacts that are a minimum of one hundred years old to better fit the definitions used by many other countries, and it would have permitted other countries that are not party to the UNESCO Convention to receive emergency protection.

The art market community marshaled its lobbying forces to oppose H.R. 2009.[18] In response, Congressman English attempted to forge compromise legislation, H.R. 3497, which was introduced in November 17, 2003. As a compromise, H.R. 3497 left the definition of coins that could be covered by CPIA import restrictions as a minimum of 250 years old. H.R. 3497 also proposed adding an additional seat to the Cultural Property Advisory Committee for a third museum representative in a bid to win support from the museum community. However, support was not forthcoming and neither H.R. 3497 nor H.R. 2009 was acted on in committee.

By late May 2003 and while H.R. 2009 was stalled in the House, the international community took action to ban trade in illegally exported cultural materials from Iraq. All goods, including cultural objects, from Iraq had been barred from entry into the United States since August of 1990 under the general sanctions.[19] United Nations Security Council Resolution 1483, passed on May 22, 2003, called for the lifting of those sanctions. However, it also provides in paragraph 7 that the Security Council

> [d]ecides that all Member States shall take appropriate steps to facilitate the safe return to Iraqi institutions of Iraqi cultural property and other items of archaeological, historical, cultural, rare scientific, and religious importance illegally removed from the Iraq National Museum, the National Library, and other locations in Iraq since the adoption of Resolution 661 (1990) of 6 August 1990, including by establishing a prohibition on trade in or transfer of such items and items with respect to which reasonable suspicion exists that they have been illegally removed, and calls upon the United Nations Educational, Scientific, and Cultural Organization, Interpol, and other international organizations, as appropriate, to assist in the implementation of this paragraph.[20]

This provision calls on all United Nations member states to prohibit trade in and to adopt other means to ensure return to Iraq of all cultural objects, not just those taken from the museums and other public institutions, but also those taken from other locations including archaeological sites.

On May 23, 2003, the day after UNSCR 1483 was passed, the United States lifted trade sanctions on goods from Iraq by granting a general license for such goods. However, certain goods were exempted from this general license, including "Iraqi cultural property or other items of archaeological, historical, cultural, rare scientific, and religious importance. . . . Any trade in or transfer of such items remains prohibited."[21]

A more permanent means of prohibiting import of stolen or illegally removed Iraqi cultural materials was provided by passage of the Emergency Protection for Iraqi Cultural Antiquities Act (EPIC Antiquities Act) in late 2004.[22] Senator Charles Grassley, Republican of Iowa and chair of the Senate Finance Committee, introduced S. 1291 in June 2003. As a narrower competing bill to H.R. 2009, the Senate bill received less support from the archaeological community but also less objection from the market community. This legislation authorizes the president to exercise his authority under the CPIA to prohibit import of designated archaeological and ethnological materials from Iraq without need for Iraq to bring a request under the CPIA for a bilateral agreement.[23] This legislation is notable for adapting the CPIA definitions of the archaeological and ethnological materials of Iraq so that they would be in accord with UNSCR 1483 in place of the normal CPIA definitions of these types of materials.[24] Only coin collectors and dealers openly opposed the Senate bill because it failed to exclude coins and other numismatic materials from coverage. This legislation fulfills the United States' obligations under Article 48 of the United Nations Charter to implement this Security Council Resolution.[25]

S. 1291 was ultimately enacted with minor modifications as part of the Miscellaneous Trade and Technical Corrections Act, S. 671. The only remarks on the legislation came from Senator Grassley when he proposed the legislation in the Senate and again in the Senate conference report:

> The purpose of this bill is simply to close a legal loophole which could allow looted Iraqi antiquities to be brought into the U.S. If Congress does not act to provide the means for establishing an interim ban on trade, the door may be opened to imports of looted Iraqi antiquities into the United States. Already the press has reported allegations that European auction houses have traded in looted Iraqi antiquities. The last thing that we in Congress want to do is to fail to act to prevent trade in looted Iraqi artifacts here in the United States.[26]

While Congress did act with deliberate speed, the Bush administration has dragged its feet with regard to implementing the new law. In interpreting this legislation, a new delegation of authority from the president to the assistant secretary of state for educational and cultural affairs was required. This delegation was not completed until February of 2007.[27] One can only assume that the authority to impose import restrictions will be exercised soon. If a comparable crisis situation were to occur in Iran, Syria, or some other country, of course, this legislation would be useful only as a model, as it applies only to Iraq.

The only non-trade-related congressional action in response to the looting in Iraq was a recommendation, tucked into the Senate report accompanying the appropriations bill, for the creation of a cultural antiquities task force. The Appropriations Committee suggested $500,000 for this task force to help prevent further looting, to create a database of those involved in the looting, to aid in cataloguing lost objects, and to ensure the United States was in cooperation with similar international efforts.[28] With Democrats now in charge of Congress, a much more generous funding measure has been offered. In an appropriations bill introduced in this Congress, the Bring the Troops Home and Iraq Sovereignty Restoration Act of 2007, the president would be authorized to provide assistance in recovering ancient artifacts and restoring sites of cultural, historical, and archaeological significance in Iraq. The bill would appropriate $250 million in fiscal year 2008 for these purposes.[29]

LESSONS LEARNED FOR THE FUTURE

Several lessons have been learned from these legislative efforts and we may formulate some suggestions for quicker and more appropriate responses on the part of the U.S. government in case of a future emergency situation. The first lesson is that the CPIA is entirely inadequate as a response to an emergency situation involving looting of either cultural institutions or archaeological sites. Despite its name, the emergency provision of the CPIA is a misnomer in that it does not permit the president to impose import restrictions in a timely and efficacious manner as a response to an emergency situation. H.R. 2009 was an attempt not only to respond to the crisis situation in Iraq but to give the president the flexibility and authority to impose import restrictions in case of a future crisis. However, the lobbying efforts of those who represent the market community were too powerful to overcome, and so the EPIC Antiquities Act applies only to Iraq and will not be useful in a future situation. The second lesson is that the preservationist community can and will be out-lobbied by the market community and so relying on the enactment of new legislation is not a sufficient response. The only thing that prevented the import of looted artifacts from Iraq into the United States and other market nations was the enactment of the UN Security Council Resolution and the pre-existing sanctions. One cannot rely on these fortuitous circumstances in the future.

A third lesson is the difficulty of distinguishing cultural artifacts from ordinary commodities and thereby convincing the trade subcommittees in Congress that a free trade philosophy is not appropriately applied to cultural objects. Because the initial goal is to prevent looted artifacts from entering the United States thereby denying a major market outlet, the problem has been addressed through trade legislation and interdiction at the border. This creates the anomaly that the CPIA is administered by the State Department, but oversight of the legislation is from the two trade subcommittees—of the Ways and Means Committee in the House and the Finance Committee in the Senate. This creates conflict and tension as to the goals of such legislation and the best means of achieving those goals. For example, the House subcommittee staff in particular were resistant to providing assistance through trade restrictions on looted artifacts and were reluctant to permit H.R. 2009 to move forward.

It is likely that the Senate Foreign Relations Committee and the House Committee on International Relations would be more sympathetic to the concerns of nations whose heritage is subject to pillage and looting, but it is very difficult to change congressional committee oversight. The most that one could perhaps do is to create concurrent oversight jurisdiction to include both the respective House and Senate trade and foreign relations committees. However, this additional oversight would not remove the free trade bias of the trade subcommittees and might make any legislative improvements subject to even more bureaucratic entanglement and additional lobbying efforts by those in opposition. Finally, it is very difficult to get the committee and subcommittee chairs to commit time for hearings on legislation involving cultural heritage, because this is simply not seen as a sufficiently high priority. On the other hand, it is unlikely that any substantive change to the CPIA or comparable legislation would be considered without hearings, giving all parties the opportunity to voice their views. This creates a Catch-22 situation in which the likelihood of legislative progress seems dim.

Perhaps the most substantive congressional action would be Senate ratification of the 1954 Hague Convention on the Protection of Cultural Property in the Event of Armed Conflict and the full First Protocol.[30] Ratification of the main convention would clarify to the U.S. military its obligations to train and educate the troops about cultural heritage preservation, would require the U.S. military to maintain personnel who are equipped and trained to help in preservation efforts, and would require the U.S. military to incorporate cultural heritage preservation priorities into the earliest stages of all its planning. The First Protocol prohibits the illegal removal of cultural objects from occupied territory and obligates nations to return illegally removed cultural objects, thereby discouraging trade in looted artifacts and reducing the incentive to loot sites. U.S. obligations under the First Protocol would apply to any other country that is a State Party and would solve the dilemma of trying to enact country-specific legislation in the midst of a crisis situation.

Another positive action that Congress could take would be the permanent funding of the Cultural Antiquities Task Force. Such permanent funding would permit the task force to plan for cultural heritage protection on a more consistent basis. The profile of the task force within the government could be raised so that it would play a respected role in planning for the protection of cultural heritage in future military actions and postwar stabilization.

Other actions could also be taken to raise the profile of cultural heritage issues in Congress. Probably the most useful would be formation of a congressional caucus on international cultural heritage preservation. While such a caucus has no direct authority, it would provide a group of sympathetic senators and representatives to whom lobbying overtures could be made when legislation is pending, and it would help bring public attention to these issues.

Although there is currently little congressional interest in holding hearings on the issue of cultural heritage preservation, a cultural heritage caucus could help raise congressional awareness and interest levels with hearings as a future goal. Congressional hearings would offer the opportunity to assess threatened cultural heritage prior to an armed conflict. For example, a congressional hearing in the armed services committee would be able to investigate the number of trained civil affairs cultural heritage specialists and their funding. Another possibility would be a congressional committee requesting a funding report, such as an Appropriations Committee request of the Department of Defense or State Department.

The biggest obstacle to achieving any change is that of relative importance; for any action to occur, the public must view the issues of stolen and looted cultural property as important. Now in the midst of intense and escalating violence, Iraq's cultural property has disappeared from public attention. Why should legislators concern themselves with some "old pots" when the human tragedy is so pressing?

Although not well known by the general public, the potential benefits of preserving Iraq's cultural property should persuade popular opinion to include it as a priority in U.S. policy. From the scientific, historical, and cultural perspective, artifacts are irreplaceable objects of archaeological significance that can shed light on a myriad of questions about the ancient world as well as the present. When looted or otherwise taken out of context, artifacts irretrievably lose their historic, cultural, and scientific value, retaining only their commercial and aesthetic value as art objects.

NOTE

1. November 17, 1970, 823 U.N.T.S. 231, 10 I.L.M. 289 (1971). The text is available at http://portal.unesco.org/en/ev.phpURL_ID=13039&URL_DO=DO_TOPIC&URL_SECTION=201.html.

2. 19 U.S.C. §§ 2601–13.

3. The CPIA states: "No article of cultural property documented as appertaining to the inventory of a museum or religious or secular public monument or similar institution in any State Party which is stolen from such institution after the effective date of this title, or after the date of entry into force of the Convention for the State Party, whichever date is later, may be imported into the United States." 19 U.S.C. § 2607.

4. Iraq ratified the 1970 UNESCO Convention in 1973. Therefore objects stolen from museums after 1983 fit the criteria of this provision.

5. Article 9 states:

Any State Party to this Convention whose cultural patrimony is in jeopardy from pillage of archaeological or ethnological materials may call upon other States Parties who are affected. The States Parties to this Convention undertake, in these circumstances, to participate in a concerted international effort to determine and to carry out the necessary concrete measures, including the control of exports and imports and international commerce in the specific materials concerned. Pending agreement each State concerned shall take provisional measures to the extent feasible to prevent irremediable injury to the cultural heritage of the requesting State.

6. 19 U.S.C. § 2602. The four determinations are (1) whether the cultural patrimony of the requesting nation is in jeopardy from the pillage of archaeological or ethnological materials; (2) whether the requesting nation has taken measures consistent with the UNESCO Convention to protect its cultural patrimony; (3) whether other nations with an import trade in the archaeological or ethnological materials are taking similar measures to restrict the import of such materials, and (4) whether the imposition of import restrictions will further the exchange of cultural materials between the requesting nation and the United States (19 U.S.C. § 2602 (a)(1)(A)-(D)). There is an exception to the third determination that allows the United States to take action even in the absence of other nations' actions if the U.S. import restrictions by themselves would be of substantial benefit in deterring the situation of pillage (19 U.S.C. § 2602 (c)(2)).

7. The Cultural Property Advisory Committee consists of eleven members, appointed by the president. Three represent the interests of the archaeological/anthropological community, three represent dealers, two represent museums, and three represent the public.

8. For a list of current and expired import restrictions, see the website of the U.S. State Department: http://www.exchanges.state.gov/culprop.

9. The CPIA provides:

[T]he term "emergency condition" means, with respect to any archaeological or ethnological material of any State Party, that such material is—
   1. a newly discovered type of material which is of importance for the understanding of the history of mankind and is in jeopardy from pillage, dismantling, dispersal, or fragmentation;
   2. identifiable as coming from any site recognized to be of high cultural significance if such site is in jeopardy from pillage, dismantling, dispersal, or fragmentation which is, or threatens to be, of crisis proportions; or
   3. a part of the remains of a particular culture or civilization, the record of which is in jeopardy from pillage, dismantling, dispersal, or fragmentation which is, or threatens to be, of crisis proportions;
   and application of the import restrictions . . . on a temporary basis would, in whole or in part, reduce the incentive for such pillage, dismantling, dispersal or fragmentation. (19 U.S.C. § 2603(a))

The other requirements for a bilateral agreement, such as the concerted action requirement, do not apply to emergency actions. Import restrictions pursuant to an emergency action may last initially only five years; they may be renewed for a maximum of three additional years only one time, in contrast with a bilateral agreement which can have an unlimited number of renewals.

10. The National Stolen Property Act states:

Whoever receives, possesses, conceals, stores, barters, sells, or disposes of any goods, wares, or merchandise, securities or money of the value of $5000 or more . . . which have crossed a State or United States boundary after being stolen, unlawfully converted, or taken, knowing the same to have been stolen, unlawfully converted, or taken . . . shall be fined under this title or imprisoned not more than ten years, or both. (18 U.S.C. § 2315)

The other section of the National Stolen Property Act states:

Whoever transports, transmits, or transfers in interstate or foreign commerce any goods, wares, merchandise, securities or money, of the value of $5,000 or more, knowing the same to have been stolen, converted or taken by fraud . . . shall be fined under this title or imprisoned not more than ten years, or both. (18 U.S.C. § 2314)

11. 545 F.2d 988 (5th Cir. 1977), 593 F.2d 658 (5th Cir. 1979). The *McClain* decision was presaged by the conviction of a dealer in *United States v. Hollinshead*, 495 F.2d 1154 (9th Cir. 1974), which involved the transport of portions of a Maya stele from Guatemala.

12. *United States v. Schultz*, 333 F.3d 393 (2d Cir. 2003).

13. Antiquities Law No. 59 of 1936, and the Two Amendments, No. 120 of 1974 and No. 164 of 1975. Article 3 states: "All antiquities in Iraq whether movable or immovable that are now on or under the surface of the soil shall be considered to be the common property of the State. No individuals or groups are allowed to dispose of such property or claim the ownership thereof except under the provisions of this Law." *Antiquities* are defined as "Movable and Immovable possessions which were erected, made, produced, sculptured, written, drawn or photographed by man, if they are two hundred years old or more" (Article 1(1)(e)). Movable and immovable property less than 200 years old may be considered antiquities "if the public interest requires its protection, due to its historical, national, religious or artistic value" (Article 1(2)).

14. 19 U.S.C. §1595(a)(c); 18 U.S.C. § 545. These provisions are relevant if the merchandise is considered to be stolen property under the NSPA or if some other illegal act is involved in the importation.

15. 18 U.S.C. § 542. The American author Joseph Braude was charged with three counts for smuggling and making false statements in violation of 18 U.S.C. § 545. When he entered the United States on June 11, 2003, Braude was found to be carrying three cylinder seals of the Akkadian period (ca. 2340–2180 B.C.), which were taken from the collection of the Iraq Museum in Baghdad. The seals still carried the partially preserved registration numbers used by the Iraq Museum's cataloguing system. Although the seals were undoubtedly stolen property, Braude was not charged under the National Stolen Property Act, nor was he charged for violating the sanctions against importing illegally removed Iraqi cultural materials. When questioned, Braude initially denied having traveled to Iraq, but he later admitted that he had been to Iraq where he had purchased the seals. He was therefore charged under the Customs statute for making false statements. Braude ultimately pled guilty and was sentenced to six months of house arrest and two years of probation. The three seals were returned to his Excellency Samir Sumaidaie, the ambassador of Iraq to the United Nations, on January 18, 2005 (U.S. Immigration and Customs Enforcement, news release of January 18, 2005, http://www.ice.gov/graphics/news/newsreleases/articles/iraqiartifact_011805.htm).

16. Representative English had introduced a Concurrent Resolution on March 25, 2003, calling on the military to avoid damage to the cultural heritage of Iraq (H. Con. Res. 113). This resolution received little attention in Congress or the media, but it drew the attention of the archaeological community to Congressman English's interest in preserving cultural heritage.

17. There was some initial question as to whether the new government of Iraq that would emerge after the war would be considered a successor state and assume all of Iraq's international commitments and memberships in international bodies and conventions. Despite the fact that Iraq was and continued to be a party to the 1970 UNESCO Convention, it still could not bring a request under the CPIA because, at first, there were still no diplomatic relations between the two nations and subsequently, under the Bremer administration, it was not clear whether a U.S. administrator could present such a request. In addition, the burdensome process required for a CPIA request does not seem feasible in light of the ongoing chaos in Iraq.

18. Dealers and collectors, including but not limited to coin dealers and collectors, as well as the Association of Art Museum Directors, were among those who opposed H.R. 2009.

19. In fulfillment of obligations under Security Council Resolution 661 of August 1990, the President of the United States imposed sanctions against Iraq under the International Emergency Economic Powers Act, 50 U.S.C. §§ 1701–7, pursuant to Executive Orders 12722 and 12744. The Office of Foreign Assets Control of the Department of the Treasury administers the sanctions.

20. The resolution was adopted under Chapter VII of the United Nations Charter and is therefore legally binding on all UN member states. The full text of UNSCR 1483 may be found at http://daccessdds.un.org/doc/UNDOC/GEN/N03/368/53/PDF/N0336853.pdf?OpenElement.

21. 31 CFR 575.533 (b)(4) states in full:

This transaction does not authorize any transactions with respect to Iraqi cultural property or other items of archaeological, historical, cultural, rare scientific, and religious importance illegally removed from the Iraq National Museum, the National Library, and other locations in Iraq since August 6, 1990. Any trade in or transfer of such items, including items with respect to which reasonable suspicion exists that they have been illegally removed, remains prohibited by subpart B of 31 CFR part 575.

These sanctions were extended in 2004 and subsequently on May 20, 2005, when President Bush issued Executive Order 13350, declaring that a state of emergency exists with respect to Iraq (70 Fed. Reg. 29435, 2005 WL 1243182). The sanctions were not specifically extended in 2006 because EO 13350 continues in effect.

22. Sections 3001–3, P.L. 108–429.

23. *Id.* § 3002(a).

24. *Id.* § 3002(b). The act states: "the term 'archaeological or ethnological material of Iraq' means cultural property of Iraq and other items of archaeological, historical, cultural, rare scientific, or religious importance illegally removed from the Iraq

National Museum, the National Library of Iraq, and other locations in Iraq, since the adoption of United Nations Security Council Resolution 661 of 1990." The CPIA requires that archaeological objects be at least 250 years old and that ethnological material be the product of a nonindustrial or tribal society (19 U.S.C. § 2601(4)). Without a change in definition, there clearly would have been gaps between the materials that could be protected under the CPIA and those that the UN Security Council resolution required to be protected.

25. Chapter 7, Article 48, Charter of the United Nations, http://www.un.org/aboutun/charter/chapter7.htm.
26. Senator Grassley Floor Statement, *Congressional Record*, S. 2188, March 4, 2004.
27. Federal Register, Vol. 72, No. 25. February 22, 2007.
28. S. 1585, Senate Appropriations Committee Report 108-144: Department of State and Related Agencies.
29. H.R. 508. The bill was introduced by Representative Lynn Woolsey of California on January 17, 2007, and currently has forty-four cosponsors.
30. President Clinton transmitted the Hague Convention and First Protocol to the Senate in 1999. However, a State Department memo, accompanying the transmittal, recommended that the United States opt out of the first section of the First Protocol because of its requirement that occupying powers compensate good faith purchasers who are required to relinquish cultural objects illegally exported from occupied territory. The first section contains most of the substantive provisions of the First Protocol. See Letter of Transmittal, 106th Cong., Senate Treaty Doc. 106-1 (January 6, 1999), http://frwebgate.access.gpo.gov/cgi-bin/getdoc.cgi?dbname=106_cong_documents&docid=f:td001.106. It is not clear, at this time, what action the Senate is likely to take with respect to the First Protocol.

CHAPTER 10

The Chain of Command

J. HOLMES ARMSTEAD, JR.

NATIONAL MILITARY ORGANIZATIONS ARE LED BY A STRUCTURE REFERRED TO AS THE chain of command. The U.S. iteration of this principle, as expressed within the country's Constitution, has the president as commander in chief of all U.S. military forces. Our current command structure divides global responsibilities into regional combatant commands: European Command (EUCOM), Pacific Command (PACOM), Southern Command (SOUTHCOM), and Central Command (CENTCOM), which includes the Middle East. The CENTCOM commander is responsible for directing designated components, conducting operations, and developing war plans for his or her particular region of responsibility. The services, led separately and collectively by the Joint Chiefs of Staff, are to organize, train, maintain, and equip forces so that they will be ready for deployment to the battle theatre and assigned to the respective regional combatant commander. The forces are led by the combatant commander under direction of the president of the United States in the constitutional role of commander in chief.

This second phase of operations is complex and difficult, involving coordination with our allies, and the employment of nonmilitary branches of government, such as the State Department. The victorious CENTCOM commander, General Tommy Franks, noted in his recent book that he was not advised as to the depth and intensity of any anticipated insurgency and that he was instructed that stability operations and the development of new governing institutions in Iraq would be handled by various supporting elements, including the State Department.

With the hindsight of four years enlightening the current debate, much has been written about mistakes in judgment, poor planning, and confused policies. It will suffice here to restate the obvious, but it is unnecessary for the purposes of this article to dissect the reasons why. In short, the forces deployed and committed to the operation in Iraq were insufficient to police and stabilize a nation of 27.5 million people following the cessation of combat operations after the defeat of Saddam Hussein's regular armed forces. A brief respite for U.S. and coalition forces, following the president's official announcement of the completion of "major combat operations," witnessed the organization of militias, splintered political factions vying for power, religious and sectarian violence developing within the population, and infiltration by external terrorist factions.[1] The responses to Iraqi instability and successive employments of forces were woefully inadequate to establish stable internal governance and normalize the civil life of Iraq.

Stability operations were not (and as of this writing, are not) meeting with the success needed to normalize everyday life in Iraq. The protection of cultural property immediately following combat operations, and later, suffered as a result of the failure to employ forces, establish local governance, and develop priorities that would identify, protect, and preserve important architectural sites. The fog of war lasted longer than it should have, U.S. forces were not present in sufficient numbers to undertake the past combat phase of operations, and we fell short in a number of ways. Civil Affairs planning and staffing did not anticipate the rapidity of our advance upon the enemy or the state of unrest and instability among the Iraq population. Insufficient forces were employed in-theatre to pacify and police Iraq, given its volatile tribal, religious, ethnic, and political situation. Commanders on the ground were unable to provide protection at cultural sites, given the level of violence. Deployments of additional military and civilian assets were insufficient to forestall the wanton destruction and criminal looting that took place subsequent to the United States' establishment of interim governing authority.

The foregoing must be understood in light of pressing combat operations; civil strife; deteriorating infrastructure that caused problems with the distribution of essentials such as food, water, and fuel; frequent interruption of electrical power generation; an intensive search for Iraqi government and military leaders; and a widespread investigation attempting to uncover weapons of mass destruction. This was a busy period for U.S. forces, with an intensive tempo of operations that saw full-scale deployments of active and reserve components. Given the low priority assigned to cultural property protection, it should come as no surprise that adequate measures to protect the numerous and diverse sites were not undertaken.

A basic principle of military operations is unity of command: the organization and employment of military force must be subject to a single guiding authority. This supports the chain of command and fixes both authority and responsibility onto the chain for the conduct and success of operations. The chain is a system devised to both command and control the employment of forces prepared to execute or impose political will by means of violence, under the auspices of international law. The various levels of command—from the commander in chief to the newest private—allow for clear creation and execution of orders to accomplish the designated mission: obedience to orders is the paramount imperative if this system is to be successful.

The priorities of combat are quite simple and are well expressed in the army's mission statement: "to close with and destroy the enemy." In the case of Iraq, that was done in twenty-seven days and with ruthless efficiency. That coalition forces did not simultaneously resolve an age-old conflict stretching back over a millennia should come as no surprise. Versailles was an attempt to address the same subset of problems earlier in the twentieth century by creating modern multiparty states in Iraq and the Balkans. The same result occurred in both places, and for the same reasons: These states were artificially created by external forces and no polity developed or matured that would supplant tribal or ethnic identities, allowing a modern stable nation-state to develop. These states never created a positive national identity and the removal of weak monarchs, followed by a generation or more of strong dictators resulted in rapid disintegration of any body politic capable of holding the state after the demise of strong authoritarian regimes. Even a casual observer should be little surprised that the same process was applied to nation-state creation by the allies in 1919 in both regions and brought similar results—a failed state when a strong dictator passes from the scene. The breakdown of Iraqi society has been a long time coming and our military command, foreign policy structure, and intelligence apparatus failed to fully appreciate the level of animosity that would be released by Saddam's dislocation. The tragic loss at the sites and museums is the direct result of the deterioration of Iraqi society into anarchy and increase of ethnic strife to levels closely approximating civil war. U.S. policymakers, both civilian and military, failed to anticipate such chaos and hence were not ready and prepared to protect the massive amount of cultural property in the country.

Ultimately, a commander is responsible for everything his unit does or fails to do. This is the basic principle of command authority and responsibility. This principle is supported by the institutional framework of the chain of command and the full weight of legal authority of the Uniform Code of Military Justice and the customary law of war. Command responsibility is a unique feature of the military institution and is without a functional equivalent in civilian life. An entire body of law exists that supports this special relationship. In many ways it is essential to the military way of life. In effect, it is how the military functions and does business—the essence of its being.

Leadership within the military relies upon this command authority for the organization to function. A commander must be able to compel obedience in a fashion totally distinct from organizations recognized in civil society. Hierarchical military organizations rely upon obedience to orders, issued by superiors to subordinates, so that assigned missions may be accomplished. An accepted definition of military leadership is "the art of influencing and directing [people] towards an assigned goal in such a manner as to elicit their willing obedience and loyal cooperation."[2] Obviously, as can be easily seen, the operative term under this definition is *obedience*. Military organizations are instituted to organize human and material resources dedicated to inflict violence upon the enemies of a state so as to affect political will. Such organizations are decidedly undemocratic and agents must have the authority to achieve the assigned goals. U.S. military law is actually an executive function, exercised by commanders to impose good order and discipline upon those under their command. Therefore, commanders have lawful authority to direct both function and behavior derived through the command relationship. The commander both assigns roles and duties as a command function and enforces criminal law upon the military personnel under his or her command. This is purposefully a powerful relationship and is in many ways anathema to the constitutionally guaranteed individual liberty we so jealously guard through the many institutions of civil society. Some of the basic tenets of the Constitution do not apply to military persons, where such would weaken or abrogate the command relationships that require almost absolute obedience to any lawful order.

There is a complex and comprehensive system for preparing war plans and issuing orders to units conducting combat operations in the field. This system involves the preparation of orders by senior commanders, which are supported by staff and issued to subordinate units responsible for their execution. Such orders specify the following:

- designate the enemy's situation, weather, and terrain
- describe the mission
- define the concept of the operation
- allocate logistical support
- define and describe command responsibilities and prescription of signal and communication imperatives

The policies, procedures, and legal requirements affecting a particular combat operation are addressed in the planning process and identified in the orders issued. Such requirements necessarily include the applicable international law as reflected in FM 27-10, the Law of Land Warfare, and other official publications, as well as customary law. While the United States is not a signatory to the 1954 Hague Convention, the 1954 First Protocol, or the 1999 Second Protocol, the last of which addresses the international protection of cultural property, official United States policy has for some time supported international norms as addressed in the aforementioned documents.

To effectuate U.S. policy (e.g., the principle enunciated in the aforesaid treaties and addenda), the military operational plans and orders must reflect those principles and requirements in a precise manner consistent with the military planning process and integrated into the field orders so that the specifics of execution will be clear and concise.

THE ROLE OF MILITARY COMMANDERS FOR THE PROTECTION OF CULTURAL PROPERTY

Commanders are responsible for the protection of cultural property within their operational area and must take pains to issue orders that will meet specified international law requirements. At a minimum, orders and planning should include the following to insure proper execution by subordinate units where cultural property is, or is likely, to be encountered:

1. Identify: Provide personnel and resources reasonably capable of identifying items of cultural property and national heritage prior to commencing combat operations.
2. Record: Prepare and maintain a thorough record of cultural property sites and items of interest; provide for retrieval and distribution of such data so that it is available for international inspection.
3. Secure: Designate and provide resources to provide for the physical protection and removal (if necessary) of cultural property.
4. Protect: Designate and provide personnel and resources, including combat units and military police units responsible for the physical securing of cultural property.
5. Preserve: Secure and maintain the necessary resources for specialized preservation of cultural property artifacts, locations, etc., including procurement of specialists or transfer and shipment to a secure location.
6. Restore: Secure personnel and resources to ameliorate damage caused either directly or indirectly by military operations and restore to previous conditions those items or locales suffering damage as soon as practical given the tactical situation.

The responsible commander must ensure these tasks are accomplished. Timely anticipation of requirements prior to undertaking combat operations will be an essential element to meeting the requirement to protect cultural property. Such issues as outlined above will of course require specialized assistance from Civil Affairs units, civilian contractors, international and professional organizations, and other assets that will not be organic to combatant or theatre commanders. UNESCO has a program that designates both cultural and national heritage property deemed protected by international law. Efforts should be made to familiarize and update military units with the appropriate databases to insure that current data is available to military commanders and personnel when necessary.

THE UNITED STATES AND THE ROME STATUTE OF
THE INTERNATIONAL CRIMINAL COURT

Since the Rome Statute of the International Criminal Court has come into force, one must recognize this growing body of international jurisprudence. Although the United States is not a signatory to this agreement and hence does not recognize its jurisdiction, a great majority of our allies have joined the International Criminal Court and will be required to comply as regards the conduct of military operations. While the legal precepts of the Rome Statute are essentially customary law, and hence recognized by the United States as applicable to U.S. operations, we must at least recognize the possibility that our allies will or may seek compliance of the requisite applications of law and may even seek our compliance as a matter of policy, despite our nonsignatory status. In actuality, by virtue of preexisting treaties, UN membership, and recognized customary practice, we are bound to voluntarily comply with the great majority of the substantive law expressed therein; we just don't accept jurisdiction of the International Criminal Court over U.S. personnel.

NEXT STEPS

At Pocantico in 2006,[3] the foregoing information was discussed and the results achieved during and following combat during Operation Iraqi Freedom were deliberated upon. A number of recommendations came out of this conference concerning military responsibilities and operations.

Cultural heritage protection should be included in military planning during all operational phases, including combat and postcombat stability and security. Initial war plans must include tailoring operational forces, providing logistical support, developing specialized training, and designating civilian support resources. In addition, these plans must include provisions for cultural property protection so that necessary resources, personnel, and material are available so that all operational imperatives recognize the legal requirement to protect and preserve both cultural and natural heritage. This will require special training for operations, planners, civil affairs, and civilian export augmentees and commanders at every level. Before target lists, mission objectives, and major routes of advance are designated, elements on the ground, in the air, and at sea must be made aware of protected sites, buildings, and areas so that a maximum effort, consistent with the operational mission, can be put forth to protect, preserve, and secure designated cultural and natural heritage property.

Theatre commanders, as part of their ongoing mission-planning process, should develop after-action reports and integrate lessons learned into all contingency planning. This should reflect the multiplicity of challenges involved in protecting cultural and natural heritage property. This planning should emphasize such concerns as an integral part of the combat mission—a requirement of international law—and be defined as standard operating procedure. The experience of previous operations may serve as a guide when the planning process begins to address the number and type of resources needed, the appropriate troop elements, the size and source of auxiliary funding, logistical support to and from local authorities, and necessary augmentation from civilian expert personnel. Such considerations must be fully integrated so the maximum effect may be achieved from our forces. We demand and expect victory from our forces. We must also demand aggressive compliance with our international obligations.

A DoD-level joint task force should be developed with responsibility for setting policy guidelines, establishing procedures, and reviewing operations that will insure U.S. forces possess operational doctrine, adequate training, sufficient resources, and well-defined mission priorities regarding cultural and national heritage property protection. Such a task force should be led by an under secretary of defense, designated as the executive agent for an interagency coordinating committee that includes the State Department, the Justice Department, and others, as necessary, so that all appropriate resources may be brought to bear in a timely manner when U.S. forces are employed and cultural or natural heritage property are determined to be at risk. Such interagency planning is particularly important when the United States is undertaking coalition operations. Additional efforts may be necessary so that international legal obligations are understood and complied with as responsibilities are determined for the various allied elements deployed to an active operational theatre. Predeployment planning may very well allow for the development and use of specialized military units or other organizational assets, such as Spain's Guardia Civil, France's Gendarmes, or Italy's Carabinieri, where such paramilitary organizations have developed unique skill sets and capabilities that could prove useful to the theatre commander responsible for planning and executing combat operations where cultural property is or may be endangered.

Much has been learned that will help military planners improve future operations. Perhaps the more pressing issue is whether we have the will and interest to make cultural property protection an important part of our operational concept. International organizations are keen to see better results in further operations; our own citizens are keenly aware of the failures that have occurred in Iraq. The United States must take action to improve our efforts at cultural heritage protection in future military actions. Our common shared heritage deserves no less.

NOTES

1. Office of the Press Secretary of the President of the United States, "President Bush Announces Major Combat Operations in Iraq Have Ended," Remarks by the President from the USS *Abraham Lincoln* at Sea off the Coast of San Diego, California, May 1, 2003, http://www.whitehouse.gov/news/releases/2003/05/20030501-15.html.
2. Pershing Rifles Constitutional Preamble
3. "Protecting Cultural Heritage during Wartime: Learning the Lessons of Iraq," conference of the Cultural Policy Center at the University of Chicago, Tarrytown, NY, August 11–13, 2006.

THE WAY FORWARD

For Military and Civilian War Planners

LEGISLATIVE ACTIONS CAN CONSTRAIN GOVERNMENTS AND THEIR MILITARIES TO PAY attention to the problem of securing and protecting cultural heritage from looting. The actualities of operational planning, however, require not only the will to do the right thing, but also the way to do it. In this section, contributors describe the forces, weaponry, equipment, and infrastructure that could be brought to bear in support of this mission—but which the military has not invested in to date.

CHAPTER 11

Bridging the Public Security Gap

Stability Police Units in Contemporary Peace Operations and the Center of Excellence for Stability Police Units

MICHAEL DZIEDZIC AND CHRISTINE STARK

THE PROBLEM OF PROTECTING CULTURAL PROPERTY FROM LOOTING IN THE immediate aftermath of combat is a small part of the overall challenge of providing security during the postcombat stabilization phase of war fighting. Peace and stability operations invariably confront a public security gap in the aftermath of combat operations, when local police functions backed by the power of the state are destroyed or suspended, leaving persons and institutions—including cultural institutions such as the Iraq Museum—unshielded. The task of filling the public security gap during stability operations has increasingly been handed to stability police units (SPUs). In this chapter, we describe the makeup, capacities, and costs of such units, which could be deployed for cultural protection purposes even if not trained specifically to perform that function. (The specialization of SPUs for cultural heritage protection, which has been done by the Italian Carabinieri, is discussed in the following chapter.)

THE PUBLIC SECURITY GAP AND THE ROLE OF STABILITY POLICE

Stability police are robust, armed police units that are capable of performing specialized law enforcement and public order functions that require disciplined group action. They are trained in and have the flexibility to use either less-than-lethal or lethal force, as circumstances dictate. They are rapidly deployable, logistically self-sustainable, and able to collaborate effectively with both the military and the police components of a peace mission.

Peace and stability operations have historically been plagued by dire lapses in public security, leaving an inadequate foundation for all other aspects of

127

these missions to build upon. At the inception of most such operations, there is likely to be an immediate need to combat rampant lawlessness, revenge killings, or major civil disturbances.

Initially, the military is often the only source of order: domestic police forces in most states do not have a surplus capacity that can be readily tapped for international contingencies. Since peace missions are apt to be severely tested during the initial deployment phase, this can be a crippling deficiency.

To address this aspect of the public security gap, qualified law enforcement personnel, such as the Italian Carabinieri, need to be organized in rapidly deployable units. Stability police units, owing to their disciplined command and control structure and autonomous logistical support capability, are capable of rapid mobilization. Unlike individual police, moreover, they are able to survive in the anarchic conditions that often prevail during the early stages of most missions.

In addition to their rapid deployability, stability police are able to fill a critical gap in capabilities that arises between military contingents, that are proficient in the use of lethal force, and individual international police, who have very limited force options and may even be unarmed.

Lethal force is of limited value in preventing loss of life and destruction of property, making military units blunt instruments for coping with public disorder and lawlessness. Among the most decisive public security tasks, moreover, may be confronting threats in the form of political-criminal power structures, rogue intelligence organizations, warlords, fanatical religious groups, global terrorists, and combinations of the above. Orchestrated civil disturbances, or "rent-a-mobs," are typically symptoms of such underlying sources of opposition to a peace process. Individual police are not capable of handling either large-scale civil disorders or the illicit, criminalized power structures that instigate them. Bridging the gap in law enforcement capability requires proficiency in the use of less-than-lethal force, as well as in criminal intelligence and investigations.

Stability police fill this gap by performing specialized law enforcement and public order functions that require disciplined group action to counter a broad scope of criminal activities. The types of activities they can undertake include the following:

- civil disturbance management
- VIP protection
- hard entry and high-risk arrest
- territorial patrolling
- criminal intelligence and evidence gathering
- countering organized crime, terrorism, and insurgency
- mobile and static security of vulnerable areas
- election security

- prison security
- border patrol

Stability police thus perform vital roles complementary to those of military forces and have demonstrated their effectiveness in a variety of mission areas. Given the range of robust policing functions that stability police can perform and their rapid deployabiltiy, they would be well suited to curb looting and perform a cultural heritage protection mission.

Stability police bridge the public security gap both through timely deployment and by performing heavy-duty law enforcement functions that require proficiency in the organized use of less-than-lethal force. When these units are deployed in support of UN peacekeeping operations they are called formed police units (FPUs). With a standard strength of 125 personnel, they operate under the command of the UN police commissioner. In the NATO context, stability police are called multinational specialized units (MSUs). Their unit strength ranges from 250 to 600 personnel, and they operate under the operational control of the NATO force commander. The European Union has also developed a readily deployable stability policing capability. Called integrated police units (IPUs), they are capable of performing executive law enforcement tasks under either the international police commissioner or senior military authority.

In addition to their vital role in establishing public security, stability police units are surprisingly cost-effective. According to reimbursement formulas used by the UN, the annual costs for a 125-member formed police unit, compared with the costs of an equivalent number of troops and individual UN police, are as follows:

Formed police unit (including contingent-owned equipment)	$4,189,325
Military contingent (including contingent-owned equipment)	$4,827,657
UN police (personnel only—not including UN-provided equipment)	$6,315,500[1]

FPUs are thus 50 percent less costly than individual UN police, owing to the difference in personnel costs (the annual mission subsistence allowance for UN police is $50,000, while the annual personnel cost for each FPU member is only $13,000). Although FPUs are only slightly less expensive than an equivalent number of soldiers, they are considerably more cost-effective. While 90 percent of FPU members can be tasked to perform daily mission requirements, only about 50 to 60 percent of soldiers may be available for duties "outside the wire."[2] Thus FPU personnel are more economical in the performance of their mandated policing functions than individual UN police and more available to perform public-security-related functions than soldiers.

STABILITY POLICE UNITS IN PAST CONFLICTS

International policing has undergone a profound transformation as a result of the introduction and widespread use of stability police units (SPUs). Since their initial deployment by NATO in Bosnia in 1998, demand for this heavy-duty policing capability has expanded to the point that SPUs now constitute almost half of international police personnel. This growth has been most dramatic in United Nations' missions. As of November 2005, the number of FPUs fielded by the UN stood at twenty-seven, accounting for 3,105 of its total of 7,160 police personnel.

Stability police have become an indispensable partner alongside traditional military contingents and individual police because they are vital for overcoming the public security gap that invariably confronts—and frequently confounds—peace and stability operations. SPUs have already made vital contributions to efforts to bring peace and stability in places like Bosnia, Côte d'Ivoire, the Democratic Republic of the Congo, Haiti, Iraq, Kosovo, and Liberia. (In the case of Iraq, Italy deployed an MSU that was populated with officers of the Carabinieri. Romanians, Argentines, and others also comprised the unit that deployed to Bosnia.)

UN police commissioners continue to petition for additional SPUs to bolster existing missions. Future operations, such as the potential UN mission in Darfur that is anticipated to require nineteen SPUs, are likely to depend heavily on stability police to establish and maintain public order. Thus the success of current and future missions undertaken by the UN, NATO, European Union, other international organizations, and ad hoc coalitions of the willing has become increasingly dependent on generating the required quality and quantity of SPUs.

THE CENTER OF EXCELLENCE FOR STABILITY POLICE UNITS

To address the burgeoning demand for a robust and rapidly deployable policing capability, G-8 members in June 2004 called for the creation of "an international training center that would serve as a Center of Excellence to provide training and skills for peace support operations." Accordingly, the Center of Excellence for Stability Police Units (CoESPU) was established in Vicenza, Italy, in March 2005 to serve as a doctrinal hub for stability policing and to provide training for future SPU commanders, midgrade officers, and noncommissioned officers (NCOs).

Owing to the prominent role that SPUs have come to play in international peace missions, it is imperative that properly trained and equipped units can be generated in sufficient numbers to meet the increasing demand. International capacity to provide SPUs, however, has been hard-pressed to keep pace. Specialized training programs are required to prepare units for the rigors of peace and stability operations, and international doctrine for their use must be developed and standardized. These are the core missions that have been assigned to the Center of Excellence for Stability Police Units. In the G-8 Action Plan on Expanding Global Capacity for Peace Support Operations, CoESPU was charged with

- Operating training programs, including "train-the-trainer" courses and pre-deployment training for specific missions; and
- Developing a common doctrine and common operational standards for employing carabinieri/gendarmerie-like forces in peace support operations.[3]

Funded and managed by the Italian government with assistance and funding from the United States under the global peace operations initiative, the intention of CoESPU is to "train the trainers" who will return to their home countries to prepare their own stability police units for international deployment. Units that have received training assistance from CoESPU may be deployed on UN missions as formed police units or as components of other international peace or stability operations.

TRAINING

The CoESPU curriculum covers stability policing concepts and doctrine, operational planning, international and humanitarian law, and negotiation and mediation. The faculty includes Italian Carabinieri, university professors, and military officers (active and retired). Initially all instruction was provided in English, but the first course in French was offered at the end of 2007. There is specific instruction on cultural awareness and territorial protection that are relevant to protection of cultural heritage sites.

In December 2005, the first class graduated from CoESPU, less than eighteen months after the G-8 proposed that the center come into existence. Twenty-nine senior officers from India, Jordan, Kenya, Morocco, and Senegal completed the first high-level course. This was followed in March 2006 by graduation of ninety-eight company-grade offices and NCOs from India, Jordan, Kenya, Morocco, Senegal, and Cameroon from the midlevel course. CoESPU has an annual capacity to offer four high-level courses (forty students per class) and five midlevel courses (one hundred students per class), which equates to a maximum capacity of 660 students per year. The goal is to train 3,000 stability police trainers at CoESPU who will subsequently train at least 4,500 SPU personnel in their home countries, achieving the G-8 target of 7,500 stability police by 2010.

In addition, the United Nations Department of Peacekeeping Operations has teamed with CoESPU to conduct command development seminars for its formed police unit commanders and their police commissioners. The first two seminars were held in March and November 2006 for current FPU commanders. Future seminars are envisioned every six to twelve months so that FPU commanders can attend either prior to deployment or shortly after arrival on mission. Thus CoESPU has succeeded not only in developing and conducting a full training curriculum, but it has formed a partnership with the UN to instill the leadership and command skills required for successful international service for all current and future FPU commanders.

DOCTRINE

In April 2005, CoESPU conducted an assessment of the March 2004 riots in Kosovo (with support from the National Defense University, U.S. Army Peacekeeping and Stability Operations Institute, and the U.S. Institute of Peace). The ensuing report, "The Future Roles for Stability Police Units," summarized current SPU doctrine, suggested how the Kosovo experience might inform that doctrine, and identified doctrinal gaps.

Bridging the intelligence-to-evidence gap—the ability to use intelligence to develop admissible evidence about violent spoilers and obstructionists—was the most critical area of doctrinal concern identified in the report. In December 2005, CoESPU organized a workshop on the role of stability police units in completing the intelligence-to-evidence sequence. The workshop was attended by representatives of the UN, NATO, and the European Union. The concepts developed at that event are currently being circulated by CoESPU among those organizations. With these activities the center has established itself as a reputable clearinghouse for ideas across all international organizations that field SPUs, while advancing the development of common doctrine and identifying lessons for responding to emerging challenges.

NEXT STEPS: HOW TO IMPROVE SPUs IN
ADVANCE OF FUTURE CONFLICTS

Sustaining the Training

The train-the-trainer concept presumes that, having attended CoESPU's courses, sending countries will commit themselves to use the graduates to prepare SPUs in their respective nations. A number of steps should be taken to ensure that this happens, some of which may entail a modest increase in resources available to CoESPU:

- A diplomatic publicity campaign should be undertaken to inform countries that have the potential to contribute SPUs to future missions about the prospects for training at CoESPU. These countries should be made a priority for training.

- Countries that send students to CoESPU for training should certify that graduates will actually return and conduct training for deployable units or be made available for international duty in some other capacity.
- Mobile training teams (MTTs) or mobile evaluation teams (METs) from Co-ESPU should be available to support potential SPU contributing countries in establishing and conducting in-country training programs.
- MTTs or METs could be used to assist current and prospective SPU contributing countries in conducting exercises that are designed to maintain the readiness of their units and enhance their interoperability with military contingents.

Undertaking these steps would help protect cultural heritage and stop looting during conflict or in the aftermath of conflict because more SPUs would be available for general purposes in stability operations.

Equipping New Units

The total cost to purchase all contingent-owned equipment items required by the UN to outfit one FPU is a little more than $6 million. At present, there is no mechanism to assist countries that have the personnel and political will to organize additional SPUs but lack the resources to procure all the necessary equipment. Even though the UN reimburses SPU contributing countries for the use of contingent-owned equipment at the rate of almost $750,000 per year through UN peacekeeping assessments, the up-front cost of equipping new FPUs is liable to be a serious limiting factor. This is a particular concern for African countries that are a priority for CoESPU training under the Global Peace Operations Initiative.

G-8 members, other bilateral donors, and the more affluent police contributing countries should consider providing assistance to potential SPU contributing countries that lack financial resources to purchase the equipment required to meet UN standards (e.g., armored personnel carriers). One no-cost option would be to donate the equipment or provide up-front funding to equip units committed to serve on UN missions. The donor would be reimbursed over time by the UN from peacekeeping assessments.

CONCLUSION

Establishing public security is essential to the success of a peace or stability operation and to the protection of cultural heritage sites. Stability police units have demonstrated their critical contribution to overcoming the public security gap that inevitably arises during these missions. If future international mandates include the prevention of looting of cultural artifacts and protection of cultural heritage sites, training modules or DVDs could be developed by CoESPU and made part of predeployment training for units deploying to those missions. Assuming the steps suggested above are undertaken, the capacity to mobilize the number of stability police could be expanded to meet growing international requirements, greatly enhancing the ability to protect cultural heritage and stop looting in the aftermath of conflict.

NOTES
1. Mark Kroeker, "Contingent Owned Equipment (COE) Reimbursement," briefing at conference on "Overcoming Challenges to Stability Policing," Center of Excellence for Stability Police Units, Vicenza, Italy, December 7, 2005.
2. Kroeker, "Contingent Owned Equipment (COE) Reimbursement."
3. G-8 Summit G8 Information Center, "Summit Documents: G8 Action Plan: Expanding Global Capability for Peace Support Operations," http://www.g8.utoronto.ca/summit/2004seaisland/peace.html.

Image P1. The Children's Museum, after the initial combat in Baghdad in April 2003. Countless Web sites and articles feature a similar picture showing the front of the Children's Museum with the hole created by the tank round. What they usually fail to mention is that the tank had fired in response to two rocket-propelled grenade shooters who had fired on the tank. Photo courtesy of Matthew Bogdanos

Image P2. Front of the museum compound taken from the roof of the library in April 2003, showing the galleries (straight ahead), two of the firing positions (in the middle), and the team's white SUVs with supplies. The administrative offices are to the right. Photo courtesy of Matthew Bogdanos

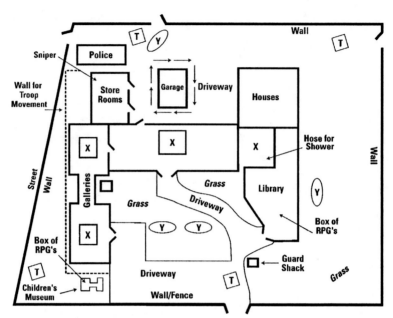

Y = Fighting Position   T = American Tanks   X = Courtyard

Image P3.   Sketch of the 11-acre compound of the Iraq Museum prepared by Colonel Matthew Bogdanos and Senior Master Sergeant Piñiero; drawing not to scale. Courtesy of Matthew Bogdanos

Image P4.   Two of the four firing positions, complete with dirt ramparts, aiming sticks to provide interlocking fire, and boxes of hand grenades—all of which had been prepared prior to April 2003. Photo courtesy of Matthew Bogdanos

Image P5.   One of a dozen Iraqi Army–issued rocket-propelled grenades discovered in the museum compound in April 2003 that had already been fired. Another two dozen were also found that had not yet been fired. Photo courtesy of Matthew Bogdanos

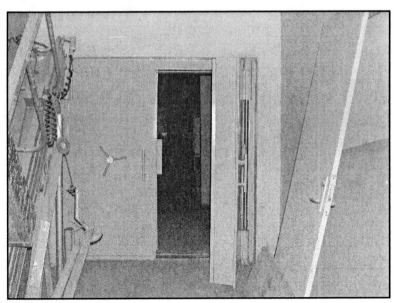

Image P6.   Door that led to two of the three looted storage rooms of the Iraq Museum. The lack of any sign of forced entry strongly suggests that the doors were opened with keys by museum staff—whether that was done voluntarily, negligently, or at gun-point remains an open question. Photo courtesy of Matthew Bogdanos

Image P7.   Parts of a sculpture lie among rubble after a mob ransacked and looted the Iraq Museum in Baghdad. Photo courtesy of Yannis Kontos/Polaris

Image P8. Exhibit of cuneiform-inscribed bricks with nine missing. Iraq Museum, May 2003. Photo courtesy of John Russell

Image P9. Lion from Tell Harmal c. 1900 B.C.E., damaged during the looting of the Iraq Museum in 2003. Photo courtesy of Corine Wegener

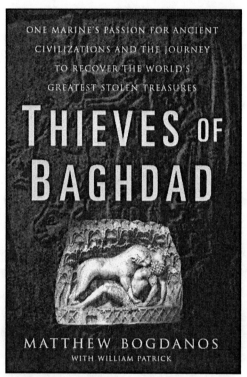

ONE MARINE'S PASSION FOR ANCIENT
CIVILIZATIONS AND THE JOURNEY
TO RECOVER THE WORLD'S
GREATEST STOLEN TREASURES

THIEVES OF
BAGHDAD

MATTHEW BOGDANOS
WITH WILLIAM PATRICK

*Image P10.   The figure of a "Lioness Attacking a
Nubian Boy" as shown on the cover of the hard-
cover edition of* Thieves of Baghdad. *Colonel Bogdanos considers it the single most exquisite and
historically significant piece that is still missing.
Courtesy of Matthew Bogdanos and Bloomsbury*

Image P11. Looters living in a tent at Jokha, the Sumerian capital. Umm al-Aqarib, Dhi Qar province Iraq, April 2003. Photo courtesy Joanne Farchakh-Bajjaly, archaeologist and journalist

Image P12. This young man used to work with Iraqi archaeologists during their excavation at Jokha, Umm al-Aqarib, Dhi Qar province, Iraq, April 2003. After the war, he became a "professional looter." His need for money was the motive for his illicit digging on the site. Photo courtesy of Joanne Farchakh-Bajjaly, archaeologist and journalist

Image P13.   Looters' tools recovered by the director of antiquities for Dhi Qar province outside the Nasiriyah Museum, May 2004. Photo courtesy of Micah Garen/Four Corners Media

Image P14.   Marine from the 3rd Civil Affairs Group displaying an archaeological artifact recovered from looters operating near Babylon, Iraq, June 2003. The artifact was returned to the custody of the Iraq Museum for conservation. Photo courtesy William Sumner

Image P15. "The dealers are not interested in fragmented objects; we throw them away," explains one of the looters digging at Jokha, Umm al-Aqarib, Dhi Qar province Iraq, April 2003. Photo courtesy of Joanne Farchakh-Bajjaly, archaeologist and journalist

Image P16. A Carabinieri officer presents a clay bowl, found near a looted archaeological site, to a high officer of the Italian Carabinieri Paratroops. Tell el-Lahm, Iraq, February 2004. Photo courtesy of the Italian Carabinieri Department for the Protection of Cultural Heritage

Image P17. A Carabinieri officer inspects an archaeological site just looted by illegal diggers. Tell el-Lahm, Iraq, February 2004. Photo courtesy of the Italian Carabinieri Department for the Protection of Cultural Heritage

Image P18. Italian Carabinieri officers with Iraqi police officers, after having recovered archaeological objects and illegal diggers' weapons. Photo courtesy of the Italian Carabinieri Department for the Protection of Cultural Heritage

Image P19. Italian Carabinieri prepare for an archaeological helicopter patrol in Dhi Qar province, Iraq, June 2004. Photo courtesy of Micah Garen/Four Corners Media

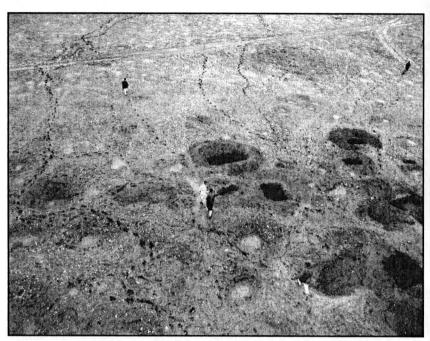

Image P20. Looters running away from a helicopter patrol at the archaeological site of Isin, southern Iraq, January 2004. Photo courtesy of John Russell

Image P21. Vukovar, Croatia, following the city's eighty-seven-day siege in 1991 by Serbian forces. The Blue Shield of the Hague Convention is displayed on the colonnade. Photo courtesy of the World Monuments Fund

CHAPTER 12

Italian Carabinieri and the Protection of Iraq's Cultural Heritage

CARABINIERI UNIT FOR THE PROTECTION AND SAFEGUARDING OF ITALIAN CULTURAL HERITAGE

WHILE SPECIALIZED POLICE UNITS (SPUs) MAY BE ABLE TO PROVIDE SOME BASIC protection to museums and archaeological sites even without additional training, the problems associated with cultural heritage protection are distinct enough from run-of-the-mill policing challenges to require a specialized response, even during peacetime. Countries with rich archaeological holdings, such as Italy and Spain, have evolved specialized policing capacities within their national police forces, the Carabinieri and the Guardia Civil, to combat the illicit looting of their own heritage. As part of the coalition effort in Iraq, the Italians sent Carabinieri units that were able to contribute their decades of experience and expertise toward combating the problem of looting. Their success provides a model for how they—or similar units that could be created by other nations, including the United States—could be deployed in future conflict situations.

THE CARABINIERI—A BRIEF HISTORY

The Comando Carabinieri Tutela Patrimonio Culturale (the Carabinieri Unit for the Protection and Safeguarding of Italian Cultural Heritage, hereafter referred to as Carabinieri) has operated for more than thirty-seven years to protect and safeguard the extraordinary cultural assets of Italy.

In 1969, the Nucleo Tutela Patrimonio Artistico (Group for the Protection of Artistic Heritage) was established, beginning as a concentrated operational unit much smaller than its present size. It is the only department expressly charged by law with its specific duty and is in the service of Italy's Ministero per i Beni e le Attività Culturali (Ministry of Arts and Culture). Remarkably, it was established a full year before the sixteenth session of the UNESCO General Conference, held in Paris from October 12–14, 1970, which mandated that each member state set up its own governmental department devoted exclusively to safeguarding and protecting cultural heritage.

The Carabinieri, which now has about three hundred specialized officers in this field, is headquartered in Rome with an operating division consisting of sections in archaeology, antiques, forgery, and contemporary art. It also has twelve squads with regional or interregional jurisdiction throughout the country.

The principal duties of the Carabinieri in Italy include

- prevention of crimes against cultural heritage
- prosecutions carried out by Italy's criminal investigation department, the Polizia Giudiziaria
- recovery of cultural assets and artistic objects
- management of a database of stolen cultural assets

Moreover, the Carabinieri actively and frequently participate in initiatives and projects promoted by UNESCO.

With regard to international peace missions, the Carabinieri have assisted in protecting and safeguarding historic and artistic objects in accordance with the 1954 Hague Convention for the Protection of Cultural Property in the Event of Armed Conflict and its First and Second Protocols (specifically in accordance with article 7, which requires States Parties to the convention and its protocols to provide services and personnel to armed forces that specialize in operations to respect and safeguard cultural assets).[1]

It was under these articles and protocols that the Carabinieri were requested to participate in Iraq in the mission organized after the wartime events of March 2003. The Carabinieri's support was requested in two distinct areas:

- in the multinational forces (multinational specialized unit, or MSU), with Carabinieri joining the Italian military contingent for the operation Ancient Babylon
- at the Iraq Museum

The Carabinieri also provided support through international interdiction actions and through the training of Iraqi site-protection forces.

ACTIVITIES AT MSU HEADQUARTERS IN NASIRIYAH
From July 2003, Carabinieri collaborated with local authorities and Iraqi police in the southwestern Iraqi province of Dhi Qar to catalogue at-risk archae-

ological sites, to provide for their protection, and to actively oppose illicit excavation and trafficking in archaeological finds. Widespread looting had affected the whole region after the collapse of the regime in 2003. As of early 2007, grave robbers still combed archaeological sites, hunting for gold jewels, gems, and cuneiform tablets, using rudimentary equipment in their excavations, and often causing irreparable harm to precious archaeological finds. These illicit finds, which often provided looters with little compensation, flowed to the Iraqi capital and then toward the principal black markets in Europe and the United States. (For more on these black markets, see the chapters by Neil Brodie, Joanne Farchakh-Bajjaly, and Matthew Bogdanos in part I.)

Since the beginning of the operations in Nasiriyah, 621 archaeological sites have been catalogued; 25 reconnaissance missions, using helicopters from the multinational forces, have been completed; 1,636 looted archaeological objects have been seized; 127 suspected people have been identified and 53 arrested; and 6 specialization courses have been organized for Iraqi guards within the Archaeological Site Protection (ASP) Force, an Iraqi policing unit for the protection of archaeological sites. (See images P16–P19 for images of the diverse work of the Carabinieri in Iraq.)

The numerous land and air patrols have enabled some at-risk archaeological sites to be monitored for illicit digging. Surveillance and active operations by officers have resulted in the recovery of numerous archaeological finds; their restitution to Iraqi institutions responsible for safeguarding cultural assets; the seizing of excavating instruments, many of them primitive in nature (see image P13); and the arrest and transfer to Iraqi police of numerous perpetrators.

The Carabinieri have also striven to catalogue the most at-risk archaeological sites and have created an archaeological map of Dhi Qar province. In fact, fourteen types of topographical maps of the province have been created that contain all 621 catalogued sites and their essential data (size, importance, ancient and modern names, coordinates, civilization, period, state of conservation, rate of looting, and catalog number).

The site maps, satellite photographs, and aerial reconnaissance missions of the Italian military contingent have been utilized by the Consiglio Nazionale delle Ricerche[2] (CNR, or Italy's National Research Council) for specific scientific studies, as well as to design a virtual version of the Iraq Museum, which is now under development. The CNR has also used these photographs to study the sites of Ur, Eridu, and Ubaid, which have uncovered both a Sumerian library and a commemorative stone dating back to 2100 B.C. (only the second ever found).

On many occasions, the Carabinieri have been featured in the Iraqi press for their protection of Iraq's great cultural wealth.

OPERATIONS AT THE IRAQ MUSEUM

Another project involved two Carabinieri officers who worked at the Iraq Museum in Baghdad. In conjunction with the Governing Italian Mission in the Iraqi provisional government, Italy's Ministry of Foreign Affairs, and Italy's Ministry of Arts and Culture, these two officers spent seven months gathering and cataloguing data on artifacts looted from the Iraq Museum. Documentation on and images of more than three thousand archaeological finds, compiled in collaboration with Italian archaeologists of the Centro Ricerche Archeologiche e Scavi di Torino (the Turin Center for Archaeological Research and Excavation) and Iraqi personnel, were transmitted electronically to the Carabinieri's headquarters in Rome. The information was then sent through Interpol's Rome office to its headquarters in Lyon, France, and then on to UNESCO.

To publicize Iraq's missing archaeological objects and obstruct their illegal trade, images of all missing archaeological objects were uploaded to the Carabinieri's website (www.carabinieri.it).

The officers filled out simple and efficient forms to acquire information on the cataloguing of archaeological finds, analogous to the forms already used in Italy. This form, called Object ID, adheres to international standards established by UNESCO, can be downloaded from the Carabinieri website, and constitutes a useful instrument for preventative care for works of art in private collections.

INTERNATIONAL COOPERATION

Carabinieri officers have not limited themselves to operating in Iraqi territory, but have carried out a well-constructed series of international interventions to hinder the illegal trade in archaeological objects looted from Iraq. In 2003, international meetings were held at Interpol headquarters in Lyon and at Carabinieri headquarters in Rome. Roundtable discussions among a panel of experts led to the analysis of the illegal trade emanating from Iraq and to the writing of guidelines and recommendations for the international community to prevent trade in looted Iraqi antiquities.

These field operations and intelligence gathering permitted the Carabinieri to carry out in Sardinia in 2003 a series of recoveries of illegally excavated Middle Eastern archaeological objects that had made their way onto the international black market. Among the recovered objects were eighty-six tablets from the archaeological site of Nippur and forty-three from the ancient area of Mesopotamia; five of these Mesopotamian tablets most certainly came from Iraqi archaeological sites.

TRAINING

Another important function of Carabinieri officers in Iraq was to train Iraqis responsible for supervising archaeological sites and to provide them with equipment.

The Carabinieri have dedicated particular attention to the training of local police in the safeguarding of archaeological objects, especially teaching them how to act when first intervening against an illicit excavation.

In September 2004, UNESCO requested that four Carabinieri officers and an official from Iraq's State Board of Antiquities and Heritage work in Amman, Jordan, to train Iraqi personnel of the Facility Protection Service (FPS), a specialized police force that had been instituted but not yet officially recognized. Its mission was to protect archaeological sites, prevent and halt specific crimes, and oppose illicit trafficking in archaeological objects.

The Italian delegation organized the training to be practical and technically oriented and provided FPS members with information to carry out the protection and safeguarding of cultural sites in Iraq.

As of this writing, the Carabinieri who had been engaged in the mission Ancient Babylon have already trained 140 out of 200 archaeological guards on duty in the province of Dhi Qar, teaching them how to utilize and set up surveillance systems at archaeological sites, how to prevent the looting of Iraq's cultural heritage, and how to catalogue seized archaeological finds.

In the course of training, Iraqis have learned the following:

- the strictly military concepts of the use and handling of weapons, arrest techniques, target practice, and intervention simulations
- methods for recognizing, describing, and cataloguing archaeological finds
- techniques for intervening to protect archaeological sites and to prevent specific crimes
- methods for the transportation of confiscated archaeological objects
- training to raise their sensitivity and consciousness of their invaluable cultural heritage

On January 26, 2006, the Nasiriyah Museum was inaugurated. On this occasion, the archaeological superintendent of the province of Dhi Qar dedicated a room to the Carabinieri to honor their operations and efforts to protect one of the regions richest in Mesopotamian archaeological objects.

Carabinieri operations in Iraqi territory are part of the larger action of protection and safeguarding that Italy offers in areas of the world in which armed conflicts or natural disasters put cultural heritage at risk. Thus, thanks to the recognized experience in the area of defense and restoration of cultural assets, Italy has become the point of reference for urgent interventions by the international community dealing with crisis situations.

To this effect, an agreement was signed in Paris on October 26, 2004, by the director general of UNESCO and on behalf of Italy by the Italian minister of arts and culture. This pact provides for the establishment of an Italian-UNESCO rapid intervention joint group called the Emergency Action Group. This group would consist of highly qualified experts—such as architects, engineers, art historians, archaeologists, and restorers—who would be supplied by Italy's Ministry of Arts and Culture, Ministry of Foreign Affairs, and other organizations. These experts would then intervene in countries in states of crisis or emergency.

From this perspective, the experiences and competencies of the Carabinieri Unit for the Protection and Safeguarding of Italian Cultural Heritage will certainly be useful on such occasions.

NOTES

1. Article 7 of the UNESCO Hague Convention:

   Military Measures:
   1. The High Contracting Parties undertake to introduce in time of peace into their military regulations or instructions such provisions as may ensure observance of the present Convention, and to foster in the members of their armed forces a spirit of respect for the culture and cultural property of all peoples.
   2. The High Contracting Parties undertake to plan or establish in peacetime, within their armed forces, services or specialist personnel whose purpose will be to secure respect for cultural property and to co-operate with the civilian authorities responsible for safeguarding it.

2. Il Consiglio Nazionale delle Ricerche, or CNR, is a public organization; its duty is to carry out, promote, spread, transfer, and improve research activities in the main fields of knowledge growth and its applications for the scientific, technological, economic, and social development of the country. To this end, the activities of the organization are divided into macro areas of interdisciplinary scientific and technological research concerning several fields: biotechnology, medicine, materials, environment and land, information and communications, advanced systems of production, judicial and socioeconomic sciences, classical studies, and arts. CNR is present throughout Italy through a network of institutes that promote its competencies throughout the country and facilitate contact and cooperation with local firms and organizations.

CHAPTER 13

Technology for the Prevention of Cultural Theft

John B. Alexander

There are numerous technologies that can assist in efforts to protect cultural heritage, many of which will be described in this chapter. However, the applicable technologies will vary significantly based on the nature of the problem to be addressed. Variants might include securing a building or fixed locations, surveillance and protection of large open areas, interdiction of the transportation and delivery process of illegal items, or recovery of stolen artifacts. (Please see appendix E for a chart that lists technologies and details their characteristics.)

Most importantly, technology can play only a supporting role in this ongoing struggle. As with illicit drugs, the fundamental problem is that expropriation of cultural artifacts is user-driven. The difference between drugs and cultural artifacts is that the underground market for exotic collectibles is limited by their expense and the recipient's flair for mystique and danger.

All technological applications require some level of human intervention to be successful in protection of heritage. Technical systems can deter, delay, inhibit, document, trace, or identify cultural artifacts. At some point, however, guards, custodians, or law enforcement must intercept the items and, in many cases, interact with persons who are either in possession of the artifacts or attempting to gain possession of them. There is no technology that can block theft for a long period of time. Therefore, technology should be employed based on a fully integrated concept of operations that includes human intervention.

RANGE OF SITUATIONS

Technical support for the safeguarding of cultural heritage is situationally dependent. The scenarios for protection that are most often presented include the following:

- technology for the protection of fixed sites, such as the Iraq Museum
- technology for the coverage of open and accessible archaeological sites that have not been fully explored
- technology to track or locate illegal artifacts that have been illegally excavated and removed from their country or place of origin.

With ten thousand registered archaeological sites in Iraq, their sheer volume represents a significant challenge. Providing equal protection for all sites would be both expensive and infeasible.

TYPES OF TECHNOLOGY: DELAY AND DENIAL

The purpose of delay and denial technologies is to slow or prevent access to fixed physical locations such as buildings. As with protection of any installation, if the perpetrators have the time, energy, and resources, they can overcome any barrier, including relatively secure vaults. Therefore, protection should begin with construction of a facility that can withstand common assaults, such as simply driving a car or truck through the outer walls. In general, these technologies are designed both to dissuade people from attempting to enter the building and to buy time for an external response to arrive.

Foams

Foam technology has advanced significantly in the past decade. Examples include foams that are sticky, slippery, or fast-hardening. Inside a building, any of these may serve to provide temporary barriers. Even water-based foams employing soap can greatly inhibit movement for a short period of time. Used in substantial quantities, sticky foams would be very effect in keeping artifacts in place. The most aggressive of these were originally designed to secure nuclear devices; they are extremely adherent and would keep items safe. However, the cleanup process would be extensive. Care would also have to be taken to ensure that the chemicals in the sticky foam did not damage or destroy the artifacts.

Slippery foams that inhibit intruders' movements can be quickly spread on surfaces. The slippery effects can be countered by a number of simple measures such as covering the area with sufficient sand. Still, they are effective against an unprepared person.

Fast-hardening foams can be used to reinforce doors, seal windows, or block other orifices such as air-conditioning vents. These foams are now available in spray cans, making them easy to apply by even untrained personnel.

They will set in about fifteen minutes and will require substantial effort to remove.

Visual Obscurants

Visual obscurants will work to inhibit movement on a temporary basis. A standard smoke grenade can be effective, although care must be taken to ensure the incendiary materials do not ignite unwanted fires. Again, care must be taken so the smoke does not damage the displays being defended. There are also cold smokes that can be used. Smokes will spread very quickly and provide limited protection. However, they also dissipate based on the airflow. Smokes will be effective when help can arrive relatively quickly.

Use of riot control agents, such as CS or OC chemicals, commonly known as tear gas, can be effective in temporary area denial for both buildings and open areas. In addition to quickly dissipating gases, residual agents have been developed that remain in the area until they are physically removed or washed away. While there are questions about the legality of riot control agents in combat operations, they are generally acceptable in domestic and peace support situations.

Physical Impediments

Physical impediments such as barbed wire and transportable barriers are already employed in many areas of the world. Combining these with the use of foams can enhance the effectiveness of both systems. In addition, there are new remote-controlled portable road barriers that are effective in controlling access in areas where vehicles are restricted to established roads. These barriers consist of extremely strong straps that are capable of catching a speeding truck and bringing it to a halt in a few feet. To be effective, these must be placed on roads that the vehicles cannot easily circumvent.

Illumination

Illumination is one of the simplest and most effective protective measures, provided the criminals know that a physical response will follow. Lights can either remain on during periods of darkness or be activated by sensors that spot movement in the area. These lights can be combined with cameras that both relay exact information about the intrusion and provide a record of the perpetrators that can be used should prosecution be required. An even cheaper alternative could be to launch flares. However, these would provide only very short-term protection.

Olfactory Agents

Recently available are olfactory agents, or "stink bombs," which provide temporary deterrence. They actually smell bad enough to have short-term effectiveness in keeping unprotected personnel away from the area.

However, there are two issues with olfactory agents. First, the source must continue to release the substance during the desired period of protection. The other is that olfactory sensors in the nose can become saturated within a period of about fifteen minutes. If the intruder can last that long in an extremely unpleasant environment, then the deterrent effect will be neutralized.

One of the more innovative proposals is the application of pheromones that attract indigenous insects. Throughout the world there are many insects that make human habitation uncomfortable. While archaeologists at the Pocantico conference indicated that archaeological thieves in the desert can accommodate occasional scorpions, the levels of pheromones proposed would cause an infestation that would make working in that area very challenging. Again, it would be necessary to renew the source of the pheromones on a repeated basis.

TYPES OF TECHNOLOGY: SENSOR SYSTEMS

Sensor systems will be an essential part of any security system and will be incorporated into security for both buildings and open areas. The most commonly used system involves small television cameras that transmit the pictures to a central monitoring station. This process allows for wide coverage with relatively inexpensive technology. This provides for conservation of personnel resources and around-the-clock observation of any designated area.

There are many other sensor systems that can be employed. In addition to staring TV cameras, there are both ambient light and infrared cameras that provide excellent coverage both day and night. Motion and thermal detectors can also be very effective. However, in open areas they require attention as indigenous animals or even blowing objects may activate them. Along roads, magnetic detectors that identify trucks or heavy metal objects could be effective.

TYPES OF TECHNOLOGY: NONLETHAL WEAPONS

Armed Guards

Armed guards offer the best protection, provided that they are capable of adequately responding to a wide range of possible intrusions. Deterring professional criminals takes more than mere personal presence. Those guarding the locations containing cultural heritage must have explicit rules of engagement that provide for escalating use of force. They must know what levels of force they are authorized to employ, as well as when they should desist. Conversely, it is beneficial that criminals not know what levels of force are authorized. In these situations, ambiguity works in favor of the defender. However, those guarding the site must have options between doing nothing and responding with deadly force.

Nonlethal, sometimes known as less-than-lethal, weapons provide such options. These weapons come in a wide variety. They are not perfect weapons and they can be misused. Therefore training and supervision are absolutely critical and nonlethal weapons must not be used indiscriminately.

Munitions with Low Kinetic Impact

Munitions with low kinetic impact are widely used. While sometimes known as rubber or beanbag bullets, they come in a variety of materials. One factor in favor of low-impact shotgun rounds is the availability of these weapons. The 12-gauge shotgun is found universally and is often used by security firms. Therefore, organizations will usually need only to buy new rounds, not new weapons. These shotguns are accurate at short ranges, and pack a very decisive punch. However, there is a minimum safe distance at which they can be fired at an individual. Close to the muzzle, a round is fired with sufficient force to cause serious damage and, on occasion, death. Further, there are specific areas of the body that should not be hit. The upper body, especially the head, must be avoided.

Baton Rounds

In addition to shotgun rounds, there are a variety of baton rounds that can be fired from a 37-mm or 40-mm launcher. These weapons are used by both military and law enforcement agencies. In recent years, substantial advances have been made to make the rounds less likely to cause serious injury.

Stun Guns

Stun guns, or electronic control devices that impart an electrical charge, are also widely used. The top brand, TASER, is now employed by more than nine thousand law enforcement agencies in the United States. Contrary to excessive, often inaccurate news media publicity, they have been proven to be both safe and effective. No one has ever died from a TASER. Range is a limiting factor, as the current versions have trailing wires that are twenty-one feet in length. A new version is due shortly that will allow much greater distance.

Police forces are gaining experience in using TASERs in situations with gangs. Street-smart gang members know that police will not shoot them when fleeing, nor will they fire on them for minor provocation. However, they quickly learned that police would use the TASER under such situations. While only 0.0036 amperes in strength, the jolt is sufficient to paralyze muscle groups and initiate considerable pain. As soon as the weapon is turned off, the pain ceases. Gangs confronted with TASERs are far less likely to remain confrontational. This lesson can be transferred to guards employed in protection of cultural heritage sites, and TASERs would be an excellent choice for those situations.

A Failed Security Plan for Iraq

LAURA PAGE

Although the kinds of policing forces and emerging technologies described in this sidebar and the previous chapter offer great promise for protecting museums and sites in future conflicts, their costs may be prohibitively high. A cheaper alternative using off-the-shelf technologies and indigenous forces to protect Iraq's archaeological sites was developed by Wathiq and Nader Hindo, Iraqi businessmen whose security firm has branches in Baghdad and Chicago, with help from associates at Motorola, Inc.

The plan involved stationing guards at numerous sites in southern Iraq and equipping them with handheld radios that would be used to

Figure 13.1. Map of Iraq with Ring of Archaeological Sites in Southern Mesopotamia (base station locations are marked by circles) Source: Nader Hindo.

communicate with a central office. Each province in the region would have its own central office with a base station and tower and could easily communicate with other provinces. Mobile supervisors would circulate through the region, driving pickup trucks outfitted with long-range communication capabilities to relay information from the field back to the base stations. This coordinated effort between sites, base stations, and provinces would create a ring of coverage for many of Iraq's most important archaeological sites.

Under this ring of coverage, more than eight hundred and sixty sites would be protected at a cost of $1.35 million. The companies committed to designing and implementing the security system did not stand to make a profit.

According to McGuire Gibson, the Italian government and military cribbed from this plan to develop their own proposal in 2003. The Italian ambassador to the CPA, Mario Bondioli Osio, selected the Italian plan over the Hindo plan, even though it provided less coverage than the Hindo plan and cost twice as much. Unable to secure sufficient funding from the Italian government, Bondioli Osio turned the plan over to the U.S. military, where it languished and eventually disappeared.

The sites the plan was meant to secure remain unprotected at the time of this writing.

Table 13.1. List of Required Materials for Security System and Associated Costs

Description	Quantity Required	Unit Price ($)	Extended Unit Price ($)	Total ($)
Motorola radios	160	504	630	100,800
Extra radio batteries	160	68	85	13,600
Mobile radios plus installation	20	962	1,203	24,060
Battery charger	1	598	748	748
Base station plus installation	20	3,542	4,428	88,560
Guiding mast plus installation	20	9,400	11,750	235,000
Generators	20	10,000	12,500	250,000
Motorola repeaters plus installation	20	6,425	8,031	160,620
Pickup trucks	20	18,500	24,050	481,000
TOTAL				1,354,373

Source: Nader Hindo and personal communication with McGuire Gibson.

Re-engineered Paintball Guns

There are other applications of OC that have been proven effective. Several companies, including PepperBall and FN Herstal, have re-engineered paintball guns and made them into nonlethal weapons. Instead of a spray, the OC in powder form is delivered in a small capsule. This provides a combined kinetic and chemical effect on the target. The impact is significant and causes bruising. The unsuspecting may actually think they have been shot with a bullet. A cloud of OC quickly forms and is usually inhaled. This provides the suspect with a feeling of burning and suffocation. In reality, the powder is safe and the person is drawing in adequate oxygen. The FN303, a less-lethal launcher made by FN Herstal, was employed by the U.S. military in the Iraqi prisons and was found to be very successful in breaking up potential riots.[1]

A Brazilian company, Condor, has specialized in making and distributing nonlethal weapons, with emphasis on OC systems. Condor has been instrumental in gaining acceptance of nonlethal weapons throughout South America and has worked to introduce these systems in many other countries.

Heat Ray

At the high end of evolving nonlethal weapons is a millimeter beam device called the active denial systems (ADS). The ADS projects a beam at about ninety-three gigahertz that strikes the nerve endings in the skin. In a matter of a few seconds there is a sensation of extreme heating that causes the suspect to move out of the beam. As soon as one is no longer exposed, the pain stops immediately. The beam only penetrates a few millimeters and cannot cause any extensive damage. The range, which is dependent on the power supply, is in hundreds of meters. Smaller devices are being developed. While the ADS would be excellent for point protection, at this stage of development the system is cost-prohibitive for protection of cultural artifacts.

Acoustic Systems

Acoustic systems are rapidly advancing. They offer a unique advantage in that they may also be employed as hailing or warning devices. Highly directional, they ensure that any intruders are warned before the use of force is escalated. These systems can be turned up so that the sound emitted is painful and forces the suspects to leave the area. Cruise liners have employed these systems to repel pirates.[2]

Nonlethal Mines

The protection of open sites can be enhanced by the use of nonlethal mines. There are several varieties either available or under development. Research for this technology has been conducted in response to a military need to deny access to certain areas without the negative consequences of explosive mines. Among the technologies in development are systems that deploy TASER-like darts. They are smart enough to sense an intruder and then aim and launch the darts. Incapacitation is short but memorable.

Alternative Chemical Munitions

Similarly, alternative area denial munitions can use any combination of chemical agents, including OC, CS, or even microencapsulated malodorants. Additionally, indelible dyes can be employed to mark intruders for later identification. These dyes may be visible, thus alerting the suspect and, with luck, causing him to flee. Or invisible dyes can be used that reflect when exposed to black light. Rather than deterrence, this approach would facilitate later arrest or interrogation of the tagged suspect. These alternative munitions can be spread throughout a protected site and activated only upon intrusion.

Incapacitating Agents

While highly controversial, there do exist incapacitating agents that will render intruders unconscious. The most notable case was the use of M-99 by the Russians during the 2002 takeover of the Dubrovka Theater in Moscow. Several hundred hostages were rescued in that action. Unfortunately, more than one hundred died. There is no totally safe chemical incapacitating agent. For very high-value assets, it may be useful to know that technology exists that can protect the sites, albeit with some risk to humans.

Tracking Technologies

One final approach is to use tracking technology to follow looted items. There are a number of small, cost-effective RFID (radio frequency identification) devices that can be implanted. These could be used to track high-value artifacts if they are stolen. Since the trail of many of the stolen artifacts is unknown, fake objects could be introduced through the underground labyrinth into which they seem to disappear. By tracking the movement and resting points, it would be possible to identify thieves, transporters, storage facilities, marketers, and, in the end, the buyers of these illicit artifacts.

There are a number of technologies that could assist in protecting cultural heritage. The real question is one of commitment. The limiting factors are cost and providing the personnel necessary to support the process. Which technologies are best suited will be based primarily upon the response time that can be supported. There are no technologies that can prevent theft for an indefinite period of time. However, the use of nonlethal weapons can add a degree of security as they provide options between passive observation and use of deadly force. Experience with nonlethal weapons in a variety of peace support operations has shown them to be an effective deterrent.

NOTES

1. Master Sergeant (P) Jonathan Godwin, presentation in "From the Front," Current Operations Forum, Non-Lethal Defense VI, Non-Lethal Weapon Options in the Global Fight Against Terrorism conference, Reston, VA, March 14, 2005.
2. Andrew Sheves, "Dangerous Consequences," website of Drum Cussac, business risk consultants, August 2006, http://www.drum-cussac.com/news/News4_dangerous_consequences.html.

THE WAY FORWARD
For Postwar Reconstruction Planners

PLANNING FOR COMBAT AND IMMEDIATE POSTCOMBAT OPERATIONS SHOULD INCLUDE the deployment of stability police units—and, if possible, units specialized for the task of cultural heritage protection—equipped with site-deterrence technologies. However, planning for the longer-term reconstruction phase must rely on different assets. In order to tamp down on looting in the countryside before it becomes regularized and tied in to an international network of smugglers, postwar planners must be able to deploy skilled law enforcement and civil-military affairs experts. As the following chapters make clear, all of these potentially powerful resources need to be better integrated and funded than they are at present if they are to be of real use in a future conflict.

CHAPTER 14

The Way Ahead
A Five-Point Plan for Future Action

MATTHEW BOGDANOS

AS THE HEAD OF THE INVESTIGATION INTO ONE OF THE GREATEST ART CRIMES IN recent memory—the looting of the Iraq Museum in 2003—I have spent more than four years attempting to recover and return to the Iraqi people their priceless heritage. I have spent almost as much time, however, attempting to correct the almost universal misconceptions about what happened at the museum in those fateful days in April 2003, to increase awareness of the continuing cultural catastrophe that is represented by the illegal trade in stolen antiquities, and to highlight the need for the concerted and cooperative efforts of the international community to preserve, protect, and recover the shared cultural heritage of all humanity.

Indeed, in more than one hundred and seventy-five speeches in almost one hundred cities in nine countries—in venues ranging from universities, museums, and governmental organizations to law-enforcement agencies, Interpol (the International Criminal Police Organization) and both houses of the British Parliament—I have urged a more active role for governments, international organizations, cultural organizations and foundations, and the art community.

I have not been very successful. Most governments have their hands full combating terrorism, with few resources left to spare for tracking down stolen artifacts. Most international organizations are content to issue proclamations, preferring to hit the conference center rather than the streets. Many cultural organizations and foundations are equally content to issue a call for papers rather than a call to action.

As for the art community, some members wash their hands of unpleasant realities and argue that, while technically illegal, the market in purloined antiquities is benign—victimless—as long as it brings the art to those who can properly protect it and appreciate it (namely, themselves). The nexus between art theft and the insurgency in Iraq that I have discussed previously in this volume gives the lie to this self-deception: the trade helps to fund the roadside bombs that kill so many, and the plunder of Iraq's 10,000 poorly guarded archaeological sites—as of early 2007, there was roughly one guard for every four sites—continues. As a result, the desert night is filled with the roar of bulldozers ripping into the ancient mounds of clay that were once thriving cities.

All the while, the situation in Iraq has deteriorated dramatically, seemingly descending into chaos—with a majority of the U.S. electorate increasingly reluctant to risk American blood to save Iraqi lives. So it's a pretty tough sell to ask people to care about a bunch of old rocks with funny writing. Finding the political will to divert resources to saving cultural artifacts, no matter how precious, seems like cutting funding for police and fire in order to expand the public library. There might be a case for it, but when? After all, looting has always been a cottage industry in Iraq, the region that gave birth not just to agriculture, cities, the wheel, and pottery, but to war and conquest as well.

The argument for protecting artifacts takes on added strength when we recognize that we are where we are today, not just because of our failure to provide sufficient security to overcome the long-festering tribal and religious animosities, but also because of our continuing failure to appreciate the importance Iraqis place on the preservation of their history. This failure to protect a rich heritage going back to the dawn of civilization has convinced many in Iraq and the Middle East that we do not care about any culture other than our own. And their belief is continually reinforced: four years after the initial looting—and despite having recovered almost 6,000 antiquities since then—we cannot keep pace with the artifacts that are being looted every day.

RECOMMENDATIONS FOR STOPPING TRAFFICKING IN LOOTED ANTIQUITIES

Protect Archaeological Sites

Based on my experience in both counterterrorism and law enforcement—and as a result of the time I have spent in Iraq and throughout the world in tracking down the stolen antiquities—I submit that the first order of business in addressing this catastrophe must be to protect the archaeological sites. Some of these, such as Babylon and Nimrud, require several hundred guards and support staff for protection around the clock. The math is daunting: country-wide more than 50,000 personnel are required, along with the necessary vehicles, radios, weapons, and logistical needs. But there is an immediate solution.

In other contexts, the United Nations (UN) and the North Atlantic Treaty Organization (NATO) have acted to address catastrophic situations. In Bosnia, Cyprus, and Afghanistan, for example, many countries have provided contingents for specific missions under UN or NATO auspices. But not in Iraq. The reasons are much-argued, and I will not revisit them here. Recalling Voltaire's observation that "everyone is guilty of the good he didn't do," I will focus instead on what we can do now.

So who might act? In the past, most archaeological digs in Iraq have had foreign sponsorship—the Germans at Babylon and Uruk, the British at Ur and Nimrud, the French at Kish and Lagash, the Italians at Hatra and Nimrud, the Americans at Nippur and Ur. Leveraging this history, I propose that these (and eventually other) countries provide forces to protect Iraq's archaeological sites until a professional Iraqi security force dedicated to the sites can be recruited, equipped, and trained.

Provide International Training for Iraqi Forces
Under this proposal, and with the permission of the Iraqi government, facilitated by the U.S military, and under the authority of the UN or NATO, each country would "adopt" a site. After sending an assessment team to the assigned sites to determine the precise numbers and type of personnel and equipment required, each donor nation would then draft and sign bilateral status of forces agreements with Iraq, outlining the rules of engagement, funding, billeting, and the standard logistical issues. Then, each country would deploy its security forces (military, police, private contractors, or a combination of all three) to the agreed-upon archaeological sites around the perimeter and around the clock.

Upon arrival, each country's contingent would also be assigned a group of Iraqi recruits (who would live and work with them) to train at their chosen site. Once those Iraqi security forces were fully trained—that ordinarily takes six months—the donor nation would recall (or reassign) its forces on a site-by-site basis. In half a year, every archaeological site of consequence in Iraq could be completely protected from the looters. Mesopotamia's cultural patrimony would be safe, al-Jezeera would have to find other ways to show Western indifference to Arab culture, and the terrorists would have to find another income source.

Unfortunately, neither NATO nor the UN has such plans in the works. NATO opened a training center in Iraq in 2005, but has trained only 1,500 Iraqi security personnel, none of whom have been assigned to archaeological sites. The UN has never trained guards for the sites. Even the UN's cultural arm, the United Nations Educational, Scientific and Cultural Organization (UNESCO) has failed to act, claiming it has no such mandate from its member nations.

Assuming that to be true, UNESCO ought to convince its member nations to support such an initiative. It is time for the UN to seize the mantle of international leadership and convince its members to support such a plan. As our best hope, UNESCO ought to step into the vacuum of international leadership, seize the bully pulpit, and become relevant again. "Man should share the action and passion of his time," former Supreme Court justice Oliver Wendell Holmes once noted, "at peril of being judged never to have lived."

Individual countries are also slow to respond. Only the Italians, Danes, Dutch, and Poles have joined the Americans and British in protecting these sites—and the Danes, Dutch, and Italians have already left. Other countries have argued that the level of violence does not permit deployment of their forces. The circular nature of this rationalization is underscored by the fact that it is the failure to protect these sites that is partly funding those who are creating the unsafe environment. "If you were to take account of everything that could go wrong," Herodotus advised long ago, "you would never act." Of course there is risk. I know this first-hand. But the risks of the failure to act are far worse: more money for the insurgents, more propaganda for al-Jezeera, and the loss of these extraordinary testaments to our common beginnings.

Rise above the Politics of the Iraq War to
Save Humankind's Cultural Heritage
Equally risky are the politics: most elected officials view involvement in Iraq as political suicide. But an internationally coordinated contribution of personnel would not be a statement about the war or the Bush administration's policies in Iraq. It would be a humanitarian effort to protect a cultural heritage rich with a common ancestry that transcends the current violence. Real leaders should have no difficulty convincing their electorate of the distinction between politics and culture. It is, of course, the very definition of leadership to educate, inform, and motivate into action those who might otherwise be inclined to do nothing.

THE NEXT STEPS: A FIVE-POINT ACTION PLAN TO
COMBAT GLOBAL TRAFFIC IN STOLEN ANTIQUITIES
The incomparable works of art unearthed in the land between the rivers predate the split between Sunni and Shiite. They predate the three competing traditions that have brought so much bloodshed to the Middle East—Islam, Christianity, and Judaism. Attending to this cultural heritage from the very dawn of civilization reminds us of our common humanity, our common aspiration to make sense of life on this planet. I have seen these pieces of alabaster and limestone with funny writing on them work their magic through a language that is both immediate and universal, visceral and transcendent.

While protecting the archaeological sites in Iraq is a vital beginning, much more needs to be done. To stop the rampant looting and the black market that funnels money into terrorist hands, we must adopt a comprehensive global strategy using all of the elements of international power. Toward this end, I propose a five-step plan of action to combat the global traffic in antiquities.

1. Mount a Public Relations Campaign for Mainstream Society

The cornerstone to any comprehensive approach must take into account that real, measurable, and lasting progress in stopping the illegal trade depends on increasing public awareness of the importance of cultural property and of the magnitude of the current crisis. First, then, we must develop and communicate a message that resonates with *mainstream* society—not just with academics. We must create a climate of universal condemnation, rather than sophisticated indulgence, for trafficking in undocumented antiquities.

But this call to arms needs to avoid the sky-is-falling quotes so beloved by the media, while steering clear of the debilitating rhetoric of red state vs. blue state politics. It also has to keep the discussion of the *illegal* trade separate from broader issues such as repatriation of objects acquired prior to 1970 and whether there should be any trade in antiquities at all. The Parthenon Marbles *are* in the British Museum, but their return is a diplomatic or public relations issue, not a matter for the criminal courts. Similarly, there *is* a legal trade in antiquities that is completely fair, regulated, and above board. And it is simply unproven (and unfair) to argue that the legal trade somehow encourages an illegal trade. Most dealers and museums scrupulously *do* avoid trading in antiquities with a murky origin. Repatriation for pre-1970 transfers and the question of whether all trade in antiquities should be banned are legitimate issues, but they are not my issues. Every time the discussion about stopping the *illegal* trade in antiquities veers off into these broader realms we lose focus, we lose the attention of mainstream society, and it makes the job of recovering stolen antiquities that much harder.

2. Provide Funding to Establish or Upgrade Antiquities Task Forces

Second, although several countries—including the United States, Britain, Italy, and Japan—have pledged millions of dollars to upgrade the Iraq Museum, to improve its conservation capacity, and enhance the training of the Iraq State Board of Antiquities and Heritage's archaeological staff, not a single government, international organization, or private foundation anywhere in the world has provided additional funding for investigative purposes. Reluctant to be seen cooperating with police and military forces, many cultural leaders and organizations seem oblivious to the fact that a stolen artifact cannot be *restored* until it has been *recovered*. To put it more clearly: money for conservators is pointless without first providing the money to track down the missing objects to be conserved.

This ivory-tower distortion of priorities affects investigative efforts worldwide. Interpol can afford to assign only two officers to its Iraqi Antiquities Tracking Task Force—and both have other responsibilities as well. Scotland Yard's art and antiquities squad has four officers covering the entire world—and in January of 2007, their budget was slashed in half. The Federal Bureau of Investigation's (FBI) Rapid Deployment National Art Crime Team has eight people. Regardless of the exceptional dedication and talent of these personnel, no law-enforcement agency can operate effectively at such levels.

Thus, as a second component, all countries—but most especially the countries of origin, transit, and destination—must establish robust, specialized art and antiquities task forces, with particular attention paid to the borders and the ports of entry. Where such forces already exist, we must increase their size and scope, with cultural foundations providing art-theft squads with vehicles, computers, communications equipment, and training.

3. Create a Coordinated International Law-Enforcement Response

Among the many dirty secrets of the looted antiquities market is that "open" borders are as profitable as they are dangerous. Many countries, especially those with free ports or free-trade zones, generate sizeable customs and excise fees from shipping and—despite their public protestations to the contrary—are not eager to impose any increase in inspection rates that might reduce such revenue. Even if willing, the sheer tonnage passing through certain international ports and free-trade zones makes 100 percent inspection rates impossible. Nor does the improved technology installed as a result of September 11 solve the problem: devices that detect weapons and explosives do not detect alabaster, lapis lazuli, and carnelian. Further exacerbating the problem, most high-end smugglers are simply too sophisticated, and the questionable acquisition practices of some dealers, collectors, and museums, too entrenched to be defeated by improved border inspections and heightened public consciousness alone.

The sine qua non for effective interdiction, then, is an organized, systematized, and seamlessly collaborative law-enforcement effort by the entire international community. We need coordinated simultaneous investigations of smugglers, sellers, and buyers in different countries. And—just as important—prosecution and incarceration need to be credible threats.

Thus, as a third component, the United Nations, through UNESCO, should establish a commission to continue the Iraq Museum investigation, expanding it to include other pillaged countries as well. Interpol, the International Criminal Police Organization, must also become more active, entering into agreements with its 191 member nations stipulating that each country forward to them immediately, along a secure network (that already exists), a digital photograph and the particulars (who, what, when, and where) of all antiquities encountered by law enforcement or military forces anywhere in the world—including those items that were seized, as well as those that were inspected and not seized because there was insufficient evidence of criminality at the time of the inspection.

The global criminal enterprise that is antiquities smuggling must be defeated globally through international cooperation (promoted by UNESCO) and real-time dissemination of information (enabled by Interpol). The consequent ability to conduct monitored deliveries of illegal shipments to their destinations (a tactic long used against drug smugglers) would enable legal authorities to incriminate and thereafter prosecute each culpable party along the trail. It would also serve as a deterrent to those collectors or curators who could never be sure that the next shipment was not being monitored by law-enforcement officials.

4. Establish a Code of Conduct for Trading in Antiquities

Fourth, museums, archaeologists, and dealers should establish a strict and uniform code of conduct. Similar to ethics rules for lawyers and doctors, this code of conduct would clarify the documentation and diligence required for an artifact to change hands legally. If they refuse such self-regulation, then Congress should impose regulation. Although many argue that the interests of dealers, collectors, museums, and archaeologists differ from each other so dramatically that any single code of conduct acceptable to all is impossible, I point out that the differences within the art world are no greater than those existing between prosecutors and criminal defense attorneys. Yet, the American Bar Association has adopted and actively enforces a single Code of Ethics applicable to every attorney admitted to the bar. Until then, I continue to urge academics, curators, and dealers to abandon their self-serving complacency about—if not complicity in—irregularities of documentation.

5. Increase Cooperation between the Cultural Heritage Community and Law Enforcement

Finally, the art community must break down barriers and assist investigators by serving as law enforcement's eyes and ears. We need scholars and knowledgeable dealers as on-call experts to identify and authenticate intercepted shipments, and to provide crucial in-court expert testimony. They should also request appropriate law-enforcement personnel (depending on country and focus) to provide detailed, factual briefings at every conference purporting to address art or antiquities smuggling. The call for up-to-date investigative facts should become as standard as the call for papers.

But the education and information exchange should run in both directions. In 2004, Dr. C. Brian Rose, then First Vice-President of the Archaeological Institute of America, developed and conducted cultural-awareness training in half-a-dozen pilot locations around the country for military personnel scheduled to deploy to Iraq or Afghanistan. The program should be expanded to include every unit deploying overseas. A similar program should be offered to the FBI and the Department of Homeland Security on a regular basis. Such cooperation between the art and archaeological communities and the law enforcement and military presents a real chance of winning a fight we cannot afford to lose.

FUTURE MILITARY CONFLICTS

The U.S. military has lessons to be learned as well. Looking to the future, we must never again cede the moral high ground on issues of cultural sensitivity and national patrimony. Thus, before the U.S. military takes action in any country, our commanders must clearly articulate our recognition of that country's proud cultural heritage and our intent to protect such property, to the extent possible, during the conflict and postconflict stage. Not just the message, but the actions that flow from it, must convince the world that the United States and, in particular, the U.S. military are committed to honoring and preserving the heritage of all nations and religious traditions.

To do so, military leaders must plan before any action for the protection of cultural property in the proposed area of operations. This protection must go beyond merely putting the site on the no-strike list. It must include the securing of significant sites (as identified by members of the archaeological community) and the immediate deployment, if needed, of on-call security forces (identified in advance of the operation) upon reports of looting. Where such forces already exist, U.S. forces should assist by providing them with vehicles, radios, and training. Where no such forces exist, the U.S. military must protect the sites until trained forces are available. Such preparation would enable planners to identify shortfalls and—where appropriate—attempt to fill such needs from international organizations or coalition countries before the conflict.

Diverting resources to save cultural artifacts during a time of war may seem trivial considering the human cost of war. But some wise soldiers before us have seen the wisdom. "Inevitably, in the path of our advance will be found historical monuments and cultural centers which symbolize to the world all that we are fighting to preserve," said General Dwight Eisenhower, just before D-Day during the deadliest war of the last one hundred years, one that threatened our nation's existence. "It is the responsibility of every commander to protect and respect these symbols whenever possible."

CONCLUSION

Antiquities trafficking will never merit the same attention or resources as terrorism, drugs, human trafficking, or violent street crime. But, at the very least, it deserves to be on the same list. From government corridors, precinct headquarters, and media newsrooms to faculty lounges, museum boardrooms, and galleries on Madison Avenue, this cultural catastrophe must be confronted and debated. We must expose those who engage in the illegal trade for what they are: criminals.

On my first tour in Iraq, our mission was to track down illegal arms and terrorist networks. My decision to expand our mission to include investigating the looting of the Iraq Museum and tracking down the stolen artifacts was characterized by many as a distraction. I regret that I did not pursue that distraction even more.

CHAPTER 15

Assignment Blue Shield

The Looting of the Iraq Museum and Cultural Property at War

CORINE WEGENER

IN APRIL 2003, PEOPLE OF THE WORLD WATCHED THEIR TELEVISIONS IN HORROR AS looters ransacked the Iraq Museum, carrying off some of the most important treasures of our shared cultural heritage. As a long-time member of the U.S. Army Reserve, I was worried about my fellow service members fighting to take Baghdad, but I was also surprised and angered by the museum looting. I knew from media reports that cultural heritage professionals had met with military personnel at the Pentagon to provide the coordinates of important cultural and religious sites for the no-strike list included in all operations orders. As an art museum curator, I was appalled by the senseless loss of the world's cultural heritage.

The failure to provide security and stability after the invasion of Iraq set the stage for looting and damage to cultural property throughout the country, including the looting of the Iraq Museum, the burning of the Iraq National Library and Archives, and the looting of archaeological sites across the country. While this tragedy can be attributed to a number of sources, the problem was certainly exacerbated by the lack of coordination and communication within and between the cultural heritage and military communities.

This paper will outline the difficulties faced by the cultural heritage community when attempting to coordinate with the military prior to the war, as well as when trying to provide an emergency response for the Iraq Museum after it was looted. Second, we will examine the military stance on cultural property protection and suggest that placing a higher priority on culture might reap both strategic and tactical benefits. Finally, I will describe the development of the U.S. Committee of the Blue Shield, an organization committed to the protection of cultural property during armed conflict, and argue that it is the best hope for improving coordination between U.S. cultural heritage organizations and the military in any future conflicts.

THE CULTURAL HERITAGE COMMUNITY: WHAT WENT WRONG?

In his chapter in this volume, "Preserving Iraq's Heritage from Looting: What Went Wrong (within the United States)," Lawrence Rothfield recounts a number of challenges faced by the cultural heritage community when trying to coordinate with the military to protect cultural property in Iraq. First among them was that the cultural heritage organizations trying to advocate for the protection of Iraqi cultural heritage had much less experience dealing with armed conflict than their humanitarian aid counterparts did, and they had no plan for a coordinated advocacy effort. There were even old conflicts between cultural organizations, such as between archaeologists and collectors groups, that decreased their ability to coordinate among themselves. When groups did meet with military planners they were not able to turn the focus from potential combat damage and looting by U.S. military personnel to looting by Iraqis, even though most in the cultural heritage community agreed the latter was the greatest risk to cultural property. They lacked an umbrella organization bringing together all U.S. cultural heritage organizations committed to protecting cultural property during armed conflict in a strong, united front able to coordinate effectively with military planners. This need would become even more apparent in the aftermath of the looting.

I was mobilized by the U.S. Army as a subject matter expert soon after the museum looting. I arrived at the Iraq Museum on May 16, 2003, and was dismayed to learn that there were no international cultural heritage organizations or object conservation experts on the ground to help conserve damaged objects. The first UNESCO team of observers arrived that same day to survey the damage and prepare a report, but they were not allowed to stay longer than a few days due to security concerns. The lack of object conservation expertise was particularly distressing. In addition to damaging the museum's offices, equipment, and infrastructure, looters shattered sculpture, clay vessels, archaeological materials, and display cases, both in the galleries and in storage. These actions aggravated an already existing problem—many objects had been in need of conservation even before the looting. The Iraqi conservation staff, a small but dedicated team of five women, had very little training in current methods of object conservation because the economic sanctions in place before the war did not allow them to travel abroad for education. I hoped that other organizations in the cultural heritage community would arrive to help the museum staff, but it took much longer than anyone anticipated.

The International Committee of the Blue Shield (ICBS), a nongovernmental organization (NGO) founded by a number of international cultural heritage organizations, was the logical choice to field a team of experts to help at the museum.[1] The mission of the ICBS is "to work for the protection of the world's cultural heritage by coordinating preparations to meet and respond to emergency situations."[2] However, staff at the museum and I were disappointed to learn the ICBS was not working in Iraq and had no plans for fielding such a team of cultural property rescue experts.

In those early days and weeks I received e-mails from conservators and museum colleagues in the United States volunteering to travel to Iraq to assist the museum, but any plans along these lines were frustrated by the bureaucratic realities of the war zone. Individual civilian volunteers were not welcome because they might become logistical and security burdens on the military. Similarly, national governments rarely issue visas to individuals seeking entrance to countries experiencing armed conflict. Such was certainly the case with Iraq. Those few cultural heritage professionals and archaeologists that made it into Iraq were admitted as part of a media team or as members of one of the established humanitarian NGOs.

Ideally, the ICBS or a U.S. Committee of the Blue Shield would have responded to the situation with the same type of emergency response capabilities of established humanitarian organizations such as the Red Cross or Doctors Without Borders. Humanitarian NGOs are routinely allowed access to a military theater of operations by the United States because they provide services for which the military has scant resources. They also usually have established their credibility with the military prior to the conflict by clearly demonstrating a professional capability to assist without becoming a logistical or security burden. In fact, military units often invite NGOs to training exercises to provide realism and coordination for future real world missions. Unfortunately, no U.S. NGO dedicated to cultural property protection during armed conflict existed to assist in Iraq.

Another problem that plagued the cultural heritage community's efforts to protect cultural property during the Iraq invasion was a general lack of knowledge about dealing with the military. This problem is understandable, as the bureaucracy of the military is legendary. However, an NGO hoping to advocate for the protection of cultural property during armed conflict could work to establish and maintain military contacts during peacetime so that it would later be invited into the military planning process. Some cultural heritage professionals may refuse to coordinate with the military on ethical grounds; however, this approach merely provides an excuse for military planners to downplay cultural property concerns and may potentially impede the ability to provide emergency cultural property conservation assistance to our colleagues in the war zone.

But who in the military should cultural heritage organizations coordinate with on an ongoing basis? One of the best places to start is with U.S. Army civil affairs units, which have primary responsibility for cultural property issues in the theater of operations.

Civil affairs units are the field commander's link to civilian authorities of the host nation, as well as to any international and nongovernmental organizations working in the area. The U.S. Army Civil Affairs and Psychological Operations Command has both active duty and reserve units, but 95 percent of civil affairs soldiers are reservists who are subject matter experts in every area of government, including judges, physicians, bankers, health inspectors, fire chiefs, and even a few cultural heritage professionals.[3] In fact, Civil Affairs has a proud history of protecting cultural property dating back to the Monuments, Fine Arts, and Archives (MFA&A) teams of World War II. These teams, comprised of museum curators and directors, art historians, and conservators, developed cultural property assessments throughout Europe and repatriated thousands of works of art looted by the Nazis. Unfortunately, in today's all-volunteer force there are few cultural heritage professionals serving in civil affairs units, though the units still bear the primary responsibility for cultural property issues. In view of the military's need for expert advice, an important mission of an umbrella cultural heritage NGO would be to offer training and expertise during peacetime, developing relationships and coordination that might also be called upon during wartime.

U.S. cultural property organizations must develop a better means of coordinating with each other and the military if they hope to protect cultural property during current and future armed conflicts, particularly those involving the United States. The most logical vehicle is an umbrella NGO that will represent their commitment to the protection of cultural property during armed conflict. This NGO must make an effort at better coordination with the military during peacetime so that it becomes the established organization for culture during armed conflict, similar to the way that the Red Cross is the established organization for humanitarian assistance in times of conflict. Such an NGO must develop an understanding of how the military is organized and how the military planning process works if it hopes to champion cultural heritage issues during armed conflict.

THE MILITARY: WHY CULTURE MATTERS

While the United States is an original signatory to the 1954 Hague Convention for the Protection of Cultural Property in the Event of Armed Conflict, it has not ratified the treaty. However, it is U.S. Department of Defense policy to follow the provisions of the Convention as customary international law. Rothfield notes this is one of a number of issues that contributed to the military failure to protect cultural property in Iraq during the U.S.-led invasion. He shows that the military understood it had a legal obligation not to destroy cultural property without military necessity, but evaded the question of whether it was obligated to actively protect cultural property from looters. He also points out that even though it is the responsibility of Army civil affairs units to advise military commanders on cultural property issues, there are very few soldiers in the all-volunteer U.S. Army with cultural property expertise to offer. Moreover, cultural property issues were a low priority. However, after the disastrous looting of the museum and the resulting surge of negative public opinion, this author would like to suggest to the military that cultural property protection should be given a higher priority in future conflicts.

In light of the terrible tragedies that occur during wartime, it is easy to dismiss the question of protection for cultural property. Troops and resources are in short supply. Careful targeting takes time in the heat of battle. Command and control fall victim to the fog of war. However, there are also compelling reasons to preserve cultural property whenever possible, not the least of which is that the protection of culture property during armed conflict is mandated under U.S. federal and international law, including the Geneva Conventions (Protocol I, Articles 53 and 85) and the 1954 Hague Convention on the Protection of Cultural Property in the Event of Armed Conflict.[4] Those who violate these laws may be prosecuted in a court of law and risk the harsh spotlight of negative media attention.

Protecting cultural property also aligns us with our NATO and other military allies. U.S. forces are increasingly called upon to work as part of a coalition of military forces from various countries; it is unreasonable and confusing to expect military forces to carry out combat operations together when operating under different treaties, policies, and guidelines. Though both the United States and the United Kingdom signed the 1954 Hague Convention, neither has ratified it. The executive branch of the U.S. government did not transmit the treaty to the Senate for ratification, apparently due to concerns from the Joint Chiefs of Staff that it might limit its strategic bombing options during the Cold War.[5] However, more than one hundred countries around the world have ratified the Convention and more than forty have ratified the Second Protocol of 1999. In 2004, the United Kingdom, the United States' closest military ally, announced its intention to ratify the 1954 Hague Convention and its Protocols, leaving the United States as the only industrial country with a military force that has not undertaken to ratify this important treaty. In a joint environment, it is vital that U.S. forces work under the same rules of engagement and operational guidelines as their coalition partners.

Finally, the most important reason to protect cultural property during armed conflict is to contribute to stability and provide force protection, both of which further the military mission. There are a number of historical precedents for this assertion. During World War II, the Monuments, Fine Arts, and Archives teams were not established merely because protecting cultural property was the right thing to do—they were established to combat negative propaganda and win hearts and minds. When Allied leaders made the decision to enter Europe through Italy in 1943, the world was confronted with images of cultural monuments damaged by U.S. forces, courtesy of the Nazi propaganda machine. Seeking comfortable lodging, Allied soldiers wreaked havoc in Europe's palaces, museums, and churches. Military leaders recognized that protecting cultural property was not only part of their legal obligation but also critical to maintaining the goodwill of the people being liberated. They sought the help of cultural heritage professionals back in the United States to identify colleagues already serving in the military. They were then gathered together to establish several MFA&A teams under the command of the Civil Affairs Division of the Army. The teams consisted of museum curators, conservators, and art historians who worked to develop protected target lists and maps, lists of buildings and areas designated as off limits, and who, at the end of the war, catalogued and repatriated thousands of works of art looted by the Nazis.[6]

In Bosnia, the destruction of cultural property became an instrument of war as cultural property, religious and civil architecture, and other monuments became pawns in the process of civil war and ethnic cleansing. The burning of the National Library in Sarajevo, the destruction of the Mostar Bridge, built in 1566, and the razing of sixteen mosques in the Serb enclave of Banja Luka were all carefully calculated to destroy Bosnia's multicultural society, and finally, to aid and abet genocide by destroying an ethnic group and any evidence of its existence.[7] A people's self-worth is rooted in its cultural heritage, and all sides retaliated for the destruction. Cathedrals and minarets alike were bombed, cemeteries were mined, and snipers targeted museums. When NATO forces finally intervened, they not only prevented further fighting but also prohibited the further destruction of cultural property, halting the increasingly violent building-for-building and monument-for-monument retaliation that had become part of the ethnic cleansing. Military forces were prepared to stop not only the destruction of human lives, but also the destruction of the culture that identified local inhabitants as a people.

Finally, one can only speculate what might have happened in Iraq had U.S. forces stopped the looting in April 2003. It is the opinion of this author that if U.S. forces had been able to first secure major cultural landmarks like the Iraq Museum, the Iraq National Library and Archives, and the Ministry of Culture, this action might have effectively sent a signal that looting in general would not be tolerated, possibly even alleviating the need to prevent looting on every street corner. Iraqis might have interpreted this show of respect for their cultural heritage as respect for the Iraqi people as a whole and responded in kind. Instead, the looting of the museum and the Bush administration's early response to it caused a negative first impression that was very difficult to overcome.

During my tour of duty I continued to think about how the cultural heritage and military communities could better coordinate on issues of cultural property during armed conflict. At the end of my tour in Iraq, I wrote a final report to the U.S. Army Civil Affairs Command detailing successful reconstruction efforts at the Iraq Museum and Iraqi Ministry of Culture, as well as a number of opportunities for improvement. One of my strongest recommendations was for a new Civil Affairs basic soldier guide to cultural property. The project was approved just as I redeployed home, and I was invited, along with several volunteer conservators and military personnel from the John F. Kennedy Special Warfare Center and School, to coauthor the guide. In March 2005 the Department of the Army published *U.S. Army Graphic Training Aid 41-01-002, Civil Affairs Arts, Monuments, and Archives Guide*.[8] In spite of the tragic loss of cultural property in Iraq, the publication of this guide demonstrates a willingness by Civil Affairs to continue its role in protecting cultural property during armed conflict and to coordinate with civilian experts in the field. However, I remain convinced that the U.S. cultural heritage community needs to establish an umbrella NGO for cultural heritage emergency response during armed conflict in order to avoid the mistakes of the past.

THE BLUE SHIELD—A CULTURAL RED CROSS?

The Blue Shield is often compared to the Red Cross as an international symbol of protection. It is the symbol States Parties to the 1954 Hague Convention for the Protection of Cultural Property in the Event of Armed Conflict may use to mark designated cultural sites for protection during armed conflict. The International Committee of the Blue Shield (ICBS) was created by professionals from museums, archives, libraries, and monuments and sites from around the world who are dedicated to protecting cultural property during armed conflict. Four cultural heritage organizations created ICBS in 1996: ICOM (International Council of Museums), ICOMOS (International Council of Monuments and Sites), ICA (International Council on Archives), and IFLA (International Federation of Library Associations and Institutions). Another organization, CCAAA (Coordinating Council of Audiovisual Archives Associations) was added in 2005. Their mission "is to work for the protection of the world's cultural heritage by coordinating preparations to meet and respond to emergency situations."[9]

In view of this mission, why didn't the International Committee of the Blue Shield send an emergency response team to the Iraq Museum after the looting in 2003? As an established nongovernmental organization they might have been admitted, especially considering the intense media scrutiny U.S. authorities were experiencing. However, my international colleagues informed me that ICBS did not have the staff or resources for such a mission. It occurred to me that one reason the ICBS was not able to field an emergency response was that as an international organization it relied solely upon its member nations for its capabilities.

Members of ICBS are, for the most part, States Parties to the 1954 Hague Convention who have developed their own national committees of the Blue Shield. However, the United States, the most powerful and active military power in the world, had neither ratified the 1954 Hague Convention nor set up a Blue Shield national committee. If the United States had had a national committee of the Blue Shield at the time, I—or someone in a similar role— might have been able to call upon their expertise, referred individual volunteers to them, and then coordinated through military channels to obtain permission for them to enter Iraq. During my nine-month tour, I became increasingly convinced of the need to develop an NGO in the United States for cultural property emergency response during armed conflict and, furthermore, that this organization should be a U.S. national committee of the Blue Shield.

Blue Shield national committees are the key to the success of the ICBS mission. They bring together different professions, local and national governments, emergency services, and the armed forces. They provide a forum to improve emergency preparedness by sharing experiences and information. They can raise national awareness regarding threats to cultural heritage and promote the ratification and implementation by national governments of the 1954 Hague Convention. There are currently fourteen Blue Shield national committees, including Australia, Belgium, Benin, Brazil, Chile, the Czech Republic, France, Italy, the Former Yugoslav Republic of Macedonia, Madagascar, the Netherlands, Norway, Poland, and the United Kingdom and Ireland.

After consulting with colleagues from government organizations such as the U.S. Department of State, the Department of Defense, and Army Civil Affairs, as well as cultural property colleagues from the museum, archaeology, and conservation fields, I was encouraged to go forward with the basic process of establishing a Blue Shield national committee. I conferred with the board of the ICBS and staff at the International Council of Museums for advice on how to proceed. According to ICBS guidelines, national committees should support the ICBS commitment to protecting cultural property during armed conflict within the framework of the 1954 Hague Convention, should have the support of national cultural heritage organizations within their own country, and maintain a line of communication with ICBS.

In January 2006, a group of colleagues from the cultural heritage community began working to establish the framework for a U.S. national committee of the Blue Shield, which was then incorporated as the United States Committee of the Blue Shield (USCBS). Since then we have invited a number of other cultural heritage organizations to join us. The USCBS received the endorsement of the U.S. National Committee of the International Council of Museums Committee (ICOM-US), the Society of American Archivists, the Association of Moving Image Archivists, the American Library Association International Relations Committee, the Archaeological Institute of America, the American Institute for Conservation of Historic & Artistic Works, and the U.S. National Committee of the International Committee on Monuments and Sites (US/ICOMOS).

On June 19, 2007, the U.S. Committee of the Blue Shield received official recognition from the ICBS. The U.S. Committee of the Blue Shield will focus on three key program areas to accomplish its mission of protecting cultural property during armed conflict: military cultural property training, developing cultural emergency response teams, and promoting U.S. ratification of the 1954 Hague Convention. USCBS plans to provide expertise, training, and coordination regarding cultural property to the U.S. military, particularly Army Reserve civil affairs units. Large-scale U.S. deployments in Iraq and Afghanistan, countries with significant cultural property resources, mean that soldiers are often confronted with cultural property damage issues with little expertise to draw upon. USCBS is partnering with the AIC (American Institute for Conservation of Historic & Artistic Works) to offer training opportunities for Army Reserve civil affairs units beginning in 2007. Topics will include the history and role of Civil Affairs Monuments, Fine Arts, and Archives teams from World War II to Iraq; recognizing immovable and movable cultural property, tangible and intangible cultural heritage, libraries, archives, and religious sites; protection, handling, and storage of cultural property; basic documentation using Object ID, an international standard for describing works of art and other cultural property; and archaeological site recognition and protection. The hope is that courses like these will help lay the groundwork for future coordination and provide soldiers with valuable contacts to call upon in an emergency situation.

USCBS will help coordinate a worldwide emergency response to cultural property threatened by armed conflict, particularly in those areas in which U.S. forces are deployed. USCBS will partner with AIC and other U.S. cultural professional organizations to develop and maintain a list of conservators and other volunteers interested in being part of such an emergency response. We will also coordinate with and offer our assistance to colleagues in other Blue Shield national committees.

The USCBS is also committed to promoting U.S. ratification of the 1954 Hague Convention and its Protocols. The reputation of the United States suffered greatly after the looting of the Iraq Museum in 2003. U.S. ratification of the 1954 Hague Convention would codify the treaty as U.S. law and contribute greatly to restoring faith in the United States' commitment to protecting cultural property during armed conflict. USCBS will educate its members and the general public about the importance of the Convention and provide information and expertise to members of the U.S. Senate Foreign Relations Committee when they consider ratification. Finally, USCBS will assume certain responsibilities as a national Blue Shield committee. USCBS is currently considered a national committee "under construction," along with the committees of eighteen other countries, and as such was invited to attend a recent meeting of Blue Shield organizations in The Hague, the Netherlands. Representatives from ICBS and several national Blue Shield committees met on September 27–28, 2006, to discuss and agree upon the most effective way to support the new International Committee for the Protection of Cultural Property in the Event of Armed Conflict, a twelve-member intergovernmental committee set up to oversee implementation of the 1954 Hague Convention and its Protocols. The parties drafted and signed the 2006 Hague Blue Shield Accord agreeing to the creation of a new body, the Association of National Committees of the Blue Shield (ANCBS).[10] According to the accord, ANCBS will set up a new headquarters in The Hague and work to establish networks of professionals from each of our countries who can provide an emergency response for cultural heritage at risk worldwide. In addition, the national committees will work to promote ratification or implementation of the 1954 Hague Convention in each of their countries, as well as work to coordinate with and train their respective militaries in cultural heritage awareness and protection.

The establishment of the U.S. Committee of the Blue Shield, with its strong network of cultural heritage organizations, combined with the newly formed network of the ANCBS, will hopefully serve to strengthen the capabilities of the entire Blue Shield system so that it is better prepared for future contingencies. However, international organizations are only as effective as their members. The stated mission and goals of the ICBS and its national committees provide clear guidance for solutions to the problems outlined in this paper: lack of coordination, inability to facilitate an emergency response, and lack of cultural property training, both within and between the cultural property and military communities. Each Blue Shield organization must strive to improve its ability to perform its mission or once again risk helplessness in the face of the next cultural property disaster caused by armed conflict.

Since September 11, 2001, the U.S. military has been continuously deployed on a scale not seen since World War II. Through the United States Committee of the Blue Shield, cultural property professionals from a cross section of disciplines could reopen a dialogue with military planners about best practices in protecting cultural property, increase coordination between civilian experts and the military, provide training and expertise on "first aid" for cultural property, and potentially even field conservation teams to assist cultural property organizations in conflict zones controlled by the U.S. military. USCBS should become the first point of contact for the U.S. military for issues concerning cultural property. Only in this way can we hope to improve coordination between the military and cultural heritage communities in the hopes of preventing another tragedy like the looting of the Iraq Museum.

NOTES

1. For more information on ICBS, go to www.ifla.org/blueshield.htm.
2. http://www.international.icomos.org/blue_shield.htm.
3. For more on the Civil Affairs mission see www.armyreserve.army.mil/ARMYDRU/ USACAPOC/Overview.htm.
4. See the full text of the convention at www.unesco.org/culture/laws/hague/html_ eng/page1.shtml.
5. See Patrick J. Boylan, *Review of the Convention for the Protection of Cultural Property in the Event of Armed Conflict (The Hague Convention of 1954)*, 1993, UNESCO Report CLT-93/WS/12,104, http://unesdoc.unesco.org/images/0010/001001/100159eo .pdf.
6. For a comprehensive account of the MFA&A teams see Lynn Nicholas, *The Rape of Europa: The Fate of Europe's Treasures in the Third Reich and the Second World War* (New York: Knopf, 1994; Vintage, 1995) and Robert M. Edsel, *Rescuing Da Vinci* (Dallas: Laurel Publishing, LLC, 2006).
7. See chapter 2 of Robert Bevan, *The Destruction of Memory: Architecture at War* (London: Reaktion Books, 2006) for a description the destruction of mosques in Banja Luka. I witnessed the aftermath and its affects on the population during my deployment as a civil affairs officer in Banja Luka for Operation Joint Endeavor, 1997–1998.
8. http://www.au.af.mil/au/awc/awcgate/army/gta41-01-002_arts_monuments_ and_archives.pdf. The second edition will be available in the near future.
9. http://icom.museum/emergency.html#mission.
10. See at http://www.ifla.org/VI/4/admin/icbs-accord28-09-2006.htm.

CHAPTER 16

The Role of NATO and Civil Military Affairs

Joris D. Kila

WORKING WITH THE MILITARY TO EFFECTIVELY PROTECT CULTURAL HERITAGE IS A challenge that takes on a distinctive form when one turns from the context of the United States to that of Europe, where many of the militaries' rules, customs, and organizational structures differ, and where the multinational nature of military activities creates distinctive opportunities—and poses distinctive dilemmas—for promoters of heritage protection. This article will focus on the intersection of cultural and military issues in Europe (including the EU) and the role of NATO (which includes the United States). I will focus on what has been done, what is being done now, and steps to be taken in the future.

WHY SHOULD NATO DEAL WITH CULTURE?

In theory, NATO would be the ideal organization to house and support a militarized cultural emergency team.

International treaties such as the 1954 Hague Convention and its protocols require that NATO and the EU bring in expertise concerning cultural heritage protection in times of armed conflict in their organizations. In the case of NATO, this task would fall naturally to the department of Civil Emergency Planning (CEP), in particular the Senior Civil Emergency Planning Committee (SCEPC). Of course, there is also a related military intelligence element, especially in the case of the illicit traffic of artifacts. In addition, NATO's Allied Command Transformation (ACT)[1] should include cultural heritage protection in its program.

Since many countries are members of NATO, the possibility of locating and recruiting militarized experts is potentially great. Furthermore, the NATO CIMIC (Civil Military Cooperation) AJP-9 doctrine seems designed to enhance implementation of Cultural Affairs: responsibility for providing advice on cultural heritage issues to military planners and commanders of NATO forces lies with CIMIC/CA, where CA stands for Civil Affairs.

In the field, the deployment of military cultural experts must be in support of the commander's mission. This is based on NATO CIMIC doctrine AJP-9, wherein CIMIC (known in the United States and United Kingdom as Civil Affairs, or CA) is defined as:

> The co-ordination and co-operation, in support of the mission, between the NATO Commander and civil actors, including national population and local authorities, as well as international, national and non-governmental organisations and agencies.

The AJP-9 doctrine gives room for multiple interpretations. The phrase "in support of the Commander's mission" could mean in the actual area of deployment of a battle group (e.g., Al Muthanna [Iraq]), or in a wider context in support of the mission in a whole country (e.g., the NATO commander's mission in Afghanistan). It can be argued that cultural activities, including tourism and creation of national identity, are of benefit to the whole country, and should be protected. The NATO doctrine is useful as a reference since, although all the countries involved in Iraq and Afghanistan have vastly different military and civilian structures, they are mostly NATO members, including the United States, and therefore should comply with the doctrine. (For a more detailed look at NATO CIMIC doctrine, please see the related table in appendix D.)

However, each of these approaches is problematic. A major problem with getting NATO[2] involved in cultural heritage protection is the fact that member states such as France oppose the idea of creating and developing special expertise aimed at reconstruction and stabilization processes during and after missions within NATO. Their main argument is that such expertise should be implemented by the Rapid Reaction Force (RRF),[3] the EU's first military initiative.[4] Therefore, initiatives not coming directly from member states are not discussed within NATO.

However, the RRF is for now not equipped to handle such processes because it has only been partially implemented and is not very active.

If the RRF—or NATO, for that matter—were to take a more active role, there are two levels at which support could be provided—a tactical level and a strategic level. On the tactical level, projects such as improving the plumbing in a village could be undertaken by professional military personnel skilled at such tasks. On the strategic level, as pertains to cultural heritage protection, archaeologists, museum curators, librarians, and the like from civilian society should be militarized and form a multinational asset able to work with and within the military to aid in projects in which a more specialized skill set is needed and provide training in peacetime.

In order to put matters on the map, member states must request as soon as possible the implementation of Cultural Affairs within NATO. In the meantime, NATO should at least organize a special conference on the subject.[5]

PROBLEMS WITH FITTING CULTURAL HERITAGE PROTECTION INTO CIMIC/CA

With respect to Cultural Affairs, the CIMIC doctrine has led to poor results in practice due to the following:

a) *It was written with more common public policy issues in mind,* such as providing humanitarian aid, repairing electricity and sewage systems, supplying drinking water, and addressing public health concerns. In general, militaries do not want to interfere in such activities for political and economic reasons. Specifically, the military does not want to be accused of spending tax money where it is not necessary.

b) *Militaries want neither to be falsely labeled as competing with civilian players, nor to be accused of devoting resources to objectives beyond the scope of their mission.* The military does not consider knowledge and handling of cultural goods and environments to be part of its core business, and certainly not a priority.

CLASH OF CULTURES

In contrast with, for instance, the field of humanitarian emergency aid, there is not a large number of organizations active in the field of culture. In other words, the market situation in-theatre concerning Cultural Affairs differs from other branches when implementing CIMIC/CA activities. This is relevant since, in these other branches, many NGOs consider military involvement as competition.

Furthermore, rumors have arisen that funds first allocated for NGOs are redirected to the military. This has been proven not to be the case with Cultural Affairs[6] and is one of the rare advantages in the complex of matters to deal with. However, many policy- and decision-makers are not aware of this and governmental departments are also confused on this subject.

One such rumor impacted the ability of a CIMIC museum team from the Dutch government to fulfill a request by the Iraqi government to travel to Baghdad for the purpose of assisting Iraqis in solving restoration and conservation problems such as saving the collection of the former museum of modern art, restoring and preserving looted and damaged archives, and training in certain disciplines concerning issues related to museums, among others. The team's trip was halted shortly before its planned departure because of interference by the Dutch Ministry of Foreign Affairs. The development aid section of this ministry had raised questions to the military concerning fears that NGOs could regard the source and use of the funding for the trip as an apparent overlap in the purpose of the team's trip and the missions of certain NGOs. In reality, there are only a few NGOs dealing with cultural heritage protection, and they support the deployment of militarized experts.

Furthermore, it seems very hard to make a distinction between cultural and humanitarian emergency aid and exactly what constitutes cultural emergency aid. For one, neither militaries, governments, nor NGOs are willing to make the distinction. Secondly, militaries are seen as more expensive than NGOs, and militaries across much of Europe do not see cultural heritage protection as part of their core missions and only reluctantly take on these tasks. Further complicating matters is that politicians confuse cultural heritage protection with the more basic issue of cultural awareness. Nevertheless, differences must be made clear since a number of activities concerning CIMIC cultural heritage protection have been restrained or even cancelled due to these factors.[7]

COMPLICATING FACTORS AND RECOMMENDATIONS FOR DEALING WITH THEM

There are all kinds of military rules, customs, and regulations that set out to accomplish the desired end-state of a mission. All aspects primarily serve military goals. CIMIC is a tool to reach the end-state of the mission faster and easier by establishing and maintaining good relations with the civil environment, and particularly the local population. Here a contradiction may arise between a military decision allocating low priority to Cultural Affairs and an action that is mandatory according to the Hague Convention and its protocols and therefore having a high priority within the context of the treaty.

Practice shows that military commanders and decision-makers who are unfamiliar with cultural and cultural heritage matters give priority to highly visible, quick-impact projects, such as redecorating schools or starting local broadcast stations, for example. Their motto is "to win the hearts and minds." While this is an important goal, advice from experts representing all CIMIC/ CA functional areas is required to obtain a complete overview of civilian needs prior to selecting a course of action to achieve this goal.

On the other hand, military from a certain country may redeploy before the situation is stable enough to hand over to the proper civilian bodies and agencies. This has been the case in Iraq. For example, a political decision brought about the redeployment of the Dutch Battle Group from its area of responsibility in Iraq's Al Muthanna province. As a result, CIMIC cultural experts who had not yet finished their job had to leave as well.

Procedures must be developed to properly hand over cultural rescue activities when such events occur. An international civil liaison agency for cultural emergency response may help out in such matters and could also maintain contacts with the military in peacetime.[8]

CHOOSING A SITE TO PROTECT

First it must be determined under whose authority or in which area of responsibility (AOR) a site is located. Sometimes this is not very easy to figure out. As an example, in the case of Uruk, I used information (including coordinates) supplied by Prof. McGuire Gibson of the Oriental Institute at the University of Chicago to convince the Dutch Ministry of Defence of the fact that although located on its border, Uruk was in the Dutch AOR. In cases where there is a temporary military authority in an area, contacts must be established with this authority. Therefore, it is important that international communication concerning cultural heritage cooperation be maintained between military organizations in peacetime. After establishing contact, there is a good chance that only military personnel will be allowed access to a certain area, but in some cases locals who were already living there may stay. If an international pool of militarized cultural experts or people within the military that have certain expertise already existed, they could go in as an emergency response.

As a general rule, assessments are to be undertaken by specialized units within the military CA or CIMIC branches. Experience shows that assessments are needed in all phases—before, during, and after a conflict. If certain armies or military organizations do not have available either cultural expertise or cultural heritage expertise, or both, it must be possible to have international militarized units to make necessary assessments. It goes without saying that whenever the security and political situation allows, civilian experts should undertake such assessments. As part of the assessment process, archaeologists and cultural heritage experts should have access to military aerial and satellite pictures of important monuments and sites.

Security Guards for Sites

An ideal solution was found in the case of the archaeological site of Uruk in southern Iraq. When the Dutch Battle Group took over Al Muthanna province from the U.S. military in the summer of 2003, it soon became evident that the highly significant archaeological site of Uruk (related to the epic of Gilgamesh; the oldest known form of writing, called cuneiform, comes from Uruk[9]) was situated in its area of responsibility. While conducting a civil assessment mission on behalf of the Dutch Ministry of Defence and addressing the five key CIMIC functional areas (including Cultural Affairs), I was in a position to actually visit this site and found out that it was one of the few that had not yet been looted. The area was previously guarded by a local bedouin tribe (family size) acting as guards for the German Archaeological Institute, which had held the concession for excavating this site for many years. The German scientists had been forced to stop their work years ago when the situation in Iraq deteriorated. After the start of the 2003 war in Iraq, the payments to these bedouins initially became irregular, and then finally ceased.

The bedouins explained that Uruk (now called Warka) belonged to them, the at-Tobe clan, by virtue of an agreement with bedouins of other tribes, who ruled over other parts of Al Muthanna. They said they wanted to safeguard the site against looting, but their capabilities were limited due to lack of means of transport and money to buy food and water after German payments had stopped. Finally, it was arranged and agreed through military channels that both Dutch and German money was to be paid to the tribe every three months, allowing them to continue their very valuable work. Initially the Dutch commander, and later some of his successors, did not see the relevance of this with regard to the support of his mission, but as an officer I was in a position to gradually make them change their minds and, following an agreement with the Dutch Ministry of Defence, these payments continued until Dutch forces withdrew from Iraq in March 2005.[10]

In the case of utilizing guards from local tribes, one has to recognize that tribe members used as guards must originate from the area where the site is located. There were reports that in Iraq locals from other tribes were about to be deployed in some areas. This would be asking for trouble. On the other hand, there are tribes that prefer to loot. As such, attempts have to be made to demonstrate to these people the importance of cultural heritage as a source of income in peacetime. Likewise, CIMIC/CA funds can be temporarily used to fight poverty in these areas. Poverty remains the main motivating factor for looting by local populations. Simultaneously, the military needs experts specialized in tribal affairs and languages as part of its reach-back capability.

Other Concerns When Utilizing Locals

There is always a shortage of means of transportation in wartime; therefore, many requests will be made to CIMIC or NGOs for vehicles to get water, food, and supplies. One must take into account, however, that there is a risk of looted goods being transported out of the site with these vehicles. Careful judgment is necessary. The same goes for requests concerning ammunition and weapons. Furthermore, it is essential that CIMIC or other involved organizations allocate funds to ensure payment of wages for local guards.

Last but not least, extra research is needed on the legal status of civilian noncombatants who work with the military. Problems could potentially arise from such a situation.

Events such as the looting of the Iraq Museum and the Taliban's destruction of the Bamiyan statues in Afghanistan have shown the need for temporary military cultural activities. In the case of the destruction of the Bamiyan statues, which occurred in peacetime prior to September 11, something might have been able to have been done had there been established cultural departments within international militaries. Considering that the Taliban had announced that they planned to destroy the statues, it could have been possible to interact with the corresponding cultural department of their military, had these cultural departments existed, to advise them that the statues could be a source of tourist income or that they were worth preserving, even through (temporary) removal.

A remarkable lesson has been that cultural experts are needed during all phases of a conflict and postconflict situation. Even though cultural activities were only expected to be needed during later phases of a conflict, it has been found that most of the damage had already been done by that time. During my research I found that problems encountered in the field in places like Iraq were similar to most of the problems encountered by predecessors such as the U.S. Monuments, Fine Arts, and Archives cultural property protection teams during and immediately after World War II. Examples are lack of transportation in the field, low priority of cultural heritage protection within the complex of Civil Affairs activities, ranking, and status problems. On the other hand, technical solutions invented by these predecessors, such as using fake booby trap signs to protect monuments, should be taken into account. Another source for lessons learned, though not always positive, was the so-called Soviet Trophies Brigades military units with cultural experts that were active during and after World War II.

Using Military Resources

In general, it has to be determined if the military entities in charge of a certain AOR have funds to spend on cultural heritage protection—U.S. Commanders' Emergency Response Program (CERP) funds or embassy funds, for example. As one example of good practice, in Baghdad during 2004 a large collection of documents from the Iraq National Library and Archives (the so-called Ottoman Archive)[11] had been damaged during the Iraq war. When Baghdad was still relatively secure, civilian experts managed to deep-freeze the archive, which had suffered water and mold damage. Freezing is a commonly applied method that preserves documents for final conservation under better, safer circumstances at a later date. However, the frozen archive was located in a former officer's club of

Saddam's army, situated in the Red Zone. Due to multiple electricity failures and worsening security circumstances, the material began to deteriorate rapidly and was also exposed to the risk of looting.

Through a U.S. request and a bilateral agreement, Dutch CIMIC[12] Cultural Affairs stationed a cultural expert in Baghdad who was able (since he was in uniform) to go out in the escort of armed soldiers and personally assess the situation. Apart from this, as a military officer with the rank of major he was able to communicate with U.S. officers[13] and ask for support. As a result, the U.S. Army used CERP funds to provide equipment in the form of a generator-powered freezer truck, and the archive was refrozen in this vehicle. The truck then was parked in a safe environment in a space that was shielded from the sun. The military also provided funding for fuel and CIMIC organized training on defrosting techniques that Iraqi experts would employ at a later stage. Furthermore, other training programs were developed and implemented for archive staff.

Another example is when the CIMIC Cultural Affairs expert in Baghdad assisted with the negotiation process that led to the organization of the Audit Commission for Babylon in anticipation of the handover of the site to the Iraqis.

Likewise, the use of helicopters proved to be indispensable for assessments of looted archaeological sites. In Babylon, they were also used to remove heavy concrete slabs that had been abusively positioned on surfaces containing historical and cultural data.

Another matter of concern was the condition of the archaeological site of Hatra, severely threatened in late 2004 by the presence of one of Saddam's ammunition depots located five kilometers away. An ammunition demolition program that was under way had caused some damage to the site. As a result of CIMIC Cultural Affairs' intervention and advice, the vibrations were decreased by 50 percent, thus saving Hatra.

EFFORTS BY NATO COUNTRIES IN IRAQ AND AFGHANISTAN

NATO countries have led serious efforts to impact cultural heritage protection in Iraq. At times their efforts have lead to the protection and preservation of monuments; at others, their actions show us that cultural affairs needs to be taken as a more serious issue within the armed forces.

In the Netherlands, following the creation of a CIMIC/CA unit, progress was halted in the first half of 2006 after a reorganization of CIMIC management and a repositioning within the armed forces. The unit shrunk and was taken over by a military historian already employed by the army. Most of the serious experts left the team, and the unit is now more or less inactive until a new commander recognizes the importance and manages to attract quality experts. The training on cultural heritage protection that took place at the multinational CIMIC Group North (now Civil-Military Center of Excellence, or CCOE) was also dropped after a change of management; the new military director did not see the relevance of the subject. All this is certainly not in accordance with the contents of the Second Protocol of the Hague Convention that became effective in the Netherlands on May 1, 2007.

German military personnel assisted civilian experts in Bamiyan, Afghanistan. The Austrian National Defense Academy in Vienna, especially its Institute for Human and Social Sciences, is active with conferences, research, and publications on the subject.[14] The academy cooperates with the Austrian Society for the Protection of Cultural Property.

Poland deployed militarized archaeologists in Babylon, Iraq.[15] The Polish Multinational Division Central South (MND CS) was alternately based at the site of the ancient temple of Babylon and at the Tell al Uhaimir-Tell Ingharra site. In southern Iraq, MND CS was present near the Tell el-Muqayyar site (ancient Ur).

The Polish zone covered five provinces: An Najaf, Al Qadisiyah, Babil, Karbala', and Wasit. Polish archaeologists have been present in Iraq since November 2003 as civil specialists of the CIMIC unit of the Polish military contingent in Iraq to document and protect archaeological sites and monuments located within the MND CS area of responsibility.[16] The archaeologists cooperated with their Iraqi colleagues and the MND CS staff on issues concerning preservation and maintenance of excavated and partially reconstructed monuments.

The conditions of several archaeological sites were determined by experts embedded in military helicopters and through the use of military satellite photographs. Whenever possible, aerial and ground reconnaissance of archaeological sites was carried out. Aerial inspections of the Babylon site took place in July and November 2004. In February 2005, reconnaissance of archaeological sites located in the southeastern part of Al Qadisiyah province and in the western part of Dhi Qar province was conducted to assess the condition of sites like Shuruppak, Adab, Kisurra, Umma, Zabalam, and Isin, Sumerian cities that had been heavily looted. Other archaeological sites in the region, like Nippur and Tell es-Sadoum (ancient Marad), were visited in convoys.

Babylon suffered from damage caused by heavy vehicles and the storage of containers in the immediate neighborhood of its monuments. This damage was done by coalition forces. The most famous example involved military personnel who indiscriminately loaded huge bags with rubble from the site, and then used them for enforcements for the camp. Cultural Affairs units could have helped avoid this had military planners been trained in this subject matter in peacetime and had more cultural units been available in wartime. Another mistake was the enlargement of the existing helicopter landing ground, in which the leveling work affected an area with ancient remains. Also, pits dug into tell slopes to obtain sand needed in defensive constructions resulted in irreversible stratigraphical destruction. Because of the construction of watchtowers, part of the terrain was leveled. Fuel tanks were dug into the ground in the vicinity of the Greek theatre. Other military fortifications included the digging of ditches near the ziggurat of Babylon in February 2004.

MND CS military camps experienced problems with military personnel involved with illegal trading in ancient objects; actions were undertaken in cooperation with the military police to prevent illegal sales to military personnel. Archaeologists advised on checking baggage of military and civil personnel returning home.

Polish archaeologists and military specialists published a report in November 2004 assessing the condition of monuments in Babylon.[17] From December 11–13, 2004, a meeting of the International Audit Commission took place at the Babylon site in order to assess its condition, based on the report prepared by Polish archaeologists.[18] The document also served as a starting point for handing over the site to Iraq's Ministry of Culture.

The MND CS troops left Babylon on December 22, 2004. A document for transferring the former Camp Alpha to the Ministry of Culture was signed in Baghdad on December 31, 2004. From that date, Iraqi archaeological police were in charge of site security, utilizing part of the military infrastructure that had been donated and left behind, such as the habitable containers, watchtowers, and fencing.

In 2005, archaeological assessments were executed in the eastern part of Al Qadisiyah province. This province was secured from September 2003 until April 2004 by a Spanish brigade that was part of MND CS forces. Major archaeological sites in the region, mainly of Sumerian and Babylonian date, were inspected, with large-scale devastation observed at Ishan Bahriyat (Isin).

In March 2005, the condition of archaeological sites in the province was assessed and proposals for immediate and long-term protective actions were written.[19] Aerial reconnaissance confirmed the looting of many archaeological sites. The ruins of Tell Fara (Shuruppak), Ishan Bahriyat (Isin), and Tell Abu Hatab (Kisurra) were found to be full of craters from continuous and methodical illicit digging that neither coalition forces nor the local antiquity service was able to prevent.[20] Cultural institution infrastructure and documentation had been destroyed. In general, Iraq lacked a credible database containing information on monuments, precise locations, and general descriptions. The Al Qadisiyah Regional Office of the State Board of Antiquities (SBAH) was understaffed and almost unarmed. The local archaeological police had very limited resources at their disposal to patrol the entire province and faced the same problems as the SBAH. Consequently, operational effectiveness was low.

A follow-up inspection of the Nippur archaeological site revealed that the introduction of protective measures by the Spanish brigade at the end of 2003 eliminated plundering and illicit digging. The entire site had been encircled by more than four miles of wire entanglements. Twenty-four policemen were stationed at a new police station and have been patrolling the site twenty-four hours a day. Finally, five police stations were built for the archaeological police in Al Qadisiyah near the American Mission excavation house.

Helicopters of Spanish and Polish coalition forces flew regularly over the site. Helicopter flights over endangered archaeological sites have proven to be one of the most effective measures for preventing illicit digging.

Polish archaeologists at Camp Alpha undertook several projects in cooperation with Iraqi experts from the SBAH and Babil University in Al Hilla and Al Qadisiyah University in Ad Diwaniyah. Most activities were financed from the MND CS CERP. Since early 2004 they have also been involved in the reestablishment of the Iraqi archaeological police (i.e., Facility Protection Service, or FPS).[21] This resulted in Babil and Al Qadisiyah provinces in the creation of archaeological police units with 350 and 100 men, respectively, by early 2005. The archaeological police are intended to support a system of civil unarmed guards (*haras*, in Arabic), recruited from among local communities and living on or nearby the sites that they are supposed to take care of. The Department of Museums supervises this new unit.

Meetings with archaeological police unit commanders in several provinces helped to identify essentials, like training and the need for means of communication, cars, uniforms, and weapons. New and restored police stations were also marked as indispensable.

Archaeological sites were assessed in terms of priority. A list of twenty-eight sites in the provinces of Babil, Al Qadisiyah, Karbala', and Wasit was prepared in cooperation with Iraqi archaeologists. The most important sites were fenced off and further protected by occasional military patrols. In December 2003, provisional barbed-wire fences were installed around the most important monuments of the part of the Babylon site located inside Camp Alpha. Following consultation with the SBAH office for Babil province, the damaged and partly torn-down fence around the archaeological site at Tell al Uhaimir was rebuilt in July 2004. Warning signs were also installed, as well as a habitable shelter for the guards. Shelters and temporary protection installations were set up around the ruins of the Summer Palace of Babylon at Barnum. At the Birs Nimrud site, observation towers were erected in late 2004. Installation of a barbed wired fence around the western part of the site and a shelter to serve as a police station at Tell es-Sadoum took place in spring 2005.

Projects aimed at restoring the infrastructure of museums and local antiquity inspectorates were implemented in the Babylon Museum, the Hammurabi

Museum, and the SBAH office for Babil province. Further activities included equipping the SBAH offices with computer hardware and software (an Iraqi priority request).Twenty Iraqi workers were trained in basic computer operation. Additionally, the SBAH office in Babil received a professional theodolite and a set of multimedia equipment (a digital video camera, notebook, and multimedia projector) to facilitate inventory work. The Department of Archaeology at Babil University in Al Hilla was provided with similar equipment.

Several projects were realized to supply a detachment of the archaeological police in Babil province located at Babylon with individual equipment, including uniforms, helmets, bulletproof vests, metal detectors, and walkie-talkies. In the spring of 2005, archaeological police in Al Qadisiyah province were in the progress of being supplied with basic equipment.

There is still a debate on the question of who or what caused certain damages inflicted on the Babylon site. Both the Polish and the U.S. Army deny responsibility, but archaeologists from the United Kingdom and Poland found damage they claim was military in nature. Furthermore, considering that McGuire Gibson had attempted to supply the Pentagon with a list of important cultural heritage sites in Iraq prior to the war, had the U.S. military and coalition forces used this list, it would have known that the sites in question were historically and culturally sensitive. Had there been international military cooperation on cultural affairs issues—between the Poles and the United States, for example—then they could have agreed upon a standard operating procedure. Unfortunately, events played out as they did due to a lack of coordination between the different international units and a lack of education, awareness, and training in issues regarding archaeology, history, and cultural heritage protection.

There have been suggestions that a training program on cultural heritage protection should be designed for military organizations from countries around the Mediterranean, including Egypt, Syria, Jordan, Turkey, Palestine, Lebanon, Algeria, Morocco, Tunisia, Cyprus, and Israel. If granted, such a project could possibly be co-financed through the Euromed Heritage program and carried out in collaboration with military academies and expertise centers from at least three partner countries. The discussion of this idea is still in an early stage. In April 2005 Euromed Heritage organized a workshop in Amman on the subject of cultural heritage protection in times of armed conflict.

On September 15, 2006, some parties within the EU attempted to implement cultural heritage training within its military activities by incorporating it in a draft of *Strategy for the Development of Euro-Mediterranean Cultural Heritage: Priorities from Mediterranean Countries (2007–2013)*. The authors of this document, a reference for future regional and cross-border cultural cooperation in the Mediterranean basin, originally indicated that "promoting actions to protect cultural heritage in times of conflict in accordance with international conventions" would include introducing "protocols for civil-military cooperation for cultural heritage protection" and "awareness programmes and training" for "military commanders and troops involved in cultural heritage" so that they would be "prepared for the adequate implementation of intervention protocols." The final version of the paper focuses largely on public awareness, training of cultural heritage professionals, and planning and capacity building within cultural institutions and ministries. Although direct mentions of civil-military cooperation and military forces in general have been removed, the references to "international conventions" still support the importance of military training in the context of EU cultural heritage protection initiatives.[23]

Euromed Heritage and its successor have continued this conversation, and Europe's Rapid Reaction Force should integrate cultural heritage expertise.

NEXT STEPS: IMPROVING THE ROLE OF MILITARIZED CULTURAL AFFAIRS AS PART OF CULTURAL HERITAGE PROTECTION WITHIN THE INTERNATIONAL CONTEXT

Undoubtedly, the best chance for getting plans and methods for cultural heritage protection implemented is through international interagency coordination,[22] preferably between and across government institutions, including the military, and NGOs, including international organizations (IOs). Due to the scarcity of militarized experts, it is necessary to establish an international team of such experts to deal with cultural heritage emergency response, assessments, providing advice, and ensuring compliance with existing rules, treaties, and military issues. Utilization of international militarized experts would be especially beneficial in areas where civilian experts are not yet allowed. Potential civilian team members from universities, museums, the International Centre for the Study of the Preservation and Restoration of Cultural Property (ICCROM), and other institutions could serve as a reach-back capability for such militarized experts and could take over as soon as the situation permitted.

The International Committee of the Blue Shield (ICBS) should normally act in this regard, but it is not completely operational and is not expected to be within a reasonable period of time.

What is needed is an entity consisting of proactive and creative individuals that maintains good working relationships with militaries around the world. It could advise field commanders and politicians at any time, coordinate and initiate joint training, and act as an intermediary between civilian experts and the military. The Hague would be a good place to establish such a bureau. There are also possibilities through the 1999 Second Protocol to the 1954 Hague Convention as well as through the Constitution of UNESCO, the latter providing the director general with a general mandate for the protection of cultural heritage. Article I(2)(c) of the UNESCO Constitution stating that the organization will maintain, increase, and diffuse knowledge "by assuring the conservation and protection of the world's inheritance of books, works of art and monuments of history and science, and recommending to the nations concerned the necessary international conventions . . ." is illustrative in this respect.[24]

The control system under the convention is composed of three elements: representatives of parties to the conflict, commissioners general for cultural property, and protecting powers. The system of commissioners general interlinked with the system of the protecting powers worked only once—following the Middle East conflict. When the mandates of the two commissioners general accredited in 1967, one to Israel and the other to the Arab governments concerned (Egypt, Jordan, Lebanon, and the Syrian Arab Republic), were terminated in 1977, no new commissioner general to be accredited to the Arab governments concerned was appointed, thus de facto putting an end to further implementation of this institution. It should be revived since it creates a possibility to deal with urgent problems that need to be handled in an intensive manner, such as the cultural heritage situation in Iraq.

Additionally, the review of the Hague Convention, which resulted in the elaboration and adoption of the Second Protocol to the Hague Convention, provided for the establishment of a new supervisory body—the twelve-member Committee for the Protection of Cultural Property in the Event of Armed Conflict,[25] elected for the first time by the meeting of the parties to the Second Protocol in October 2005. The committee had its first session on October 26, 2006, during the UNESCO General Conference and met again in June 2007.

For more detailed and juridical information on this subject I refer to the excellent articles from Jan Hladik[26] and a forthcoming article by Professor Jiří Toman to be published by the Asser and Clingendael Institutes in the Netherlands following their conference entitled "The Protection of Cultural Property during Armed Conflict," which was held in April 2007 in The Hague.

That being said, I advance the following as a list of recommendations for military forces to undertake for the better protection of cultural heritage in future and existing conflicts:

- NATO member states should request that NATO implement Cultural Affairs as a multinational asset.
- Field experience shows that CIMIC Cultural Affairs is necessary in different phases of a conflict, including the early stages.
- An interagency coordination bureau must be established that creates and maintains contacts and working relationships with the military. This office should also initiate training by civilian heritage experts and the military and should serve as a cultural emergency response unit. The bureau can assist the ICBS in emergency situations. (The ICBS is currently not functioning in this regard and is not expected to do so in the near future.)

- It has yet to be determined whether CIMIC/CA can also be active during peacetime to respond to emergencies, such as major natural disasters.
- An Arabic version of a basic guide on cultural heritage must be developed as well as a guide for European soldiers. Preferably, this should happen in cooperation with civilian organizations.
- Organizations such as NATO and the EU should create Departments of Cultural Affairs and should work together with UNESCO.
- Cultural Affairs should always be included in a CIMIC/CA assessment mission. Whenever possible, an assessment mission should be executed. Ongoing aerial assessments utilizing helicopters should be carried out, considering that they have proven to be especially important in preventing looting.
- Joint field exercises and training, especially for high-ranking officers and planners, are necessary.
- Lessons learned from Iraq and Afghanistan must be shared and read by planners. The same can be said for past field experiences, especially in relation to World War II and the MFA&A officers and the Soviet Trophies brigades.
- A UNESCO medal or something similar should be created to make cultural heritage protection more appealing to the military.
- UNESCO should have someone assigned to deal with military matters and to act as a liaison with military and military organizations such as NATO and military academies.
- An international survey has to be performed to create a register of experts in the military who studied art history, archaeology, anthropology, cultural sciences, and other relevant disciplines. For example, I recently learned that a commander of the Irish special forces is an archaeologist and very interested in cooperation.
- After the military mission, cultural heritage matters must be properly handed over to local authorities, NGOs, or follow-on forces, as appropriate.
- The possibility to nominate a commissioner-general for cultural property should be revived and further developed in collaboration with the president of the International Court of Justice and UNESCO.

NOTES

1. ACT's mission statement includes the following goals: "Improve military effectiveness and interoperability" and "Support Alliance operations."
2. "In NATO, I see an extraordinarily valuable emergency management capability that is being underutilized. I believe that this is due to the lack of civil-military cooperation, coordination and planning at NATO." Federal Emergency Management Agency, "FEMA Director Paulison Speaks at NATO on the Importance of Civil-Military Cooperation," News Release FNF-06-017, November 16, 2006, http://www.fema.gov/news/newsrelease.fema?id=31586.
3. The Rapid Reaction Force was set in motion by the French and British. Despite some reservations by non-NATO members, EU leaders agreed at the Helsinki summit in December 1999 to establish the RRF for peacekeeping, crisis management, and humanitarian and rescue work.

4. Example: "We cannot accept an institutional structure that allows NATO exclusivity in matters of security, while at the same time confining Europe to a permanent secondary role. We don't want a division of roles that leaves the strategic direction of operations in American hands, and European forces facing the task (and the risk) of carrying them out on the ground. The principle established in Berlin in June 1996 permitting the Western European Union (WEU) to use the resources of the alliance to carry out European operations under its own direction should be put into effect." Source: Paul Quiles, deputy from Tarn in the French National Assembly and president of the Commission on National Defense and the Armed Forces. An interesting link to this is Foreign Minister Hubert Vedrine's speech to the North Atlantic Council in Brussels on December 8, 1998.

5. In October 2006, I had a discussion on this with a representative of NATO's Civil Emergency Planning Department who considered this to be a good idea that should be executed. NATO has made no further response.

6. There are few civilian organizations dealing with cultural heritage protection when compared to humanitarian aid organizations such as Médecins Sans Frontières (Doctors Without Borders), Oxfam, and the Red Cross. However, the International Committee of the Red Cross is mentioned in the Hague Convention and undertakes to provide expertise about the convention.

7. For example, in the Netherlands, all CIMIC matters have to be judged by a department within the Ministry of Development Aid. There, no distinction is made between cultural and humanitarian emergency aid, which results in cultural CIMIC projects in Iraq and Afghanistan being blocked.

8. The creation of such an office is recommended by the Amman Euromed Heritage workgroup as well as (for Iraq) by the UNESCO ICC Committee.

9. There is debate about this. I recently met an Egyptologist who claimed that older writings were discovered in the town of Abydos, Egypt.

10. See also Gary Schwartz, "Dutch Help Bedouins Guard the Sumerian Site of Uruk," *The Art Newspaper* (October 2003), http://www.theartnewspaper.com.

11. This is not an official name but a working title given by the senior cultural advisor. Funding was through CERP.

12. Officially, the deployed specialist was not on a CIMIC mission since the activity was not directly in support of the mission in the Dutch AOR. Furthermore, the officer was sent out as an architect to assist with reconstruction of the Ministry of Culture.

13. See also Gary Schwartz, "An Insider's Account of the Evacuation of Babylon," *The Art Newspaper* (April 2005), http://www.theartnewspaper.com.

14. For example, "Protection of Cultural Property in the Event of Armed Conflict: A Challenge in Peace Support Operations," ed. Edwin R. Micewski and Gerhard Sladek (Vienna: Armed Forces Printing Office, 2003).

15. The information used is based on several talks with a former CIMIC commander of the MND CS, Colonel Knoop (lent out by the Dutch army) and for a substantial part an adaptation of the article of Miroslav Olbryś, "Archaeologists on Duty in Iraq: Polish Approach to the Protection and Salvage of Archaeological Heritage

in Central South Iraq (November 2003–April 2005)," *Conservation and Management of Archaeological Heritage* 8, no. 2 (2007): 88–104. It is curious that at the time the Polish experts were active in Iraq there was no communication between them and other militarized cultural experts (such as from the Dutch army). I found out much later which experts were active for the MND CS and what they were doing, although they were part of a CIMIC unit lead by a Dutch commander. This demonstrates the need for continuous international communication on the subject, especially with the military.

16. From November 2003 to April 2005, six Polish archaeologists worked in Iraq on six-month contracts in agreement with the Polish Ministries of Culture, Foreign Affairs, and Defence. Through a bilateral request, the CIMIC unit had two Dutch commanders successively lent out as augmentees.

17. Miroslav Olbryś, T. Burda, and A. Dolatowska, "Report on the Current Condition of the Babylon Archaeological Site (The Military Camp Alpha Site)," website of the Ministry of Culture and National Heritage of Poland at http://www.mk.gov.pl/website/index.jsp.catId=340. The report was also published on CD (Warsaw, 2005).

18. Participating in the meeting were representatives of Iraq's Ministry of Culture headed by Mr. Borhan Shaker; Dr. Miriam Omran Mousa of the SBAH Babylon Regional Office; Dr. John Curtis, an expert on Mesopotamian archaeology from the British Museum; representatives of the multinational forces in Iraq; and the MND CS. Dr. Curtis was invited by the Ministry of Culture and prepared a report on his observations. See John Curtis, "Report on the Meeting at Babylon 11th–13th December 2004," British Museum, http://www.thebritishmuseum.ac.uk/iraqcrisis/reports/Babylon%report04.pdfhttp://www.thebritishmuseum.ac.uk/newsroom/current2005/Babylon_Report04.doc.

19. Miroslav Olbryś, *Raport otwarcia: Stan dziedzictwa kultury i jego ochrony w prowincji Kadisija, Irak, oraz propozycje działań pilnych i długookresowych [Opening report: The Status of Cultural Heritage and its Protection in Al Qadisiyah Province, Iraq, and Proposals of Urgent and Long-Term Activities]*, (typescript paper submitted to the MND CS command, March 2005).

20. Cindy Ho, "Heritage Lost: Looting of Archaeological Sites Continues in Iraq," *Saving Antiquities for Everyone* website (first published in 2004), http://www.savingantiquities.org/h-featureIraq.htm.

21. Olbryś, 2007

22. See as an introduction Matthew Bogdanos, "Joint Interagency Cooperation: The First Step," *Joint Force Quarterly* 37(Second Quarter 2005): 10–18, http://www.dtic.mil/doctrine/jel/jfq_pubs/0437.pdf.

23. European Commission, *Strategy for the Development of Euro-Mediterranean Cultural Heritage: Priorities from Mediterranean Countries (2007–2013)* (Luxembourg: Office for Official Publications of the European Communities, 2007); September 15, 2006, draft received courtesy of Roberto Carpano, coordinator of the Regional Management Support Unit for Euromed Heritage.

24. United Nations Educational, Scientific and Cultural Organization, *Basic Texts,* 2006 edition (Paris: UNESCO, 2006), 6.

25. The committee members elected for four years (i.e., until 2009) are Austria, El Salvador, Libyan Arab Jamahiriya, Peru, Serbia, and Switzerland. The members elected for two years (i.e., until 2007) are Argentina, Cyprus, Finland, Greece, the Islamic Republic of Iran, and Lithuania. The essential functions of the committee relate to granting, suspension, or cancellation of enhanced protection; assistance in the identification of cultural property under enhanced protection; supervision of the implementation of the protocol; and consideration and distribution of international assistance and the use of the Fund for the Protection of Cultural Property in the Event of Armed Conflict.

26. Jan Hladík, "Reporting System under the 1954 Convention for the Protection of Cultural Property in the Event of Armed Conflict," *International Review of the Red Cross* 840 (December 31, 2000): 1001–16, http://www.icrc.org/Web/eng/siteeng0.nsf/html/57JQTD. Mr. Hladik provided me with juridical information on the subject.

THE WAY FORWARD

For Governmental and Intergovernmental Agencies

WHILE MILITARIES CAN AND MUST ASSUME PRIMARY RESPONSIBILITY TO PREPARE FOR protecting museums and archaeological sites against the looting that may result from the breakdown in law and order created by their actions, civilian agencies involved in postwar reconstruction have both a duty and an interest in cultural heritage protection. What steps should foreign services and intergovernmental organizations take to address the threat of cultural looting, and how should they coordinate their efforts with the military to ensure a unity of effort?

CHAPTER 17

Practical and Policy Considerations in Protecting Cultural Heritage and Preventing Looting during International Peace and Stability Operations

CHRISTOPHER J. HOH

ALTHOUGH SCHOLARS AND LEGAL EXPERTS HAVE DEVELOPED A SUBSTANTIAL BODY of international law to protect cultural heritage in situations of conflict, recent experience shows that practitioners have some catching up to do, both to incorporate these norms into planning and to give them practical effect in execution. Now is an opportune moment to tackle this problem, given the worldwide effort to improve planning and response for peace and stability operations.

First, however, comes the question to be expected from harried peacekeepers—whether they be diplomats, soldiers, aid workers, or other officials—Why devote energy and funding to the "luxury" of safeguarding cultural artifacts when resources are insufficient to care for refugees, control violence, or rebuild infrastructure? And even if heritage protection were made a priority for the mission, how do we organize effective action and tap the necessary expertise?

THE IMPORTANCE OF CULTURAL PROTECTION
FOR MISSION SUCCESS

Despite the obvious benefit of safeguarding cultural treasures, veterans of deployments in places like Bosnia, Kosovo, Afghanistan, Iraq, and Sri Lanka will point out that civil wars create a harsh reality for local inhabitants and international personnel. In such conflicts and their aftermath, the indigenous population suffers economic deprivation, social upheaval, and lethal violence long after the main combat is over. In these and most other cases, the international community has eventually mobilized itself to respond, but without providing sufficient military, political, or economic resources for a decisive turnaround. Furthermore, lasting stability takes time to achieve—sometimes generations—until attitudes shift and the underlying drivers of conflict are resolved.

Confronted with the daunting task of helping a war-torn society right itself and move forward with reform, international representatives may find that preserving artifacts and monuments seems not only impractical but an unjustified diversion of attention away from human emergencies. Amid chaos and starvation, local inhabitants may see looting and selling antiquities as legitimate for parents desperate to provide for their families. Under such circumstances, is it not better for the peacekeeper to turn a blind eye?

In most cases, however, the real answer is that protection of cultural heritage is essential to the success of the mission. This observation holds for both the short-term effectiveness of stability operations and the longer-term exit strategy. True, planners and operational chiefs will have to balance competing priorities in difficult circumstances. Nevertheless, they ignore the cultural dimension at their peril. Four policy elements, in addition to the legal imperatives, make heritage protection a compelling priority in peace and stability missions:

- the need to deny spoilers control over a country's cultural heritage
- the importance of understanding and respecting local culture during the mission
- the responsibility of the mission to act swiftly and decisively with regard to culture
- the powerful effects that demonstrating respect for cultural heritage has on postconflict reconciliation

These can apply before and during combat operations, as well as in the postconflict period.

Denying Spoilers Control

First and foremost is the need to deny to "spoilers" the benefit of controlling historical treasures, be it for political, economic, military, or propaganda purposes. Spoilers are defined by political scientist Stephen J. Stedman as parties who believe that "peace emerging from negotiations threatens their power, worldview, and interests, and [who] use violence to undermine attempts to achieve it."[1] Almost always, postwar situations give rise to bands of militants who seek to undermine the international mission or local authorities, or both. Variously called warlords, insurgents, separatists, nationalists, mafia, or war criminals, these militants reject the new order being established and are prone to using violence and intimidation to gain influence and to protect their freedom of action.

Cultural heritage is a tempting target for spoilers, as well as those who loot out of economic necessity without realizing the impact of their actions. Politically, libraries and museums can offer historical evidence that an antagonist wishes to make disappear of the presence of a particular ethnic group or tribe. The Serb firebombing of Sarajevo's libraries in 1992 is a case in point, when the centuries-old records of ethnic diversity were deliberately destroyed. Economically, selling off valuable antiquities to unscrupulous traders can provide spoilers with ready cash. In Iraq today, middlemen in criminal networks are making substantial profits, while frontline looters benefit relatively little.

In military and operational terms, religious sites and other prized institutions can provide a protected base for operations, even though using them for military advantage is a blatant violation of international law. It was reported, for instance, that Hezbollah guerrillas used Christian churches in southern Lebanon to shield rocket launchers from attack by Israel in 2006. Propaganda abuses abound too, whether the spoilers seek to derive legitimacy as the guardians of tradition or to showcase defiance of the old ways. The Taliban's destruction of the Bamiyan Buddhas in 2001 was a calculated and shocking demonstration of determination and ruthlessness. Clearly, warlords will often seek to control heritage sites, so international planners must prepare to counter them.

Demonstrating Respect for Local Culture

Peace and stability operations will also be more successful if they demonstrate respect and understanding for local culture. This element is not just a matter of putting a benign face on military occupation. It goes to the heart of strategic communication requirements: international overseers and new local leaders must show they are organized for the greater good of the society in question.

In recent years, these interventions have tended not to seek limited military ends but to promote transition to a new society. Often pursuant to a broad UN mandate, the international presence is organized to foster democratic elections, the rule of law, economic liberalization, and international security arrangements. An ambitious reform agenda results, well beyond traditional peacekeeping. It is, to use Secretary of State Condoleezza Rice's term, "transformational diplomacy," aimed at creating conditions for stable, locally led peace.

Getting that message across is a complicated business, especially to populations traumatized by dictatorship, war, and poverty. The words and actions of the international mission should reflect a vision of a better society for all its members, rather than one that replaces one set of exploitative elites with another. The effort will benefit greatly from awareness of the country's history and values, seeking to build on what was glorious in the past and taking time-honored traditions into account.

Conversely, failure to protect cultural heritage can create a cognitive dissonance, undermining the strategic communication goal. A case in point is the recent building in Iraq of coalition military bases on the sites of ancient Babylon (in modern Babil province) and Ur (known today as Tell el-Muqayyar). This action needlessly fueled resentment and suspicion among the local population and beyond. A positive example is NATO's 1999 bombing in Serbia and Kosovo. It avoided Serbian Orthodox holy places, showing respect for the Serbian people despite a bitter confrontation with its leaders.

The Responsibility to Act Swiftly and Decisively
An additional policy element is closely related, demonstrating the international mission's strength. After all, it does no good to profess respect for a country's people and then appear powerless to protect the things they hold dear. Since international forces are supposed to safeguard cultural treasure, they had better do so successfully or risk looking weak. The looting of the Iraq Museum in Baghdad in 2003 provides a dramatic illustration. Live reports and video footage portrayed a mission in disarray—even if it wasn't—and fueled rumors of everything from U.S. government corruption to military incompetence. It does not matter whether soldiers in fact knew where the museum was, that their commanders had an explanation for what transpired, or that actual losses were less than reported. This apparent loss of control did damage to the coalition's credibility that was prompt and profound. Ethically, the appearance of impropriety is the operative standard whether or not an action is illegal. So too must peacekeepers worry about image as much as reality and avoid the appearance of impotence. Had these forces' situational awareness encompassed the cultural dimension, they would not have been on the defensive when they should have been projecting strength and resolve.

Effects on Postconflict Resolution
Finally, demonstrated appreciation of the local culture can provide a powerful tool to promote reconciliation. Some will regard this statement as a starry-eyed sentiment. The fact remains, however, that people emerging from civil strife can find a rallying point in their culture's contribution to the heritage of mankind, a reminder of common pride and perhaps shared traditions. Seeing eminent scholars from abroad coming to examine local treasures can be a tonic: a reminder of universal values like beauty and faith, an example of respect for diversity, and a bridge to build understanding.

The story of the Sarajevo Haggadah is worth recalling here. A medieval illuminated manuscript from Sephardic Jews, it was hidden (by Muslims) when the Nazis occupied Yugoslavia in World War II. Spirited away again for protection in the 1992–1995 Bosnia war, it had been rumored destroyed or sold, but was readied for display as the National Museum of Bosnia and Herzegovina was being repaired in 2001–2002. Thanks largely to the UN mission in that country, the Sarajevo Haggadah is now the centerpiece of a world-class interpretive display, alongside contemporaneous Islamic, Orthodox, and Catholic volumes. The result is a persuasive case of multiculturalism in Bosnian history, an honest but shrewd initiative by international peacekeepers who understood cultural history and its power.

THE STATE OF SYSTEMIC REORGANIZATION FOR PEACE AND STABILITY OPERATIONS

An Overview of U.S. Government Efforts since the Iraq War
Having explored the "why" of protecting cultural heritage and preventing looting in peace and stability operations, it remains to address the "how" of turning good intentions into reality on the ground. Before trying to do so, however, it is worthwhile to summarize recent developments in planning and preparation for these missions. This field has been in ferment, spurred by frustration with Iraq, but reflecting a pre-existing desire to draw lessons from the many international interventions since the Cold War's end and to apply them in future operations. This article will review the main U.S. government developments and then touch on aspects of planning, contingency preparation, and communities of practice.

To paraphrase the Cheshire Cat in Lewis Carroll's *Alice in Wonderland*, "if you don't know where you are going, any road will get you there." This situation unfortunately characterizes the international response to many recent conflicts abroad. This is not to disparage the good results and heroic measures that have gone into postconflict missions in places like Bosnia, Haiti, Kosovo, Afghanistan, and Iraq. Rather, it is to observe that these efforts have been ad hoc and improvised, largely reinventing the wheel every time. In Washington, a bipartisan consensus emerged in 2003 that the United States should organize itself better for future operations. A major contribution to the discussion was the *Winning the Peace* study resulting from the Center for Strategic & International Studies–Association of the United States Army (CSIS-AUSA) Post-Conflict Reconstruction Project.[2] A milestone reflecting this consensus was the Stabilization and Reconstruction Civilian Management Act of 2004, referred to as the Lugar-Biden bill, which has since passed the Senate unanimously.[3]

The CSIS-AUSA study argued for increased civilian and military capacity and examined how postconflict missions could better promote security, governance, economic well-being, and justice. The Lugar-Biden bill sought to strengthen nonmilitary structures by creating a civilian coordinator for postconflict response within the State Department, a Response Readiness Corps and Response Readiness Reserve of prepositioned specialists, an emergency fund for postconflict assistance, and related initiatives to improve planning, training, and cooperation among government agencies.

Later in 2004, then Secretary of State Colin Powell established a coordinator for reconstruction and stabilization to spearhead U.S. efforts along these lines.[4] In December of 2005, President Bush signed a presidential directive to improve coordination, planning, and implementation within the U.S. government for assisting foreign states and regions facing conflict or civil strife.[5] Meanwhile, the Department of Defense (DoD) commissioned the Defense Science Board to review the subject, which offered comprehensive recommendations on the transition to and from hostilities, with implications for civilian agencies and NGOs as well as the military.[6] DoD's guidance for security, stability, transition, and reconstruction operations (SSTR), issued in November 2005 and partly based on a subsequent Defense Science Board report, designated stability operations a core mission comparable in priority to combat operations.[7]

In the more than three years that this initiative has been under way within the U.S. government, much has been accomplished and much more remains to be done. Institutional change comes slowly, particularly when it requires significant new resources and new ways of thinking and managing. The work is complicated, with many interlocking aspects—planning systems, response cadres, flexible funding, sectoral best practices, operational models, training, exercises, interagency coordination, international consultation, civil-military integration, and NGO outreach, to name the main ones.

In addition, budgetary stringency and the press of current crises make funding for future contingencies less attractive within both the executive branch and Congress. So the ambitious documents described above are being implemented piecemeal. Nevertheless, significant change is afoot, not only in the United States but also with many allies undertaking similar efforts and in the new United Nations Peacebuilding Commission and staff.

The U.S. government's draft planning framework[8] structures an approach to conflict transformation that would identify the few overarching goals, the interdisciplinary major mission elements that support them, and the component essential tasks (and subtasks) for each major mission element. The tasks can then be mapped to a responsible agency (U.S. or foreign), tied to resources, and plotted on a timeline. This framework helps policymakers identify strategic options and tradeoffs, and it lends itself to sound metrics for tracking progress.

The Potential Role of Cultural Heritage Professionals

For the cultural protection community, the essential tasks list may be the most interesting tool in the box.[9] These tasks describe the substance of what is to be accomplished (e.g. "protection of indigenous individuals, infrastructure and institutions," which could include museums, libraries, and religious sites). This job is part of the initial response of establishing a safe and secure environment. Over time, the objective is to develop legitimate and stable security institutions by creating indigenous capacity to protect the institutions and sites. Similarly, tasks related to police training, border control, customs inspection, and community rebuilding all could play a role in protecting religious and cultural heritage.

Contingency preparation encompasses several ways to improve U.S. capacity to respond effectively on short notice. They are aimed at replacing ad hoc approaches with suitable and available resources. Several of these efforts involve preparing cadres of expert personnel. One is a proposed civilian reserve of specialists who could train ahead of time in postconflict matters and then be mobilized as needed into temporary government service to supplement a particular mission with their nonfederal skills. President Bush has called for such a reserve; initial funding has been included in administration budget requests; and the Lugar-Biden bill would authorize a similar reserve. Congress has been reluctant to appropriate funds for this purpose, although prospects for an appropriation were reportedly improving in the spring of 2007.

If it were established, such a reserve system could provide an efficient way of including in the planning and operational phases experts in the heritage of the territory in question and also personnel experienced in assessment and preservation of artifacts. An organized reserve system would help ensure the availability of trained and motivated specialists as part of the official U.S. contribution to an international effort. Although in theory the desired staff might be found within U.S. government ranks, in practice there is little likelihood of the right people being available or prepared for such duty. This same situation applies also in most other disciplines of reconstruction and stabilization.

A further area for systemic reform involves sectoral communities of practice—knowledgeable and experienced people who should provide input on standards for essential tasks in a given sector and on related aspects of U.S. and international planning. The need here is not to create such communities from whole cloth. Across the board, they are generally well established, as is the case for instance with archaeology and cultural heritage. The question is how to get these experts in touch with the officials who will be planning and carrying out upcoming peace and stability operations and how to do so on a less ad hoc basis. This is a mission for the overextended staff of the reconstruction and stabilization coordinator in the State Department. In fact, discussions have been under way among the United States Institute of Peace, the U.S. Army War College, and the State Department to link up various communities of practice through technological and other approaches. However, this effort is not likely to be a current priority.

So it is incumbent upon the cultural protection community to take the initiative—as the University of Chicago's Cultural Policy Center has been doing—and help ensure these issues receive due consideration. A telling example is that two years into the presidential initiative to establish the Office of the Coordinator for Reconstruction and Stabilization, its staff and the staff in the State Department's Office for International Cultural Property Protection were unaware of each other's existence. It took the Cultural Policy Center's Pocantico Conference to bring them together.[10] Obviously, there is scope to improve these networks.

The Role of U.S. Foreign Policy Personnel

Similarly, U.S. foreign policy experts could and should do more to keep lines out to the cultural heritage community. This should be a matter of course, not individual interest. A U.S. embassy or diplomatic mission will typically have a cultural affairs unit that promotes contact and exchange with scholars, artists, scientists, and intellectuals in the host country. In addition, the mission's political section often follows religious affairs and human rights and therefore cultivates ties to a cross section of clerics and religious figures. Someone in the mission is usually charged with engaging the ministries of culture (or youth, sports, religion, etc.), another important source for understanding the country's heritage. Similarly, U.S. relationships with UNESCO and other international cultural institutions will be nurtured both by diplomatic missions abroad and relevant Washington offices.

So in principle, the right networks exist and the right practices are in place for U.S. planners not to go in culturally blind when organizing stability operations. In reality, however, these networks and practices can suffer neglect at a crucial time. They take time to build up and maintain. During a conflict (or preconflict period), the U.S. embassy may have closed or been drawn down to essential personnel. In such circumstances, it is obviously more important to know the coordinates and managers for the airport, refinery, or television station than the museum. Best, however, is to know these things for *both* cultural and infrastructural sites; and if the networks are tended in peacetime and the preparatory work organized in advance, then it is indeed possible to avoid the kinds of mistakes cited above.

NEXT STEPS: ADVANCING CULTURAL PROTECTION IN POSTCONFLICT ZONES

So far, this article has tried to make the case for protecting cultural heritage in peace and stability operations abroad and to sketch some of the new organizational approaches the U.S. government is using to improve its planning and response capability. Besides the longer-term, systemic improvements described above, the question arises as to what practical steps the cultural protection community—in willing partnership with military and diplomatic organizers— could take to improve the safeguarding of cultural and religious heritage when an international mission is being launched into a particular country. Regarding practical steps, some observations may be useful regarding information, networks, objectives, and coordination.

- *The basic information that mission organizers require is a list of the most important holy places, archaeological sites, museums, and libraries.* Ideally, it would contain coordinates for either geodetic latitude and longitude or the military grid reference system, along with a short description of the sites and objects that a layperson could understand. In theory, this work would be undertaken ahead of time under the auspices of the International Committee of the Blue Shield and related institutions charged with implementing the Hague Convention for the Protection of Cultural Property in the Event of Armed Conflict and its Protocols.[11] In practice, however, the information may not be agreed upon, let alone up-to-date and accessible. In this age of the Internet and ubiquitous phones, a good military or diplomatic planner can probably improvise a passable list in a couple of hours and refine it with a few consultations in subsequent days. That is a poor substitute, however, for having definitive data provided by authoritative specialists, no matter how well intentioned the midlevel planner might be.
- *Even with the best information in the world, there is no substitute for a good network of reliable experts.* Particularly needed are names of the key specialists *in country* who know the history of the objects, sites, and cultures in question and are familiar with existing measures for preservation and protection. In a stable, modern, and open society, the leading cultural and religious figures would be obvious candidates. In a state where central authority has collapsed, however, and which may be emerging from years of war or dictatorship, professional curators and others of good faith could be difficult to find. By the time a military task force or international peacekeeping mission is deployed, it is probably too late to look for them. So besides lists of important cultural objects, the heritage protection community could assist by identifying resource persons in countries experiencing civil strife who are respected for their professionalism and are available for consultation in an emergency.
- *Setting objectives for peace and stability operations sounds simple, but in practice it is about hard choices of where to concentrate effort early on.* The idea is to make the right trade-offs to maximize chances that local and international authorities will still be present to tackle bigger problems once conditions are more settled. For example, in choosing to safeguard certain sites or objects, the mission is implicitly deciding that others will go unprotected. In opting to prepare more police for upholding public order, it may defer specialized training for heritage protection workers. In instituting a buy-back program to return stolen artifacts, it could create a temporary incentive for more looting. (Similar dilemmas surround the purchase of surrendered weapons.) There are no one-size-fits-all

solutions, just best practices to be studied and adapted to specific countries. The more collaboration taking place between cultural experts and peacekeeping practitioners, the greater the odds of getting the objectives right.

- *Coordination on the ground is another essential component of stability operations.* Experience shows that good communication and consultation about future courses of action is best accomplished in the field, often through decentralized structures. The flexible provincial reconstruction teams (PRTs) in Afghanistan, which combine the military, diplomatic, and assistance arms of the NATO presence, are now being emulated for coalition efforts in Iraq and also incorporated into operational models for future missions.

There is a paradigm shift in this approach that bears attention. Military personnel are rightly concerned about operational security and deterrence. Aid workers by contrast need open collaboration with local partners and implementing agencies to succeed. Bringing the two communities into the same tent means each must adjust to the other's way of doing business. Finding a modus vivendi usually takes work, but is worth the effort to achieve unity of effort and a whole-of-government approach greater than the sum of its parts. Similarly, effective heritage protection in the field may require cultural specialists not only to be present on the ground in unfamiliar circumstances but also to adapt their methods to work with (and to tutor) military forces and international officials. Being successful is probably less a matter of preparation than approach, facing a new situation with an open mind and flexible attitude, and this goes for the peacekeepers as well as the archaeologists.

*   *   *

To summarize, in organizing international peace and stability operations, the need for knowledge of the local culture, careful planning in advance, and effective coordination on the ground is apparent, but their attainment will require dedicated effort, especially as regards the protection of religious and cultural heritage. This article has sought to make the case that such protection is essential for the success of the international mission, despite the likely lack of resources. Failure to plan and prepare for the safeguarding of cultural heritage gives spoilers an advantage and undermines the international community's strategic message.

Within the U.S. government and among our partners, a new interdisciplinary emphasis on proper planning and contingency preparation seeks to improve our capacity to respond and organize similar interventions in the future. Systemic reforms that are under way or that are being proposed offer opportunities to advance the cultural protection agenda and prepare for the next crisis, particularly as regards planning conflict-transformation tasks, preparation of personnel and other resources for ready deployment, and strengthening communities of experts who can help define best practices.

As specific interventions are being launched, the cultural protection community can take practical steps to bolster international peacekeepers' understanding and effectiveness in exercising their responsibilities in the field with respect to cultural heritage. These include development in advance of an inventory of key sites and objects, provision of expert advice in setting objectives and plans, and flexible field coordination to help keep activities mutually reinforcing.

NOTES

1. Stephen J. Stedman, "Spoiler Problems in Peace Processes," *International Security* 22 (Fall 1997): 5.
2. Robert C. Orr, ed., *Winning the Peace*, CSIS Significant Issues Series (Washington, DC: The CSIS Press, 2004).
3. Subsequently reintroduced for the 110th Congress as S. 613 and H.R. 1084. Original bill available at http://www.govtrack.us/congress/bill.xpd?bill=s108-2127. Current bill available at http://frwebgate.access.gpo.gov/cgi-bin/getdoc.cgi?dbname=110_cong_bills&docid=f:s613rs.txt.pdf.
4. U.S. Department of State, "Office of the Coordinator of Reconstruction and Stabilization," Fact Sheet, March 11, 2005, http://www.state.gov/s/crs/rls/43327.htm (accessed on January 11, 2007).
5. White House National Security Presidential Directive 44, *Management of Interagency Efforts Concerning Reconstruction and Stabilization* (Washington, DC: The White House, December 7, 2005), http://www.fas.org/irp/offdocs/nspd/nspd-44.html.
6. U.S. Department of Defense, Office of the Under Secretary of Defense for Acquisition, Technology, and Logistics, "Defense Science Board 2004 Study on Transition to and from Hostilities," http://www.acq.osd.mil/dsb/reports/2004-12-DSB_SS_Report_Final.pdf.
7. U.S. Department of Defense Directive, No. 3000.05, *Military Support for Stability, Security, Transition, and Reconstruction (SSTR) Operations* (Washington, DC: Department of Defense, November 28, 2005), http://west.dtic.mil/whs/directives/corres/pdf/300005p.pdf.
8. U.S. Joint Forces Command, *J-7 Pamphlet U.S. Government Draft Planning Framework for Reconstruction, Stabilization, and Conflict Transformation, Version 1.0* (Norfolk, VA: U.S. Joint Forces Command, 2005), http://www.dtic.mil/doctrine/jel/other_pubs/jwfcpam_draft.pdf.
9. U.S. Department of State, Office of the Coordinator for Reconstruction and Stabilization, "Post Conflict Reconstruction Essentials Tasks Matrix," Fact Sheet, April 1, 2005, http://www.state.gov/s/crs/rls/52959.htm.
10. "Protecting Cultural Heritage during Wartime: Learning the Lessons of Iraq," conference of the Cultural Policy Center at the University of Chicago, Tarrytown, NY, August 11–13, 2006.
11. http://portal.unesco.org/en/ev.php-URL_ID=13637&URL_DO=DO_TOPIC&URL_SECTION=201.html.

CHAPTER 18

UNESCO and the Safeguarding of Cultural Heritage in Postconflict Situations

Efforts at UNESCO to Establish an Intergovernmental Fund for the Protection of Cultural Property in Times of Conflict

MOUNIR BOUCHENAKI

War is the enemy of man. It is also the enemy of the best that man has made—art, culture, monuments, and the whole cultural and historic heritage. Many works of art have been destroyed over the centuries, works that we have never known and that we shall never see again.

—Jiří Toman[1]

CULTURAL HERITAGE IS INCREASINGLY PERCEIVED TO BE A PRIORITY DURING POST-conflict reconstruction. "The biggest challenge facing UNESCO," said its Director General Koïchiro Matsuura, "is to make the public authorities, the private sector and civil society as a whole realize that the cultural heritage is not only an instrument for peace and reconciliation but also a factor of development." This message dates to 2002, on the occasion of the United Nations' Year for Cultural Heritage. Five years later such a statement remains a critical point of reference.

Increasingly, conflicts target symbols of culture so as to destroy a people's identity. This destruction can often lead the international community to react. In the wake of the destruction of cultural heritage during World War II, the international community responded with the 1954 Hague Convention. Since then, the nature of warfare has changed, with conflict becoming less a matter of external belligerents and more one of internal conflict. During these internal conflicts, warring parties often specifically target cultural heritage. The Second Protocol to the 1954 Hague Convention was written to address this changing nature of conflict, and the international community must continue to identify proper mechanisms to respond to the growing demand for the preservation of heritage badly damaged during such conflicts.

This paper focuses on efforts at UNESCO to establish an intergovernmental fund for the protection of cultural property in times of conflict. We will begin with an overview of UNESCO's history, followed by several examples of funds that have been set up and actions that have been taken to safeguard cultural property in times of armed conflict, and conclude with a series of recommendations of next steps that should be taken.

EMERGENCY MEASURES WITHIN UNESCO'S INTERNATIONAL LEGAL FRAMEWORK

The five years between 1945 and 1949 saw a series of extremely important world developments and events which, though not specifically relating to the legal protection of cultural property at the international level, laid the foundations for cultural protection in the post–World War II period.

In response to the ravages of World War II, a new international organization, the United Nations and its specialized agencies, including the Educational, Scientific and Cultural Organization (UNESCO), was created in November 1945. The preamble of the UNESCO Constitution of 1945 declares: "Since wars begin in the minds of men, it is in the minds of men that the defenses of peace must be constructed." This sentiment can be seen as the basis of the first convention adopted by UNESCO in 1954 at The Hague, which specifically concerned the protection of cultural property in the case of armed conflict. (For a detailed discussion of the 1954 Hague Convention, the 1954 First Protocol, and the 1999 Second Protocol, see chapters 7 and 8.)

In the years following the adoption of the 1954 Convention, noninternational armed conflicts, particularly those relating to internal strife along national, regional, ethnic, linguistic, or religious lines, became an increasingly common feature of the world order, resulting in losses of monuments, museums, libraries, and other cultural repositories.

UNESCO's press release No. 18 of 2002,[2] on the occasion of the United Nations' Year for Cultural Heritage, stated that "from Bamiyan to Jerusalem or Sarajevo in the past few years cultural heritage has often been a military target or the flashpoint of political, ethnic and religious conflicts."

However, events such as these are not entirely unexpected. For at least two decades there has been a growing body of research and published information on the rise of ethnic, racial, and religious tensions and of the parallel rise of "internal" regionalism and *communautarisme* in many parts of the world— not the least of which has been in Europe. These trends have suggested a long-term threat to the world's stability through the breakdown of present patterns of comparatively large, often multinational and multiethnic, political, sovereign states, created between 1870 and 1920 (including most of the ex-colonial national frontiers in Africa and Asia).

Besides the target of human lives, contemporary conflicts and wars also encompass other targets such as human values, cultures, and religions, thus opening to new considerations the safeguarding of cultural heritage in post-conflict situations.

UNESCO's primary concern was the lack of specific funds in its regular budget for "urgent interventions." A first response was the possibility of allowing countries within the World Heritage Fund established by the 1972 Convention Concerning the Protection of the World Cultural and Natural Heritage to apply for technical assistance within situations linked to the rehabilitation of cultural or natural sites affected by conflicts and wars. However, this step was considered insufficient since it only covers sites on the World Heritage List, and particularly those that are on the World Heritage in Danger List.

In his article, "World Heritage Partners," published at the occasion of the thirtieth anniversary of the 1972 Convention (Paris, 2003), the director of the World Heritage Centre, Mr. Francesco Bandarin wrote:

> The World Heritage Convention established a World Heritage fund based on a contribution equal to one per cent of the Member States' contribution to UNESCO. Currently totaling about US$4 million per year, this Fund is largely used to assist States Parties in preserving the World Heritage sites on their territory. Extra-budgetary contributions, arising principally from Funds-in-Trust agreements with individual Member States and royalties from publications, add around $5.5 million per year. UNESCO covers administrative costs separately, which brings the total sum available for administering the Convention to US$12 million per year.

In the fall of 1992, the government of the Netherlands and the executive board of UNESCO entrusted Patrick Boylan, currently a professor of heritage policy and management and the head of the department of cultural policy and management at City University in London, with the review of the objectives and operations of the 1954 Hague Convention so as to identify measures for improving its application and effectiveness, and to see whether the convention required revision.[3]

One of Prof. Boylan's recommendations was to establish a fund within the convention to cover all aspects of cultural heritage. This recommendation was acted upon in the 1999 Second Protocol, which entered into force on March 9, 2004. A special fund has therefore been opened to receive voluntary contributions to enable UNESCO to react to emergency situations involving cultural heritage, whether or not the sites are inscribed on the World Heritage List. Among other uses, these funds can be used to stop or prevent looting, as the

1954 Hague Convention covers all aspects of war, including destruction and looting of cultural property.

ADDITIONAL STRATEGY FOR FUNDING EMERGENCY RESPONSE

In addition and in parallel to the international normative action, UNESCO set up other operational and ad hoc responses to emergency situations for cultural heritage.

International Safeguarding Campaign of the Monuments of Nubia

One example is the International Safeguarding Campaign of the Monuments of Nubia, Egypt, set up in 1959–1960 when construction of the high dam of Aswan began and the temples and monuments of Nubia were doomed to be submerged by the waters of the lake.

In this case, UNESCO mobilized the international community and expert groups were asked to draw up an international action plan to safeguard the whole of the Nubian heritage. In 1959, experts began their investigation, visiting all sites between Aswan and Semna. Their recommendations included a survey and archaeological excavations and research of all sites.

Several safeguarding projects were planned. On March 8, 1960, UNESCO launched an international appeal, inviting the world to give financial and technical assistance for the safeguarding of the Nubian monuments.

Almost submerged during the construction of the first Aswan dam in 1910, and threatened with total disappearance by the construction of the high dam in 1960, these monuments would not have been saved without the concerted action of states worldwide and the imagination and patient work of many specialists and experts. A special fund was established by UNESCO for the Nubia Campaign, and donations came in from all over the world. UNESCO brought together an international group of experts to ensure, along with Egyptian authorities, the sound management of the $80 million fund and proper implementation of safeguarding activities.

Cambodia: Save Angkor

Within the same spirit, and in response to the alarm sounded at the beginning of the 1990s by a rise in conflict, UNESCO launched a series of special programs to respond to increasing international needs.

Following the Paris agreement on Cambodia in October 1991, there was an appeal from the director-general of UNESCO, Mr. Federico Mayor, calling on the international community to "Save Angkor." In this country ravaged by an internal war for nearly 30 years, damages and the consequences of the war on the Khmer temples and the impact on the displaced population were assessed. In December 1992 in Santa Fe, New Mexico, the World Heritage Committee decided to inscribe the Angkor area on the World Heritage List and simultaneously on the World Heritage in Danger List, with a number of strict conditions.

In just ten years, the Angkor Special Programme had made significant progress. The success was attributed to the special UNESCO fund created through $20 million in donor contributions and to the establishment of an International Coordination Committee (ICC). This ICC was set up just one year after the inscription of the site of Angkor, and it is still functioning.

In an article published by *Museum International* in May 2002, Khmer Minister of State Vann Molyvann stressed the importance of an "international institutional machinery for managing the site of Angkor":

> Among many which responded to this campaign, two countries, for historical reasons, would play a role of first importance: France and Japan. It is in fact on their initiative, with the support of UNESCO, that the International Coordination Committee for the Safeguarding and Development of the Historic Site of Angkor was established in October 1993. The ICC holds a plenary meeting, once a year, at ambassador level, in Phnom Penh or Siem Reap. Between these plenary meetings, a Technical Committee, composed of embassy counselors who participate in the technical committee's work, meets three times a year.[4]

A fund-raising campaign raised $40 million for Angkor in twelve years, the second-largest amount ever raised through an international campaign for the safeguarding of cultural heritage. The bulk of the funding went toward the rehabilitation of temples and related cultural sites. The second-largest portion of the funding went toward the training of Cambodians at the University of Phnom Pehn, the training of technicians to catalogue objects, and the training of heritage police by the French National Police. A similar program was initiated in Iraq in 2003; however, due to the declining security situation, the program was discontinued.

Afghanistan

After Taliban leader Mullah Mohammed Omar issued an edict on February 26, 2001, stating that the Bamiyan Buddhas should be destroyed, Koïchiro Matsuura, the director general of UNESCO, launched a large number of initiatives to put pressure on the Taliban regime to reverse its order. These included meetings with representatives of Islamic countries, the mission of a special envoy (Ambassador Pierre Lafrance) to Kandahar, a call to President Hosni Mubarak of Egypt, a mission of high-level Islamic scholars to Kandahar with the support of the emir of Qatar, and a call to members of the government of Pakistan. Unfortunately, all were in vain.

In June 2001 and in October 2001, the UNESCO executive board and the general conference approved a resolution endorsing urgent activities, in particular, the creation of an international coordination committee for the safeguarding of Afghan cultural heritage. This was followed by a UNESCO conference in Doha, Qatar, in December 2001, organized in cooperation with and in the presence of the president of the Organization of the Islamic Conference (OIC); the two directors-general of the Islamic Educational, Scientific and Cultural Organization (ISESCO); and the Arab League Educational, Cultural and Scientific Organization (ALECSO); and under the chairmanship of H.H. Sheikh Hamad bin Khalifa, the emir of Qatar.

Agreements to assess and evaluate damage to Afghanistan's cultural heritage were concluded with the Society for the Preservation of Afghanistan's Cultural Heritage (SPACH) and with NGOs such as the Japanese Hirayama Foundation, chaired by Ikuo Hirayama, and the Afghanistan Institute and Museum in Exile at Bubendorf, Switzerland, chaired by Paul Bucherer, which provides for the safekeeping of cultural objects found on the international art market until they can be returned to Afghanistan. An international coordinating committee was established, which began planning for cultural protection work in Afghanistan. UNESCO created a special $6 million fund from contributions from member states and from the United Nations Development Group (UNDG).

A large number of projects has and continues to be carried out with the support of the UNESCO office in Kabul. Funding has been used to train guards and implement site protection measures to prevent illegal excavations at various locations throughout Afghanistan. Funding is also being used to rehabilitate the museum in Kabul and to train Afghani technicians in how to restore objects destroyed by the Taliban.

Iraq

When UNESCO received information regarding the impending war against Iraq, mainly through contacts with United States and the United Kingdom, I took the initiative, in my position as assistant director-general for culture, with the approval of the director-general, to send a letter in January 2003 to the observer of the United States and to the ambassador of the United Kingdom, reminding them of the provisions of the 1954 Hague Convention and the fact that Iraq is one of the richest countries in the Middle East in terms of cultural heritage. In this letter it was also mentioned that in Baghdad there was a very important museum where UNESCO's Division of Cultural Heritage worked to repair the air-conditioning damaged during the 1991 Persian Gulf War. The letter I sent to the observer of the United States received a reply requesting more information on cultural heritage in Iraq. I sent back a listing of the twenty to thirty most significant sites in Iraq, such as Babylon, Nineveh, Hatra, Ashur, Uruk, Ur, and the Iraq Museum. No further reply was received before the invasion.

During January and February 2003, I was also in contact with several foreign colleagues working in Iraq, particularly with Prof. McGuire Gibson of the University of Chicago, to provide them with the maximum of information on Iraq's cultural heritage. We were especially concerned about the archaeological sites of Ctesiphon and Babylon, as well as sites south of Babylon. Considering the extensive looting in the aftermath of the 1991 Persian Gulf War, we were especially concerned about the potential for looting of archaeological sites.

With colleagues at the World Heritage Centre, and in particular with Director Francesco Bandarin and the head of the Arab States Unit, Giovanni Boccardi, we prepared a map of the major sites of Iraq. At that time, one site—Hatra—was recognized as a World Heritage Site. Another site—Ashur—was considered to be a likely candidate for future recognition as a World Heritage Site. UNESCO had been keeping a close eye on Ashur because of concern about the impact of a dam construction project on the site.

During the Iraq war, the assessment started de facto in April 2003, and thanks to the almost live coverage of the war, we were able, together with several hundred million television viewers, to witness helplessly the destruction and looting of Iraqi cultural institutions and in particular the theft of archaeological collections from the Iraq Museum.

The whole world was outraged, but the looters continued their work, away from the cameras, on the great archaeological sites of this country.

Despite extremely difficult conditions, UNESCO conducted two missions in Iraq in mid-May and at the beginning of July 2003. Included in these missions were the heads of archaeological missions from countries such as Germany, Italy, Japan, the United Kingdom, and the United States. The missions also included museum, library, and archives specialists from Denmark, France, Iraq, and the Netherlands, as well as a representative from Interpol. These teams assessed and created the basis for an emergency plan for the rehabilitation of cultural institutions in Iraq.

After seeing the looting of the Iraq Museum, the director general of UNESCO, Koïchiro Matsuura, called a task force meeting on April 10, 2003. Considering that international organizations like UNESCO, ICCROM (the International Center for the Study of the Preservation and Restoration of Cultural Property Rome, a governmental center created by UNESCO fifty years ago and hosted by Italy), ICOM, ICOMOS (International Council of Monuments and Sites), IFLA (International Federation for Libraries and Archives), and the Blue Shield cannot be on the ground during the war to protect cultural heritage, we had been obliged to cease any action aimed at cultural heritage protection because the U.S. military would not authorize such a mission while Iraq remained a war zone. As such, UNESCO's only action immediately following the looting of the Iraq Museum was to organize a meeting on April 17, 2003, with all of the chiefs of foreign archaeological missions working in Iraq, as well as archaeologists, architects living outside of Iraq, and four Iraqi scholars in the field of heritage. (On April 17, no one could leave Iraq, despite UNESCO efforts to work with U.S. authorities to have one Iraqi expert from the museum attend this meeting.)

Ten days after this meeting in Paris, which resulted in a first appeal about the cultural heritage of Iraq, the British Museum organized a meeting—on April 29—in London, chaired by the minister of culture of the United Kingdom. It was at this meeting that, with the support of the BBC, Dr. Donny George Youkhanna, the director of antiquities and research for the State Board of Antiquities and Heritage, was able to come to London. This was the first time that direct testimony about the looting of the Iraq Museum was given by an Iraqi official.

After the meeting in London, another appeal was launched to all conservators and all institutions to impede looted objects from making their way into the art market. Coming back to Paris, I was asked by Mr. Matsuura to participate in the meeting organized by Interpol in Lyon on May 6, 2003, on the subject of the looting of Iraq Museum. In this meeting that I co-chaired with the director of Interpol, an agreement was prepared between UNESCO and Interpol for establishing a database of stolen objects. This database was then dispatched by Interpol to all police forces around the world.

It was at that moment that the war was considered officially terminated, and therefore, with the support of many ambassadors of UNESCO and in particular the ambassador of Italy Francesco Caruso, it was possible to organize a mission to Baghdad. The UN Security Office did not allow UNESCO to take a military plane either from the United Kingdom or Italy to Baghdad. In May 2003 there was no other possibility to go to Iraq, except through Amman by road, with significant difficulties and danger. Therefore, it took nearly ten days of negotiations with U.S. authorities in charge of Iraq; with the new minister of culture designated by U.S. authorities, the Italian ambassador Pietro Cordone; and with the UN security coordinator to obtain approval to go to Baghdad to obtain a direct report on cultural heritage, particularly of the Iraq Museum.

Finally, after long negotiations, a mission was carried out by a group of specialists composed of Neal McGregor, director of the British Museum; John Russell, professor at the Massachusetts College of Art; Ken Matsumoto, chief of the Japanese Archaeological Mission in Iraq; Roberto Parapetti, director of the Italian-Iraqi Centre of Baghdad; and myself. We traveled to Baghdad through Amman and we flew from Amman in a UN flight. We landed in Baghdad on May 15, 2003, and we held our first meeting with Ambassador Pietro

Cordone, who was in charge of the culture of Iraq. This mission was authorized only for Baghdad. It was during this mission that we discovered that not only the Iraq Museum had been looted but that all other museums were either looted or burned, such as the Museum of Fine Arts and the Museum of Traditional Music, and we also discovered—and this was a terrible shock—that the National Library and Archives had been burned from the first floor to the third.

The follow-up to the mission in Baghdad was considered a very important contribution from the international community: first of all, for the knowledge of damage to cultural heritage, but also because it led to the introduction in the Security Council Resolution of June 2003 of a paragraph dealing specifically with the looting of culture heritage. This was the first time that UNESCO was mentioned in these resolutions of the UN Security Council. Mr. Matsuura asked me to conduct a second mission in Iraq to have a wider look at what happened, not only in Baghdad but also in the rest of Iraq, and I did so in July 2003. I was received again by Ambassador Cordone, and also by Paul Bremer, the director of the Office of Reconstruction and Humanitarian Assistance, and I attended the opening for a half a day of the Iraq Museum where for the first time in the recent history of Iraq the Nimrud treasure was displayed.

This second mission was organized to enable us to visit major sites in southern Iraq, in particular Babylon, Kish, Uruk, Ur, the University of Basra, the regional library of Basra, and the old city of Basra. We saw looters digging illicitly on the site of Umma, which had been transformed into a cratered landscape. Then we went north from Baghdad to Erbil and Mosul, visiting Hatra, Nineveh, and Ashur, which had just been recognized as a World Heritage Site by the World Heritage Committee.

In this case again the director general of UNESCO, Koïchiro Matsuura, established an international coordination committee (ICC), in October 2003 for the safeguarding of Iraq's cultural heritage. Two meetings later took place at UNESCO Paris under the chairmanship of the minister of culture of Iraq (Mr. Mufid Al Jazaïri in May 2004 and Mr. Noori Farhan al-Rawi in June 2005) with the active participation of Donny George Youkhanna.

Contributions for the safeguarding of cultural heritage of Iraq, which amounted to more than $5 million in 2004–2005, were mainly used for the rehabilitation of the Iraq Museum, for purchasing necessary equipment, and for training Iraqi personnel. Through the mechanism of the ICC, many activities have been undertaken in close relationship with UNESCO's Baghdad office, which is temporarily based in Amman. Monies were earmarked for the training of groups of Iraqis in Amman and Cairo on how to protect cultural heritage sites, for the training of Iraqi experts on the documenting and cataloguing of objects, and for the restoration of various departments of the Iraq Museum. After the bombing of the mosque at Samarra, UNESCO began to ask how it could help with the protection of historic sites as well.

Other Funds

- A "special project" was set up in Lebanon after the Taef agreement in 1989.[5] A UNESCO report on the impact of the internal conflict in 1980s Lebanon on historic cities such as Baalbek, Tripoli, Byblos, and Tyr led to the creation of a fund-in-trust for the rehabilitation of the National Museum and archaeological research in the center of Beirut.
- The old city of Jerusalem and its cultural heritage was regularly followed by the special advisor of the director-general of UNESCO, Prof. Raymond Lemaire, who has undertaken, within the application of the Hague Convention, one or two missions per year since 1967. These reports constitute a very valuable source of information for the state of conservation of the old city of Jerusalem, subject to constant tensions between Israelis and Palestinians. A special account has been set up, with Saudi Arabia being the main donor through a $2 million contribution.
- The conflicts in Africa during the last fifteen years have particularly affected natural heritage, and UNESCO World Heritage Centre obtained from the UN Foundation a very important donation that is now nearing $40 million for the rehabilitation of the national parks in the Congo Basin that are inscribed on the World Heritage List. There are four sites which are still benefiting from the UN Foundation.

Special Programs, Revisited

As described above, the international coordination committee mechanism showed very good results in the case of Cambodia. For this reason, it was replicated in Afghanistan at the end of the war in 2002 and again in Iraq in 2003. Each committee was composed of experts and representatives of the states providing financial resources for the restoration and rehabilitation of cultural heritage.

More than $40 million has been raised for Cambodia, with different countries, such as Italy and France, adopting a different monument for restoration. In Afghanistan, cave paintings showing the life of the Buddha are in the process of being restored.

Special programs have been designed to accompany other actions at the international level, highlighting the interest of the international community. These experiences institutionalized, through their special programs, an "operational reply" to specific conflict situations that became a de facto operational mechanism. This mechanism is quite simple and consists of

- assessment missions, carried out immediately after a declared ceasefire by recognized experts[6]

- preparation of a plan of action with a list of priorities and cost estimates
- participation at UN donors' meetings
- the setting up of an international coordination committee (ICC)

The ICC is thus the international mechanism that coordinates assistance. It has the task of ensuring the consistency of the different projects proposed by various donors or institutions willing to contribute and to define any technical and financial standards. Another important aspect of the ICC contribution is the role played in avoiding duplication of efforts.

CONCLUSION

At the beginning of the twenty-first century, one of the biggest challenges for those confronted with the destruction of cultural heritage by armed conflict is to build upon a global alliance aimed at encouraging voluntary contributions so as to have, at the international level, emergency funds that can facilitate the operations for a rapid response leading to concrete activities of rehabilitation and restoration. In this context, and with the above-mentioned instruments, currently UNESCO seems to be the most adequate forum to catalyze the presence of the different stakeholders in the affected conflict areas.

Next Steps
- Create a coalition of all active, competent, and well-known bodies, such as ICOM and ICOMOS, the Blue Shield, and the World Monuments Fund, among others.
- As soon as the security situation improves in places like Iraq, send these organizations in to address problems, study the best ways to address issues, and work with Iraqi colleagues on issues of heritage, particularly archaeological sites.
- Advocate that national armies provide some type of cultural heritage training for the respect of cultural heritage.
- Move toward the signing and ratification of conventions; they are useful tools within countries to improve proper legislation.
- Investigate the disturbing trend of internal warfare, its impact on cultural heritage, and how these conflicts can be resolved.
- The mechanism put in place by UNESCO through the ICCs and their relevant technical committees is a concrete response of building partnerships with donor countries and the many institutions that are active in the field of cultural heritage, such as IGOs (the Council of Europe, ALECSO, ISESCO, and ICCROM), or NGOs (e.g., ICOMOS, ICOM, IIC, IFLA, ICA), foundations or private institutes (e.g., UN Foundation, the Getty Conservation Institute, the World Monuments Fund, the Aga Khan Trust for Culture, Europa Nostra, and the Global Heritage Fund). A possible next step would be to establish a standing fund or endowment for the general purpose of dealing with threats

to cultural heritage raised by the specter of armed conflict. Such a fund could be drawn upon *before* rather than following a conflict, or at least more expeditiously in the aftermath of a conflict.

NOTES

1. Jiří Toman, preface to *The Protection of Cultural Property in the Event of Armed Conflict* (Brookfield, VT: Dartmouth Publishing Company; Paris: UNESCO, 1996).
2. "United Nations Year for Cultural Heritage: Priority on Reconciliation and Development," *UNESCO Media Services,* February 4, 2002, http://portal.unesco.org/en/ev.php-URL_ID=2939&URL_DO=DO_TOPIC&URL_SECTION=201.html.
3. Patrick J. Boylan, *Review of the Convention for the Protection of Cultural Property in the Event of Armed Conflict (The Hague Convention of 1954),* 1993, UNESCO Report CLT-93/WS/12,104, http://unesdoc.unesco.org/images/0010/001001/100159eo.pdf.
4. Vann Molyvann, "Management of the Angkor Site: National Emblem and World Heritage Site," *Museum International* 54, no. 1/2 (May 2002): 110–16.
5. *The Official Lebanese Forces* website, http://www.lebanese-forces.org/lebanon/agreements/taef.htm.
6. On October 26, 2004 a bilateral agreement between UNESCO and the Italian Ministry for Cultural Activities and Heritage has been signed in Paris, aiming to take care of worldwide cultural heritage in case of natural calamities or actions of war and terrorism. This group of experts has been named the Blue Shield for cultural heritage. The task force will include experts from the Italian Protezione Civile. In case of need, following a request from UNESCO in coordination with the beneficiary country, a preliminary assessment of damages will be carried out, followed by a phase of recovery that previews a wide involvement of the local population.

CHAPTER 19

Engaging Interagency Processes to Protect Cultural Sites

Communities, Authorities, and Capabilities

SCOTT R. FEIL

THIS CHAPTER OUTLINES INTERAGENCY COORDINATION AMONG THOSE WHO CAN ACT to protect cultural heritage immediately before, during, and after armed conflict. In general, it also identifies the particular challenge faced by those who wish to see protection of cultural sites and artifacts accorded the appropriate priority in intervention planning and execution, and outlines a method and pathways to engage current and emerging interagency processes to achieve that goal.

Communities with an *intrinsic* interest in cultural heritage protection have few resources to dedicate to culturally significant places and objects immediately before, during, and after armed conflict within a weak or failed state. Conversely, those communities of expertise with significant resources that have jurisdiction to operate in the theater of war will only protect cultural sites and artifacts when it can be demonstrated that such protection yields benefits to their operations. In most circumstances, this community may only act in defense of cultural heritage if there is a likely *instrumental* value in protecting sites and artifacts. The challenge for the cultural heritage sector, which sees culture as an intrinsic value, is to make the case, as this volume does, to the *instrumentally oriented community* that it is in its interest to protect cultural sites and artifacts.

IDENTIFYING COMMUNITIES OF INTEREST:
INTRINSIC VERSUS INSTRUMENTAL

When engaging a large, diverse, and vertically "stovepiped" government to act in new and unfamiliar areas, it is important to consider the motivations of government organizations and bureaucracies in responding to inputs and requests for action. In the case of protecting cultural sites and artifacts, one may divide the potentially interested actors, both governmental and nongovernmental, into two categories. There are those who see the intrinsic value of the protection of cultural sites and artifacts, and those who see (or more accurately, can be informed) that the protection of cultural sites and artifacts provides instrumental value to them in the execution of their core competencies and responsibilities.

The first group, those that see the intrinsic value of protection of cultural sites and artifacts, are, like many readers of this volume, those with a personal or professional interest in the issue from the perspectives of academics, research, preservation, or economics. Unfortunately, these interested individuals and groups do not have the resources or the authority to take action to protect sites and artifacts in the absence of competent, responsible, and transparent government. Such governance provides the physical security, laws, and rules of property and provenance required for devising and implementing methods to resolve issues and hopefully satisfy the interested parties. Without competent government, sites and artifacts become "commons" that are ripe for individual exploitation, destruction, and loss.

Competent governance is, however, the purview of others who may not immediately perceive any connection between establishing governance, the rule of law, sound economic activity, and security. This community of those who may be aware, but uninterested in cultural site and artifact protection, represented in large part by the military, diplomatic, and development communities, are directly involved in providing services and developing indigenous (assisted nation) capacities in the four framework pillars. The military and civilian agencies are oriented largely on the security, economic, justice/rule-of-law, and governance tasks that confront the interveners and the assisted government. They therefore have significant resources at their disposal to devote to these issues. However, protection of cultural sites and artifacts may be viewed by these groups as either a lesser component of the central tasks, or as naturally following from the success of their efforts in the political, economic, security, and justice areas. Moreover, the instrumental community may not be aware of the contribution that protection of cultural sites and artifacts can make to success in these other areas.

The logical nexus of the two communities lies in the ability of the intrinsic community to make the case to the instrumental community that protection of cultural sites and artifacts is an important task that will yield benefits to the instrumentally oriented community directly. Only then will government agencies institutionalize the task into their plans and seek and integrate the resources necessary to accomplish the task. Such a campaign to raise the issue to the appropriate level will require dedicated and long-term engagement with government agencies that are developing new processes for managing U.S. involvement in interventions. Action is being taken now to preclude ad hoc organizations and processes and a "pickup game" for intervention and security, stability, and reconstruction operations. The intrinsic community needs to take steps to ensure that cultural protection tasks receive appropriate attention and achieve an institutionalized process that forces interagency planners and operators to integrate requirements for protection of cultural sites into their products. Without such engagement, protection of cultural sites and artifacts will probably remain an afterthought in plans and will only be considered as a result of an anecdote of the sort, "remember what happened in Iraq." As agencies institutionalize the lessons from the first four years of the Iraq conflict, protection of cultural sites and artifacts needs to be part of that process.

Other chapters in this volume have outlined the case that the intrinsic community needs to make to the instrumentally oriented community. Namely, protection of cultural sites and artifacts accomplishes the following:

- It contributes to an overall atmosphere of general security.
- It promotes the rule of law and respect for property.
- It removes a potential source of income from criminal, terrorist, and illicit power structures.[1]
- It ensures that economic benefits from tourism and legitimate exploitation of cultural sites and artifacts are distributed in accordance with international and national laws, creating a continuing benefit.
- It affords a sense of legitimacy to government, as it demonstrates its ability to protect the national cultural identity.
- It avoids the negative press and regional or worldwide backlash that are unleashed when cultural heritage is removed or destroyed.

The intrinsic community must employ a sustained effort to engage both the legislative and executive branches of government. The legislative branch has the power to direct consideration of particular elements and provide resources. Operation Enduring Freedom in Afghanistan and Operation Iraqi Freedom in Iraq have provided the impetus for congressional receptivity— and demands—for change in the executive branch's approach to intervention aftermath. For its part, the executive branch has made some encouraging changes in the processes that facilitate cooperation and coordination between military and civilian agencies. These initiatives are being institutionalized.

The intrinsic community should seize the opportunity to engage the instrumentally oriented community, make the case for protection of cultural sites and artifacts, and be willing to participate in ongoing efforts to develop and institutionalize these processes. The intrinsic community, which itself is a composite of different interests, should come together to approach, engage, and provide expertise and manpower to the government to ensure that protection of cultural sites and artifacts is an integral part of any intervention planning and execution.

THE GENERAL INTERAGENCY CHALLENGE

As is evident from previous chapters and the outline of the history of protection efforts in Iraq from 2003 onward, the issue of protecting cultural heritage sites is complex, subtle, and the direct responsibility of no single office within the U.S. government. It is a "horizontal" problem of the life cycle of discovery, identification, custodianship, and exploitation of cultural heritage sites and artifacts that cuts across the "vertical" organizations and instruments of government. As is the case with all such issues requiring interagency coordination, the real action is at the seams between organizations, and the goal of interagency coordination should be to get organizations that are concerned with their own core competencies and responsibilities to

1. Act within a conceptual framework that fosters a comprehensive understanding of the problem, the proposed solutions, and the organizations' potential contributions.
2. Recognize and take action with respect to the effects and outcomes from other organizations to which they contribute, and conversely, which impact that organization.

A general framework that has been adapted for analytical and planning use in overseas interagency involvement includes the issue areas of (1) security, (2) economic and social well-being, (3) justice, reconciliation, and the rule of law, and (4) governance.[2] Variations on this framework have been developed to guide government planning and programs for action by several different agencies, including the Departments of Defense and State and the U.S. Agency for International Development (USAID).

This framework and its derivatives can be used both to address the protection of cultural sites and artifacts, especially in a pre- or postconflict environment, and as a first cut at a program to engage government to prepare for and execute responsibilities in this area. The value of such frameworks is that they deconstruct the complexity of issues so that individual agencies can focus and target specific areas within their purview, while illustrating the interdependency of the various efforts undertaken. While there are agencies that are charged with primary responsibility for each of those major issue areas, success in any given area is predicated upon satisfactory performance in others, and issues that fall within the mission of one agency often depend upon performance in others.

Protecting cultural heritage sites requires coordinated actions that cut across government agencies that are set up to address only certain aspects of the issue. The effort must also encompass the conditions that face all assistance efforts—there are program coordination issues that exist and must be resolved within the U.S. government; there are program coordination issues that the indigenous government must address internally; and there will be coordination issues between the host country and the U.S. government. These issues often arise from cultural, political, and organizational differences, within and between governments. Rarely, if ever, is there a one-to-one match between different countries' bureaucracies in terms of authorities and capabilities. While the police or security forces under a ministry or department of defense may be responsible for securing the site, police forces and criminal investigators from the ministry of justice or ministry of the interior may be required to track and counter illicit trade in artifacts. Some countries have ministries of antiquities or culture that have additional responsibilities at a national level for the inventory and care of sites and artifacts. This paper recognizes the additional complexity of getting a U.S. government response to mesh with a host nation response and capability, but focuses on the more immediate issue of approaching the U.S. government to incorporate the protection of cultural sites and artifacts into planning, coordination, and capabilities requirements.

The issue of government response in a "vertical" or "stovepiped" fashion to complex issues that have a foreign assistance life cycle is illustrated in figure 19.1. The horizontal dimension in figure 19.1 is a life cycle time sequence of "capacity" to address an issue or requirement during an intervention. The phases are notional, but phasing has been adopted in some form by most government agencies to facilitate analysis, planning, execution, measurement, and assignment of responsibilities.[3] The issue depicted is generic, but could concern security, economics, governance, infrastructure, or protecting cultural sites and artifacts, or it could be a composite. In early phases, the *Affected Nation Capacity* (solid line) is adequate, but deteriorating (for whatever reason). Crisis intervention usually begins with an increase in outside assisting *Civilian Resources* (long dash) to shore up declining affected-nation capacity. If those initial intervention steps fail, the situation may deteriorate to the point that *Military Resources* (dash-dot) must be deployed to regain control of the situation. Those military resources often outstrip both outside civilian and affected-nation resources and may take on additional roles. Subsequently, at a given time or under predetermined conditions, military resources are supplanted in the long term by civilian resources, usually when the security situation permits. Both military and civilian outside resources are used to restore affected-nation capacity until military forces and civilian assistance reverts to "normal" levels of interaction. Replicating this description across all issue areas and overlaying the

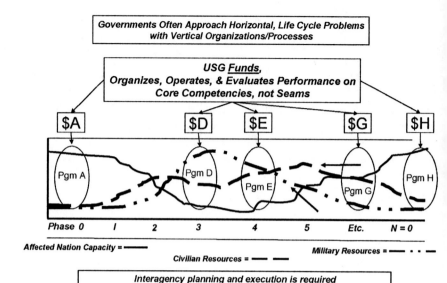

Figure 19.1. Interagency Coordination Challenges

activities of international governmental organizations (e.g., the UN or NATO), international organizations (e.g., the International Committee of the Red Cross), and nongovernmental organizations (e.g., Mercy Corps, Doctors Without Borders), one can see the complexity of gaining recognition for a particular requirement and then developing the coordinated or collaborative action to resolve the issue.[4]

The vertical dimension, however, depicts the response to crisis and intervention that is constrained by organizations operating in "routine" mode as most governments, including the U.S. government, are organized and prone to do. This is depicted by the different labeled "pots of funding" and the ovals depicting specific programs within certain phases. Authorities are often narrowly prescribed and direct actions in limited areas of endeavor and under certain conditions. They often proscribe actions. As an example, after the Vietnam War and congressional action in the 1970s, the provision of police training to assisted nations became very constrained. USAID and the Department of Defense are generally prohibited from providing any police training, which is now the purview of the Departments of State and Justice. (This constraint has been relaxed somewhat in Iraq with respect to the Department of Defense.) In parallel with authorities, appropriations are often directed to specific activities and restricted in their application. As a result of this top-down direction, from authorities in both the legislative and executive branches, organs of government

224   SCOTT R. FEIL

develop core competencies and focus on the areas and programs where they are expected to achieve success, and for which they receive continued funding. Hence, resources may be directed to component aspects of the interventions issue through different agencies with only secondary thought given to integrated application of those resources.

Accounts of interventions are replete with instances of overlaps and gaps in the application of resources coordinated through programs and projects that do not cumulate in progress toward an overall goal. Frequently, organs of government seek to optimize their own core competencies and performance with little thought given to optimizing the overall function of government.[5] The results of this method of operation played out in the squandered opportunity to protect Iraq's cultural sites and to leverage that protection to the advantage of the coalition and the future of Iraq.

CURRENT AUTHORITIES AND INITIATIVES: WHO'S BELLING THE CAT?

The Presidency

Several initiatives and statements indicate that the government will (or may) be more open to the argument that protection of cultural sites and artifacts requires attention and priority. The president's 2006 National Security Strategy states a goal of "developing a civilian reserve corps, analogous to the military reserves. The civilian reserve corps would utilize, in a flexible and timely manner, the human resources of the American people for skills and capacities needed for international disaster relief and post-conflict reconstruction," and his 2007 State of the Union message created additional emphasis and potential for more civilian input and participation in influencing the planning and execution of stability, security, transition, and reconstruction operations. Acting on the momentum established by the departments and Congress, the president stated: "A . . . task we can take on together is to design and establish a volunteer Civilian Reserve Corps. Such a corps would function much like our military reserve. It would ease the burden on the Armed Forces by allowing us to hire civilians with critical skills to serve on missions abroad when America needs them."[6]

While this was the first time the president addressed the issue directly, civilian and military departments and agencies within the U.S. government have taken initiatives to strengthen the overall capabilities of the United States to create conditions for success and sustainability in interventions. While the real momentum for these initiatives has come from operations in Afghanistan and Iraq, pressure to innovate preceded those actions and was founded in some of the lessons of peacekeeping operations in the Balkans and elsewhere in the previous decade.

The Department of State

The president is recognizing and supporting a concept that had evolved from his establishment of the Office of the Coordinator for Reconstruction and Stabilization within the State Department in the spring and summer of 2004. This office is intended to be the interagency coordination office for all U.S. government involvement in reconstruction and stabilization missions, coordinating at the national level and providing planning and implementation capabilities at the local levels. The office is described elsewhere in this volume (see chapter 17), but would fulfill its responsibilities by doing the following:

- leading policy coordinating committees
- providing the interface for other agencies
- offering additional coordination capability with the military and multilateral/ multinational organs
- providing civilian capabilities at regional and local levels

Field teams would be capable of operating independently but could also work with military headquarters. Part of the appeal of the office is the initiative to harness civilian capacity that exists within the United States, from national government agencies, state and local authorities, and experts and the civilian private sector (both commercial and nonprofit). The office explored several models for developing, training, and managing a civilian reserve, as well as developing operational concepts for executing its responsibilities and working with military units.[7]

Critical to the effort to protect cultural sites and artifacts, the Office of the Coordinator drafted a planning framework using major mission elements adopted from the previously identified CSIS/AUSA Post-Conflict Reconstruction Task Framework. These frameworks include the tasks to "protect and secure places of worship and cultural sites," and to "protect and secure strategically important institutions (e.g., government buildings, museums, religious sites, courthouses, communications, etc.)."[8] These task statements begin incorporating cultural site and artifact protection into the institutional processes of the government.

The State Department also has reorganized its foreign assistance operations under an under secretary of state who is also designated the director of foreign assistance and the administrator of the U.S. Agency for International Development. In this capacity, the State Department has created a single office for coordination of foreign assistance with the department and a single office for interacting with other government departments and agencies. Announced in January 2006,[9] this office provides an opportunity to engage on the subject of protection of cultural sites on a broader front, including but not limited to conflict and postconflict situations. Some of the steps outlined in other chapters in this volume—tasks such as documentation, location, and inventory, among others—could be undertaken with additional focus and resources directed through foreign assistance.

The Legislative Branch

The legislative branch has become engaged as well, with the Senate Foreign Relations Committee thoroughly examining in hearings and reports the need for better integration of civilian and military capacities. This resulted in several proposals to establish, through authorizing legislation, a civilian reserve and better interagency planning, coordination, and execution organizations and processes.[10] These bills have met with some success in the Senate. However, despite repeated calls from a number of sectors to establish this reserve,[11] which would provide the opportunity for participation by those interested in cultural site protection, funding has not been forthcoming.[12]

The Department of Defense

For its part, the Department of Defense articulated policies designed to recognize and institutionalize requirements for postconflict intervention management and leadership. Of interest to this issue of protecting cultural sites and artifacts, Department of Defense Directive 3000.05, adopted in November 2005,[13] instructs the department to

- prepare for and conduct stability, security, transition, and reconstruction operations as a core competency on a par with combat operations (Paragraph 4.1)
- operate and support the operation of military civilian teams, accepting participation from personnel in government agencies, international organizations, nongovernmental organizations, and the private sector with relevant expertise (Paragraph 4.5)

The commander of U.S. Joint Forces Command is directed to develop the organizational and operational concepts for these teams, in consultation with other agencies, organizations, and the private sector (Paragraph 5.10.2). Further, the under secretary of defense for policy is designated as the lead office for interaction with the private sector and nongovernmental organization, establishing a stability operations center and developing information sharing procedures (Paragraph 5.1.8 and 9).

As a result of the directive and other requirements, the under secretary of defense for policy is reorganizing the office. Two subordinate offices now could be characterized as having missions that would encompass or address the concerns of protecting cultural sites and artifacts. Under the assistant secretary of defense for global security affairs, the deputy assistant secretary of defense for building partner capacity is charged with building interagency capacity with input from nongovernmental organizations. Under the assistant secretary of defense for special operations and low-intensity conflict, the deputy assistant secretary of defense for stability operations capabilities is responsible for oversight of policy development and execution for stability, security, transition, and reconstruction operations.[14]

National Security Presidential Directive 44

Following closely on the publication of the Department of Defense directive, the president signed National Security Presidential Directive (NSPD) 44.[15] The NSPD effectively codified initiatives and accomplishments to December 2005, specified departmental authorities, and directed actions to be taken in the future. Of most interest to those who wish to protect cultural sites and artifacts, the directive designates the secretary of state as the lead cabinet-level official for postconflict reconstruction planning, coordination, and execution, and solidified the establishment of the Office of the Coordinator for Reconstruction and Stabilization.

The directive charges the office with developing plans that reflect the framework containing the task to protect and to engage those civilian experts and nongovernmental organizations who can contribute to planning and execution of postconflict reconstruction operations. Finally, the directive also instructs the coordinator to develop concepts for a civilian reserve. This directive and the statement in the president's State of the Union on the establishment of the civilian reserve represent significant support and momentum from the Office of the President for the initiative.

A caution, however, is that executive branch authorities like NSPDs and executive orders can be rescinded by subsequent administrations. Executive branch authorities establish necessary, but not sufficient, conditions for institutionalizing the processes for conducting postconflict reconstruction operations. Without congressional authorizations and appropriations the progress made to date remains at risk in subsequent administrations.

INTERACTION BETWEEN UNIFORMED MILITARY AND CIVILIAN AGENCIES

In parallel with and in response to the development of these policies, the uniformed military has also taken several conceptual and operational steps to include civilian advice and participation in operations to ensure the appropriate application of complementary resources and to recognize the central role that the military will play in task execution until civilian operational capabilities can be brought to bear. The U.S. Joint Forces Command, as the Department of Defense point organization for experimenting with new concepts and exploring new methods for interacting with civilian agencies, has recommended a number of innovations. These include establishing the Joint Interagency Coordination Group, located at military combatant command headquarters. This group works with the Departments of State, Justice, and Treasury as well as USAID to devise new planning and operational processes to achieve synergy between the military and civilian agencies of government. Experiments and exercises develop and evaluate new concepts and record initiatives and innovation to be adopted by government agencies as new operating procedures, and help justify development of new capabilities. As previously noted, U.S. Joint Forces Command worked with the coordinator for reconstruction to jointly produce the draft planning system.[16]

The Army and Marine Corps have revised their counterinsurgency doctrine and incorporated lessons learned from the current conflicts. While not specifically addressing protection of cultural sites and artifacts, the doctrinal manual recognizes the central role that culture plays in determining the success or failure of insurgencies and counterinsurgency efforts.[17]

NEXT STEPS: ENGAGING COMMUNITIES OF INTEREST

The challenge facing the intrinsic community of interest in protection of cultural sites and artifacts is to engage the U.S. government at all these entry points, take advantage of the directives that are in effect, and make the sustained case that

- protecting cultural sites and artifacts is important to the intrinsic and instrumentally oriented communities of interest
- the intrinsic community of interest is willing and able to help

This requires an organizational and advocacy effort that is focused and sustained. Organizing to make this effort will require a steering group composed of leaders of the museum, academic, and commercial interests involved with cultural sites and artifacts. Their goals should include the following:

- The steering group should convene on a regular basis to establish direction and provide guidance to working groups that conduct the engagement.
- The principals on the steering group should make themselves available to meet with congressional and executive branch leadership at appropriate times and venues to convey the importance of the issue and willingness of the community to engage in solutions and fieldwork.
- Contacts with Congress must be targeted to those staff and members working on foreign conflict and legal issues and cover both authorizing and appropriating committees.
- Working groups should engage at the concept development and operational levels with the Departments of State, Defense, and Justice as well as the uniformed

military commands and services to make the same points and work on detailed initiatives.

- The steering group must have engagement with the director of foreign assistance, the coordinator for reconstruction and stabilization, and the under secretary of defense for policy and their offices.
- The group must be involved with the service war colleges and the Foreign Service Institute to not only introduce the issue and importance of protection for cultural sites and artifacts, but also to offer subject matter expertise on a frequent and routine basis to provide direct instruction to the students.
- Working groups engaging with the Department of Justice should contact the Office of Overseas Prosecutorial Development Assistance and Training (OPDAT)[18] and the International Criminal Investigative Training and Assistance Program (ICITAP)[19] to emphasize and work with assistance and training teams in combating illicit and illegal trade in cultural artifacts.

This effort to provide information and educate policymakers and operational planners on the importance of the issue and its relevance to providing security, economic, legal, and governance benefits must be coupled with an initiative to provide expertise in the field that does not exist at the federal level. The key to successful interagency impact is the ability to engage and provide resources. The resources of most importance to government agencies involved in stability, security, transition, and reconstruction operations are people to participate and authoritative information. At the direction of the steering group, a working group should canvas the intrinsic community and develop lists of subject matter experts that could be provided to the Office of the Coordinator for Reconstruction and Stabilization. This list of subject matter experts could be tapped to participate in Department of State deployable teams. The working group on participation should examine the potential to establish a working relationship with USAID for individual work with Disaster Assistance Response Teams (DART), Response Advisor for Technical Services (RATS),[20] or under collective contracts with a corporation or nonprofit organization in the Support Which Implements Fast Transitions (SWIFT)[21] program. Such programs provided expertise to teams that deployed to earthquake sites in Bam, Iran, in 2003[22] and in Turkey in 1999.[23] Personnel systems in use by the federal government and in development by the Department of State can use this information to support the civilian reserve concept and demonstrate that communities in the United States are willing and able to support. This would benchmark the cultural protection community as a leader in partnering with government.

Those interested in getting government to protect cultural sites and artifacts can be expected to be asked to provide information on the location of sites and artifacts, the size and the quantities involved, the characteristics of the articles (easily pilfered, damageable or not, and so on), and the relative priority among the sites. Only the intrinsic community can provide that sort of information.[24] Such information exchange and update should be institutionalized for use in operational concept development and training exercises. Government recognizes that some information may be difficult to obtain, but any information that can help inform civilian and military planners would be appreciated and important.

Working groups can report back to the executive steering group on progress and milestones. The objective should be adequate funding for programs that can contribute to protection of cultural sites and artifacts, through the Departments of Defense and State (including programs executed by USAID and the Department of Justice), and an institutionalized relationship that would see the community of interest participating in concept development, planning, exercises, and deployments with subject matter experts that keep the protection of cultural sites and artifacts on priority lists and in the "bloodstream" of department, agency, and organization activities.

NOTES

The views expressed in this chapter are solely those of the author and do not necessarily reflect the policies or positions of the Institute for Defense Analyses, any departments, agencies, or organizations of the United States government, or any other organizations.

1. "The third lesson is the importance of cutting off the would-be spoilers' access to highly portable, high-value commodities that they can use to fund resistance to the peace process." U.S. Senate Committee on Foreign Relations, Testimony of William Durch, *Hearing on Afghanistan: In Pursuit of Security and Democracy*, 108th Cong., 2nd sess. (Washington, DC: U.S. Senate Committee on Foreign Relations, October 16, 2003), 3. While the comment was made with respect to drug trafficking, the same lesson can be applied to illicit and illegal trade in cultural artifacts. http://www.senate.gov/~foreign/testimony/2003/DurchTestimony031016.pdf (accessed February 2007).

2. The origins of this framework lie in the Post-Conflict Reconstruction Project conducted by the Association of the U.S. Army and the Center for Strategic and International Studies, and the associated Commission Report. This framework has been adapted by the Departments of State and Defense in various forms to assist with analysis, planning, exercises, and resource allocation in postconflict situations. The original citations are "Post-Conflict Reconstruction Task Framework," May 2002, and "Play to Win: The Commission on Post-Conflict Reconstruction," January 2003, Association of the U.S. Army, Arlington, VA, and the Center for Strategic and International Studies (CSIS), Washington, DC. CSIS continued the project and more information is available at http://www.csis.org/researchfocus/pcr. The U.S. government adaptations of the framework are referenced later in this paper.

3. See U.S. Joint Forces Command, *J-7 Pamphlet U.S. Government Draft Planning Framework for Reconstruction, Stabilization, and Conflict Transformation, Version 1.0* (Norfolk, VA: U.S. Joint Forces Command, 2005), and the U.S. Department of State, *Foreign Assistance Framework* (Washington, DC: U.S. Department of State, Chart dated October 12, 2006), and U.S. Department of State Coordinator for Reconstruction and Stabilization, *Post Conflict Reconstruction Essential Tasks* (Washington, DC: U.S. Department of State, April 2005). Phases can be numbered but are usually also defined in terms of conditions met and resources expended or elapsed.

4. This view of interagency coordination issues has been developed by Mart Lidy and other colleagues from the Institute for Defense Analyses. Other organizations and experts have conducted research into the issues and have made similar findings. The "sine wave" (or adaptations of such ebbs and flows in capabilities based on conditions and timing) of intervention progress and capabilities in military/civilian, government, multinational, and multilateral efforts has been a useful concept for analysis and policy recommendations. See Clark Murdock and Michele Flournoy, Principal Investigators, *Beyond Goldwater-Nichols: U.S. Government and Defense Reform for a New Strategic Era; Phase II Report* (Washington, DC: Center for Strategic and International Studies, July 2005), http://www.csis.org/media/csis/pubs/bgn_ph2_report.pdf (accessed December 2006); Dennis C. Jett, *Why Peacekeeping Fails* (New York: St. Martin's Press, 1992); Robert Oakley, Michael Dziedzic, and Eliot Goldberg, eds., *Policing the New World Disorder: Peace Operations and Public Security* (Washington, DC: National Defense University Press, 1998); Robert Orr, ed., *Winning the Peace: An American Strategy for Post-Conflict Reconstruction* (Washington, DC: The Center for Strategic and International Studies Press, 2004); Robert Perito, *Where Is the Lone Ranger When We Need Him?: America's Search for a Postconflict Stability Force* (Washington, DC: United States Institute of Peace Press, 2004), and Jock Covey, Michael Dziedzic, and Leonard Hawley, eds., *The Quest for Viable Peace: International Intervention and Strategies for Conflict Transformation* (Washington, DC: United States Institute of Peace Press, 2005).

5. One of the central works in this area is still found in Graham Allison and Philip Zelikow's *Essence of Decision: Explaining the Cuban Missile Crisis*, 2d (New York: Pearson Longman, 1999). Though addressing the Cuban missile crisis of 1962, it is still useful to analyze and characterize the motivations and rationale behind organizational and bureaucratic choice.

6. President George W. Bush, *The National Security Strategy of the United States* (Washington, DC: The White House, 2006) 44, http://www.whitehouse.gov/nsc/nss/2006/sectionIX.html (accessed February 2007); President George W. Bush, *State of the Union* (Washington, DC: The White House, January 2007), http://www.whitehouse.gov/news/releases/2007/01/20070123-2.html; and "Policy Initiatives" at http://www.whitehouse.gov/stateoftheunion/2007/initiatives/index.html (accessed February 2007).

7. See the coordinator website at http://www.state.gov/s/crs (accessed February 2007).

8. Office of the Coordinator for Reconstruction and Stabilization, *Post Conflict Reconstruction Essential Tasks Matrix* (Washington, DC: The Department of State) I-4 (accessed April 2005). The tasks are listed under the Initial Response Phase; Security;

Protection of Indigenous Individuals, Infrastructure and Institutions, http://www .state.gov/s/crs/rls/52959.htm#protection (accessed February 2007).

9. U.S. Secretary of State Condoleezza Rice, *Transformational Diplomacy and a New Direction for U.S. Foreign Assistance* (Washington, DC: The Department of State, January 19, 2006), http://www.state.gov/secretary/rm/2006/59408.htm (accessed February 2007).

10. Although several bills were proposed, the most successful legislative history was that of the Stabilization and Reconstruction Civilian Management Act of 2004, introduced as S. 2127 and H.R. 3996 and again in 2005 as S. 209. S. 209 can be read at http://www.theorator.com/bills109/s209.html (accessed February 2007); S. 613, the "Reconstruction and Stabilization Civilian Management Act of 2007" is the latest version of the effort, introduced by Senator Lugar, chair, and Senator Biden, ranking member, of the Senate Foreign Relations Committee on February 15, 2007. Senator Richard Lugar's "Speech to the National Defense University," at the Symposium on "Resourcing Stability Operations and Reconstruction: Past, Present and Future" at the Industrial College of the Armed Forces, National Defense University, March 23, 2006, http://lugar.senate.gov/press/record.cfm?id=253067 (accessed June 2007) provides a good synopsis of legislative progress in authorization and obstacles in securing funding.

11. A list of agencies participating in the Office of the Coordinator for Stabilization and Reconstruction and those nongovernmental organizations supporting authorization and appropriation legislation is available at http://www.sourcewatch .org/index.php?title=Office_of_the_Coordinator_for_Reconstruction_and_ Stabilization (accessed February 2007).

12. Lugar, "Speech to the National Defense University."

13. U.S. Department of Defense Directive 3000.05, *Military Support for Stability, Security, Transition, and Reconstruction (SSTR) Operations* (Washington, DC: Department of Defense, November 28, 2005).

14. Memorandum from the Under Secretary of Defense for Policy, September 25, 2006, and organization chart, USD (P), undated.

15. White House National Security Presidential Directive 44, *Management of Interagency Efforts Concerning Reconstruction and Stabilization* (Washington, DC: The White House, December 7, 2005), http://www.fas.org/irp/offdocs/nspd/nspd-44 .html (accessed February 2007).

16. See the U.S. Joint Forces Command website, http://www.jfcom.mil (accessed February 2007).

17. Headquarters Department of the Army, *Field Manual 3-24 Counterinsurgency,* Headquarters U.S. Marine Corps Marine Corps Warfighting Publication 3-33.5, (Washington, DC: Department of the Army Department of the Navy Headquarters U.S. Marine Corps, December 15, 2006), http://www.fas.org/irp/doddir/ army/fm3-24.pdf (accessed February 2007).

18. OPDAT has been tasked with the coordination of the training of judges and prosecutors abroad in coordination with various government agencies and U.S. embassies. The program uses individual contract personnel to provide these services. http://www.usdoj.gov/criminal/opdat.html (accessed February 2007).

19. ICITAP's activities encompass two principal types of assistance projects: (1) the development of police forces in the context of international peacekeeping operations and (2) the enhancement of capabilities of existing police forces in emerging democracies. Assistance is based on internationally recognized principles of human rights, rule of law, and modern police practices. ICITAP's training and assistance programs are intended to develop professional civilian-based law enforcement institutions. This assistance is designed to (1) enhance professional capabilities to carry out investigative and forensic functions; (2) assist in the development of academic instruction and curricula for law enforcement personnel; (3) improve the administrative and management capabilities of law enforcement agencies, especially their capabilities relating to career development, personnel evaluation, and internal discipline procedures; (4) improve the relationship between the police and the community it serves; and (5) create or strengthen the capability to respond to new crime and criminal justice issues. The program uses firms under contract to provide teams of personnel to provide the services. http://www.usdoj.gov/criminal/icitap (accessed February 2007).

20. USAID uses this program to solicit individuals for personal contracts to USAID to implement programs. These people are solicited on an as-needed basis. Scott Feil et al., "Joint Interagency Evaluation: Manning a Civil Reconstruction and Stabilization Response Capability," Institute for Defense Analyses Document D-3184, (Alexandria, VA: Institute for Defense Analyses, August 2006).

21. USAID uses this program to enter into Indefinite Delivery Indefinite Quantity contracts with preapproved firms to provide both individuals and teams to implement programs. Rosters are maintained by the firms and teams are assembled and deployed based on task orders from USAID. Scott Feil et al., "Joint Interagency Evaluation."

22. Reports digested at http://www.globalsecurity.org/wmd/library/news/iran/2004/1-050104.htm (accessed February 2007).

23. Press release at http://www.usaid.gov/press/releases/whrel.htm (accessed February 2007).

24. Bob Woodward, *State of Denial* (New York: Simon and Schuster, 2006), 92–96, recounts the challenges faced by military intelligence and operations staff to determine the currency of information and the relative priority of more than 700 WMD sites in Iraq from all sources prior to the initiation of the ground campaign in 2003. Similar comprehensive, authoritative, and timely information, coupled with methods to assign priorities to sites, will be required to adequately secure cultural sites and artifacts in any future intervention.

THE WAY FORWARD

For Cultural Ministries, Departments, and Agencies

AS STATES PREPARE FOR WAR AND ITS AFTERMATH, MILITARY AND OTHER GOVERNMENT postwar planners are likely to be preoccupied with humanitarian concerns. Worries about thousands of refugees; victims of biological, chemical, and conventional weapons; and mass starvation are almost certain to crowd out concerns about cultural heritage. In such a policy environment, it falls to government bodies engaged in cultural administration to make sure that plans are in place in advance to safeguard museums and archaeological sites. In a country threatened with the possibility of a disastrous loss of its patrimony, what should ministers of culture, directors of antiquities boards, and museum officials do to prevent antiquities, artifacts, archives, and art from damage— direct or collateral—during armed conflict? And in countries where invasion planning is under way, how can cultural administrators make sure their concerns are heard by postwar planners?

CHAPTER 20

Governmental Agencies and the Protection of Cultural Property in Times of War

NANCY C. WILKIE

ALTHOUGH NOTHING INDICATES THAT POLICYMAKERS MADE A CONSCIOUS DECISION to allow the looting of Iraqi antiquities, the lack of communication between government agencies created gaps in oversight that opened the door to chaos at both the Iraq Museum and archaeological sites throughout Iraq. In the run-up to the war, the division of labor between various agencies in the United States was fairly opaque, and no single agency assumed responsibility for the direction of efforts to secure Iraq's cultural heritage. Had the hierarchical structure of these agencies been better understood, more could have been done to coordinate their activities. As Francis Deblauwe, most recently director of the Iraq War and Archaeology Project, University of Vienna, has commented, "considering the public relations debacle that ensued from the looting of the museum, I would think that if they could do it over, they definitely would protect the museum."[1]

Thus, the challenge that still lies before us is to determine what steps can be taken to address the ongoing problem of looting in Iraq and to ensure that similar disasters do not occur in the course of future military conflicts. This chapter will situate the issue of cultural heritage protection within the web of government agencies charged with cultural affairs and suggest recommendations for future coordination of their activities.

THE U.S. DEPARTMENT OF STATE

Oversight of culture in the United States is decentralized and, as a consequence, highly uncoordinated. Although the National Endowment for the Arts and other agencies work primarily with arts and culture, the only cabinet-level department whose charge includes cultural affairs is the Department of State, where oversight for cultural affairs is dispersed among different bureaus.

Bureau of Educational and Cultural Affairs

Within the Department of State, the office most heavily engaged with the issue of cultural heritage protection in Iraq is the Bureau of Educational and Cultural Affairs (ECA), structurally located below the under secretary of public diplomacy. The ECA has the mission of fostering "mutual understanding between the people of the United States and the people of other countries around the world," and has several programs that deal specifically with protecting cultural heritage as a tool for international diplomacy. The Cultural Heritage Center of the ECA assists with administration of these programs, two of which are outlined below.

CULTURAL PROPERTY ADVISORY COMMITTEE. The Cultural Heritage Center is charged, among other things, with the implementation of the 1970 UNESCO Convention on the Means of Prohibiting and Preventing the Illicit Import, Export and Transfer of Ownership of Cultural Property. In this role it provides technical and administrative support to the Cultural Property Advisory Committee (CPAC), which reviews requests from foreign countries for import restrictions on specific categories of cultural property under the terms of the 1983 Cultural Property Implementation Act (CPIA). In the lead-up to the Iraq war, CPAC had no role to play since the Iraq government had not made a request for import restrictions on its antiquities.

After the looting of the Iraq Museum, however, some believed that CPAC should have started taking action to curb the devastation being done to museums and archaeological sites in Iraq. They pointed to the resignations of the chair, Martin Sullivan, as well as of two other members of the committee, which were announced shortly after the looting of the museum, as a strong statement of protest with the potential to change the course of events in Iraq. Sullivan gave as the reason for his resignation a desire to speak freely about the situation in Iraq, which he could not do as a member of CPAC, since in that capacity he was considered a special government employee. Citing the lack of planning for the protection of the cultural heritage of Iraq in what was essentially a preemptive war, Sullivan also expressed displeasure at then Secretary of Defense Donald H. Rumsfeld's insensitive characterization of the chaos in Iraq as "untidiness."[2]

Yet as Sullivan himself acknowledged, the resignations were merely symbolic gestures that carried little weight. His term, as well as the terms of all the current members of the committee, were about to end following President Bush's announcement a few months earlier that he intended to appoint nine new members to the committee, replacing all of the current members whose terms had long expired. Immediately following the invasion, CPAC also could not act since there was not an Iraqi government in place that could make a request to the U.S. government for import restrictions on its antiquities. Furthermore, even though the 1990 UN sanctions on imports from Iraq had been lifted, sanctions on the importation of cultural materials illegally removed from Iraq remained in place.[3] In order to insure that these import restrictions continued, on December 3, 2004, President Bush signed into law the Emergency Protection for Iraqi Cultural Antiquities Act of 2004. This law gives the president the authority under the CPIA to impose import restrictions on Iraq's cultural property without the need for a request from Iraq to the U.S. government. It remains in effect until September 30, 2009.

AMBASSADOR'S FUND FOR CULTURAL PRESERVATION. Another way in which the ECA works to protect cultural heritage is through the Ambassador's Fund for Cultural Preservation (AFCP), the only U.S. program that funds heritage preservation projects in less-developed countries. Administered by the Cultural Heritage Center, the AFCP permits U.S. ambassadors in these countries to apply for funds to support projects such as restoration of historic buildings, conservation of museum collections, improved storage for archives, and archaeological site preservation—the very projects that the United States should undertake both prior to and immediately following military operations. However, the budget for the AFCP is quite small. Since being established in 2001 with a budget of $1 million, a total of $9.5 million has been awarded, all in small grants typically ranging from $15,000 to $30,000. The annual budget for the program has steadily increased, however, to $3 million in 2006. Although the AFCP would, in principle, be an ideal source of support for cultural heritage in Iraq, prior to 2004 there was not a U.S. ambassador in Iraq to make a request for funds. Since then, no funds have been awarded, presumably because the U.S. ambassador has more pressing concerns than the preservation of Iraq's cultural heritage.

Future of Iraq Project
In addition to the Bureau of Educational and Cultural Affairs, other State Department agencies have had a stake in the issue of Iraq's cultural heritage. When planning for the transition from Saddam's regime, the State Department launched the Future of Iraq Project in collaboration with its Bureau of Near Eastern Affairs, Bureau of International Information Programs, the Middle East Institute in Washington, DC, and others. One of the project's seventeen working groups, called Preserving Iraq's Cultural Heritage,[4] was not part of the original project but a late addition. It met only once, which, as it developed, was inconsequential since the project as a whole was largely ignored

once the Department of Defense began to develop more concrete plans for the invasion of Iraq.

Plans developed by the Future of Iraq Project had little or no impact on the course of events following the invasion of Iraq, since as Charles Patterson, a member of the project, observed, "the primary problem was lack of . . . sharing of knowledge and information across the government."[5] A senior defense official also noted that "State has good ideas and a feel for the political landscape, but they're bad at implementing anything. Defense, on the other hand, is excellent at logistical stuff, but has blinders on when it comes to policy."[6] Therefore, the first and most important recommendation for those planning military action of this nature in the future should be that all parts of the government must find a way to share information and develop a unified plan of action. The responsibility to see that this is accomplished belongs to officials at the highest level of government (i.e., the president and the members of his cabinet).

CROSS-AGENCY EFFORTS TO MITIGATE DAMAGES TO CULTURAL PROPERTY IN IRAQ: MISSED OPPORTUNITIES AND SUCCESSES

In January 2003, President Bush directed the Department of Defense to create a postwar planning office (subsequently named the Office of Reconstruction and Humanitarian Assistance [ORHA]), and charged it with establishing links to those UN agencies and NGOs that would have a role in the postwar reconstruction of Iraq. ORHA also took over activities that had been pursued by the State Department's Future of Iraq committees. Aside from a list of sites that were to be secured as soon as possible after the invasion, which senior commanders received from the ORHA,[7] there is little evidence that plans for the protection of cultural property had been formulated prior to the invasion of Iraq. Following the looting of the Iraq Museum, however, a number of initiatives were begun by U.S. governmental agencies that were to be carried out both in the United States and abroad. Unfortunately, all of these efforts have focused on mitigation of damages that arose from lack of planning prior to the war and not on developing plans for ways to avoid similar disasters in the future.

Interagency Working Group

On July 14, 2003, the State Department announced that it would coordinate the activities of an interagency working group organized to assist in the rebuilding of the cultural heritage infrastructure in Iraq. Funding for the effort, including $2 million set aside by the State Department, was to come from governmental sources, although private donations also would be accepted as a way to circumvent the economic sanctions that continued in effect. In addition to the Department of State, other agencies included in this initiative were the National Endowment for the Humanities (NEH), U.S. Agency for International Development (USAID), the National Science Foundation (NSF), the Library of Congress, the Institute of Museum and Library Services (IMLS), and the National Endowment for the Arts (NEA).

The following is a description of some of the activities that the various governmental agencies that participated in the meetings of the Interagency Working Group agreed to fund.

NATIONAL ENDOWMENT FOR THE HUMANITIES. In July 2003, NEH announced a special initiative entitled Recovering Iraq's Past. It aimed to preserve and document Iraq's cultural heritage in its museums, archives, and libraries by funding grants to U.S. nonprofit organizations as well as to state and local agencies. The total sum of money awarded in the first year of the initiative was $559,000, much of which went toward the creation of digital inventories and catalogs of archaeological materials and archaeological and historic sites. One of these projects was the Getty Conservation Institute (GCI)-World Monuments Fund (WMF) Iraq Cultural Heritage Conservation Initiative—a joint project with the Iraq Ministry of Culture and the Iraq State Board of Antiquities and Heritage (SBAH) in which members of the National Park Service (NPS) also participated, providing instruction in methods for assessing the condition of archaeological and other heritage sites. The Recovering Iraq's Past initiative concluded in October 2005 after awarding nearly $1.5 million in grants. Not all of the funded projects could be completed, however, because of the rapidly deteriorating security situation in Iraq. Moreover, since the grants were of two years' duration, other projects are still in progress. These include the creation of digital databases of excavated materials from Iraq, the preparation of reports on previously unpublished archaeological excavations and surveys conducted in Iraq, and training for archaeologists, conservators, librarians, and archivists.

UNITED STATES AGENCY FOR INTERNATIONAL DEVELOPMENT. Although it is an independent agency, USAID receives general direction and overall foreign policy guidance from the Secretary of State. One of its goals is to build human capacity through education and training. As part of the interagency response, USAID agreed to undertake an assessment of the needs of museums and libraries in Iraq, to modernize institutions of higher education, and to explore the feasibility of cultural tourism in Iraq. A USAID grant to a consortium of U.S. universities led by State University of New York at Stony Brook, in partnership with several universities in Baghdad and Mosul, was dedicated to the modernization of archaeological research in Iraq. Because USAID has access to much larger sums of money than any of the other agencies involved in the interagency response,[8] it has the potential to make a greater impact in the postwar reconstruction and training efforts in Iraq than other agencies of the U.S. government. USAID awards stipulate, however, that funds must be spent in the United States, although goods and services purchased in the United States can then be sent overseas.

NATIONAL SCIENCE FOUNDATION. Although the NSF stated that it was prepared to provide awards for the recovery, preservation, and conservation of scientifically relevant archaeological and cultural heritage artifacts from Iraq, there is no evidence that the agency actually followed through on its commitment.

LIBRARY OF CONGRESS. A team of experts from the Library of Congress visited Baghdad in the fall of 2003 to assess the damage done to the National Library and Archives and to develop a plan for its reconstruction. Although the experts involved were from the Library of Congress, the funding for the effort was provided by the ECA.

MUSEUM ASSESSMENT PROJECT. Early in 2004, the ECA sent a team of experts to Iraq to determine what was needed in order to rehabilitate and reconstruct the Iraq Museum. One result of this project was a $700,000 grant from the State Department for repair of buildings and other infrastructure updates.

COUNCIL OF AMERICAN OVERSEAS RESEARCH CENTERS AND THE SMITHSONIAN INSTITUTION. The Council of American Overseas Research Centers (CAORC), in partnership with the Smithsonian Institution's National Museum of Natural History, received a grant from the ECA to fund a five-week training course for twenty-three Iraqi museum specialists during February and March 2004 at various locations in the United States.

PACKARD HUMANITIES INSTITUTE (PHI). In July 2003, the Department of State announced that PHI had donated up to $1 million to assist with cultural heritage preservation in Iraq. The funds were used in 2003 to purchase computers, photographic equipment, and related supplies for the Iraq Museum in Baghdad, and in 2004 to purchase twenty pickup trucks and radio communication equipment to be used as part of the Archaeological Site Protection Plan. These funds were channeled through the Department of State since sanctions that were still in place prohibited direct aid to Iraq.

CURRENT INITIATIVES BY GOVERNMENTAL AGENCIES FOR PROTECTION OF CULTURAL PROPERTY IN IRAQ

After the turnover of the government to the Iraqis in 2004, and the subsequent deterioration of the security situation throughout the country, there has been little direct effort by U.S. governmental agencies to protect Iraq's cultural heritage. Although the Cultural Heritage Center of the ECA has an ongoing project involving Iraq, its efforts are centered in Washington, DC, due to the deteriorating security situation in much of the country.

NEXT STEPS: FUTURE BUREAUCRATIC MEASURES

The Department of State should undertake increased responsibility for protection of cultural heritage worldwide. Unlike many other nations, the United States does not have a Ministry of Culture. Oversight of our own cultural heritage is vested in numerous governmental agencies on the national, state, and local levels, while cultural relations with other countries are overseen by the State Department. Some have advocated for the creation of a cabinet-level position to deal with culture so that cultural affairs would be afforded the same importance as, for example, environmental matters. Experience has shown that policy initiatives formulated and approved at the uppermost levels of government are the ones most likely to result in concrete action. Lower-level agencies, on the other hand, are better suited for implementing new and continuing policies. Since one of the major problems often alluded to in connection with the planning for the invasion of Iraq was lack of communication among various parts of the government at all but the highest levels, the creation of a Department of Culture could alleviate the problem by assigning greater importance to culture than the government currently affords it.

At the moment, however, there does not seem to be sufficient political impetus for such a radical rethinking of the role of government in the protection of culture. In fact, the low level of importance currently attached to cultural affairs is indicated by the physical location of the ECA, which is housed in the State Department Annex, far removed from the main State Department headquarters. Moreover, the oversight of cultural affairs that currently resides in the State Department is quite limited, focused mainly on educational and other exchange programs, the Ambassador's Fund for Cultural Preservation, and implementation of the 1970 UNESCO Convention.

Congress must adopt as a foreign policy priority the expansion of the government's role in the protection of the world's cultural heritage. It could do this by redefining the mission of the ECA, broadening the range of cultural heritage matters under its purview, and dedicating adequate permanent funding toward the effort. Today the main role of the ECA, as defined in its mission statement, is to promote American culture abroad, an outcome of the restructuring of the foreign affairs agencies in 1999, when the U.S. Information Agency (USIA) was merged into the Department of State. It would be entirely fitting and appropriate for Congress to expand the role of the ECA to the protection of all aspects of cultural heritage, both in the United States and abroad.

Whether or not this occurs, representatives of the Department of State should routinely participate in policy discussions that might have an effect on the world's cultural heritage, regardless of which political party is in power or who holds the office of secretary of state. As the lessons of Iraq have shown, the simple fact that the ECA resides within the Department of State has not guaranteed that its voice will be heard by those in other areas of the government, most importantly in the Department of Defense. Because all branches of the government need to participate in the planning stages of military operations, it is necessary that a mechanism be found for this to happen. We need a single governmental body whose job it is to coordinate actions that might have an impact on cultural heritage whether in peacetime or war.

To protect tangible cultural heritage, the United States needs to better understand the intangible cultural values of the nation to be occupied. One of the factors that contributed significantly to our failure to protect cultural property following the 2003 invasion of Iraq was our lack of awareness of cultural differences between the United States and Iraq, a direct result of the sanctions that were imposed at the time of the 1991 Persian Gulf War. [9] The cessation of cultural exchanges between the United States and Iraq, which might have helped to bridge some of these gaps, resulted in our lack of access to individuals with an understanding of contemporary Iraqi culture. As a result, in planning for the 2003 invasion, we were dealing with Iraqis who had an outdated understanding of their cultural values. Iraqis in the United States were, for the most part, members of the educated middle class who were unaware of the changes that had taken place in Iraqi society since they left the country. Their absence resulted in a serious shortage of bureaucrats who could have helped stabilize the situation in the immediate aftermath of the invasion. Moreover, because we had little knowledge of the expertise of those professionals who did remain in the country, we were unable to engage them sufficiently in our belated efforts to protect Iraq's cultural heritage.

Our failure to recognize that Iraqi people tend to identify more closely with their tribal origins than with the nation-state also has contributed to the looting of archaeological sites. Under Saddam's regime, residents of rural tribal areas were displaced, becoming urban dwellers whose tribal affiliations were still paramount. As a result, they have little interest in or attachment to the ancient past of the area where they currently live.[10] In addition, under Saddam's regime these displaced people would have taken their cues from the educated middle class, but their numbers, and consequently their influence, had greatly diminished since the Persian Gulf War of 1991.

The looting of museums and archaeological sites was exacerbated by the fact that, based on their past experience, most Iraqis expected the imposition of a strong government that would strictly enforce stringent rules immediately after the overthrow of Saddam's government. Our failure to understand this and to act accordingly opened the door for the looting of museums and archaeological sites. As one member of the Future of Iraq Project noted, we "predicted widespread looting. You didn't have to have a degree from a Boston university to figure that one out. . . . It was entirely predictable that in the absence of any authority in Baghdad that you'd have chaos and lawlessness."[11]

As the United States continues its military efforts in Iraq, and U.S. companies undertake reconstruction projects, all parties involved would benefit greatly from more intimate knowledge of one another's culture, both ancient and modern. Under the leadership of C. Brian Rose, the president of the Archaeological Institute of America, the organization has been conducting lectures to troops being deployed to Iraq that focus on the ancient culture of the region and the need for its protection.[12] In many cases, this has been the first opportunity for members of the military to familiarize themselves with the history of the region where they were soon to spend a year or more of their lives.

Similar efforts should be made with private contractors, especially since they are just as likely to encounter archaeological and historical materials in the course of their work. Moreover, USAID's reconstruction contracts contain requirements for the preservation of historical, archaeological, and cultural resources.[13] Immediately following the invasion of Iraq, the impact of construction projects was monitored by Dr. John M. Russell, professor of art history and archaeology at the Massachusetts College of Art. Because of the increasingly dangerous situation in Iraq, however, this position is no longer filled, so the need for contractors to be aware of the potential damage to cultural property is even more acute.

Reevaluate the effect of sanctions on cultural property protection. As noted above, UN sanctions brought an end to cultural exchanges between the United States and Iraq and caused many Iraqis to become embittered toward the United States as the country's economic situation deteriorated. Sanctions also made it difficult or even impossible for archaeologists and museum personnel to acquire the materials needed to create the kind of detailed inventories of their cultural property, both movable and immovable, that would have been useful for interdicting the trade in looted objects in the aftermath of the invasion. International standards for such inventories have been set by Object ID, a widely accepted method for describing and cataloging objects that enables law enforcement officials to recognize and track stolen cultural property more easily.[14] Yet as a result of the sanctions, museum personnel in Iraq lacked the necessary computer equipment to undertake such an inventory, and they were not able to seek expertise from those familiar with the system. Therefore, many of the items looted from the Iraq Museum that have found and will find their way onto the international art market cannot be readily identified in such a way that they can be returned without protracted legal proceedings.

Many of the objects looted before the 2003 invasion of Iraq came from remote archaeological sites that the Antiquities Department could no longer patrol by air after no-fly zones were imposed following the 1991 war. During the 2003 invasion, coalition forces generally were able to avoid bombing archaeological sites that had been identified for protection by archaeologists in the United States and abroad, but shortly thereafter many sites became attractive targets for looters. Concern for protection of cultural property among the citizens of Iraq had waned after the Gulf War because regional museums had not reopened and educational programs of the Iraqi government were largely disbanded. Whereas in the past, local people had taken pride in their cultural heritage, delivering objects that they chanced upon to local museums, they now have turned instead to looting.

It is time for the international community to reevaluate the costs and benefits of imposing economic sanctions on countries such as Iraq. Sanctions impoverished and embittered the very people whom we hoped would become our allies once we had overthrown Saddam's regime, and they caused many of those who could have helped us the most in the days immediately following the invasion of Iraq to flee the country soon after the sanctions were imposed. Sanctions also meant that we no longer had contact with or knowledge of those who staffed the various governmental departments with whom we needed to work to protect the cultural heritage of the country. In fact, in many cases we did not even know the locations of their offices.

*   *   *

Solutions to problems such as those the United States has encountered in Iraq do not come about through money alone. Only an intimate knowledge of the peoples and cultures of the world will allow us to formulate policies that can achieve the results that we desire—protection and preservation of the world's cultural heritage. Because it is culture, both tangible and intangible, that defines both groups of people and nation-states, it is in our best interest to take all possible means to preserve and understand culture in all its facets. Even in desperate times, culture is a unifying force that gives people a reason to live and hope for a better future.

NOTES

Acknowledgments. I would like to thank Lawrence Rothfield for the opportunity to contribute to this volume, even though I was not a participant in the conference from which it originated. In doing the research for this article, I have benefited greatly from discussions with a number of individuals who have asked to remain anonymous. Although I owe them a great debt, any errors or omissions are entirely mine.

1. "Iraq: Looting of Cultural Treasures" (transcript of online discussion with Francis Deblauwe, April 21, 2003), http://www.washingtonpost.com/wp-srv/liveonline/03/special/iraq/sp_iraq-deblauwe042103.htm.

2. "Martin Sullivan's Letter of Resignation as Chairman of the President's Advisory Committee on Cultural Property," April 14, 2002, in *Washington Report on Middle East Affairs* (June 2002): 15, http://www.wrmea.com/archives/june2003/0306015.html.

3. United Nations Security Council, *Resolution 1483*, 4761st meeting (May 22, 2003), http://daccessdds.un.org/doc/UNDOC/GEN/N03/368/53/PDF/N0336853.pdf?OpenElement.

4. Marc Grossman, Under Secretary for Political Affairs, "Post-Saddam Iraq," Testimony before the Senate Foreign Relations Committee, 108th Cong., 1st sess., (February 11, 2003), http://www.state.gov/p/us/rm/17616.htm.

5. Charles Patterson, "Preparing for Post-Saddam Iraq: Plans and Actions,"(presentation to the MIT Security Studies program, Cambridge, MA, October 27, 2004), http://web.mit.edu/ssp/fall04/patterson.htm.

6. Eric Schmitt and Joel Brinkley, "The Struggle for Iraq: Planning," *New York Times*, October 19, 2003.

7. Paul Martin, Ed Vulliamy, and Gaby Hinsliff, "U.S. Army Was Told to Protect Looted Museum," *The Observer*, April 20, 2003.

8. From 2003–2006, USAID provided more than $5 billion of assistance to Iraq.

9. See Farrah Hassen, "New State Department Releases on the 'Future of Iraq' Project," *National Security Archive Briefing Book* 198 (September 1, 2006), www.gwu.edu/~nsarchiv/NSAEBB/NSAEBB198/index.htm. He notes that a recurring theme in the Future of Iraq Project is the "detrimental, long-term effects of the multilateral UN sanctions imposed on Iraq in 1990," and suggests that the authors inadvertently have made "a compelling case against the future implementation of comparable sanctions."

10. See Ann Hitchcock, "Through the Fog of War in Iraq: Lessons Learned in Heritage Preservation," *The George Wright Forum* 20 (2003): 37, who argues that cultural heritage preservation will only be successful when all groups feel they have a stake in the culture.

11. David Rieff, "Blueprint for a Mess," *New York Times*, November 2, 2003.

12. Katie Vasserman, "Prof Teaches Soldiers to Fight Antiquities Theft," *The Daily Pennsylvanian*, February 15, 2006, http://media.www.dailypennsylvanian.com/media/storage/paper882/news/2006/02/15/News/ProfTeaches.Soldiers.To.Fight.Antiquities.Theft-2145460.shtml.

13. U.S. Agency for International Development, Request for Proposals No. M/OP-04-004 Iraq Reconstruction Phase II, issued October 2, 2003, http://www.usaid.gov/iraq/contracts/pdf/iirii_rfp100203.pdf.

14. "Prompt Identification Using the Object ID Standard," *Legal and Practical Measures Against Illicit Trafficking in Cultural Property*, UNESCO Handbook (Paris: UNESCO, International Standards Section, Division of Cultural Heritage, 2006).

CHAPTER 21

What Cultural Ministries and Heritage Sites Should Do to Prepare for Conflict

McGuire Gibson and Donny George Youkhanna

As a result of the events leading up to the looting of the Iraq Museum and State Board of Antiquities and Heritage (SBAH) complex in the initial days of the war with Iraq, there was clearly a need for more comprehensive plans to secure Iraq's museums and sites. During his tenure as director general of the Iraq Museum and later as president of the SBAH, Dr. Donny George Youkhanna began developing a plan for the defense of the Iraq Museum.

Thanks to actions taken before the war with Iraq in 2003, almost all of the items on public display were preserved, and artifacts left in the vault of Iraq's Central Bank survived, although some suffered water damage. Unfortunately, some important items that had been left, for various reasons, in display areas or workrooms were stolen or damaged. Furthermore, major losses occurred due to some degree of insider knowledge of the location and contents of underground storerooms. However, the use of a secret storage area and the transfer of records and manuscripts to a nuclear shelter away from the museum led to the preservation of thousands of other artifacts.

The concept of the museum defending itself arose not just because of what happened to the museum and the administrative offices of SBAH in the initial days of the Iraq war, but because in its aftermath, the situation remained insecure. The museum is situated in what is, at the time of this writing, one of Baghdad's most unstable areas, being only two blocks west of Haifa Street. Even if not subjected to direct attack, the museum's collections are still vulnerable to vibrations from gunfire and the rumbling of tanks. A major bus terminal less than two hundred meters from the museum has been the target of numerous car bombs. Museum guards, on the job since May 2003, have been attacked and wounded several times by men in cars who drive past the front of the museum and fire bursts of automatic weapons. On one occasion, a Katyusha rocket struck the museum garden.

Under these conditions, special steps have been taken to protect the museum in the event that no guards are present and that the newly installed electronic devices that control museum entrances are not functioning. Although the SBAH/museum complex, as part of the reconstruction of the antiquities complex, has been furnished with emergency generators, a very good probability exists that under certain circumstances there will be no electrical service to the museum and no fuel for the generators. To guard against losses during periods of chaos, the museum has constructed additional secure storage. It has welded shut all metal doors, and it has built more walls across doorways leading to the museum's collections. Even the administrative areas of the museum were emptied and all museum staff members distributed to other departments of the SBAH. This makes it difficult for museum staff to carry out routine tasks, much less to continue with the inventory of storerooms to gain a more definitive number of looted objects. Yet, for now, security takes precedence over all other matters.

Thanks to basic museum records having been stored in a shelter off-site before the war, museum staff were able to retrieve them and begin inventorying storerooms soon after the arrival of U.S. troops on April 17. Had there been a sizable computerized database, the inventory would have been much more efficiently carried out, but the museum had just begun creating that database in the year before the war.

As early as the 1980s, the museum was using computers for its work. So when five thousand objects were looted from regional museums, it was prepared to assemble a database to send to Interpol and other agencies. However, the museum had difficulties keeping its computers from crashing due to multiple viruses.

It was obvious from earlier efforts that photographs or detailed drawings of objects are essential to tracking down stolen items. Without a photograph, object identification is almost impossible. Yet even when the museum had negatives of objects on file, the UN sanctions regime put in place after the 1991 Persian Gulf War blocked the museum from obtaining photographic supplies to make the positives. In a few cases, records kept by foreign excavators were used to supply photographs or drawings of stolen artifacts, but the process of asking excavators for photos, receiving them, and incorporating them into a listing meant the passage of several weeks, a time span that would allow any thief to cover his tracks and leave his trail cold. Staff members charged with creating the computerized database recognized the importance of a photographic record in the years leading up to the war with Iraq that began in 2003; however, the museum's diminished staff and the fact that many of the objects were in storage for safekeeping meant that scanning for the database was limited.

As part of the rehabilitation of the museum and the State Board offices in the aftermath of looting in 2003, a computer network was installed, enabling staff to operate at a higher level of efficiency. Arrangements were made between the SBAH and UNESCO for the creation of a comprehensive digital data program for the museum's collections. UNESCO arranged for a contract with a specialized Canadian company, funded by grants from the international community. SBAH senior administrators and museum staff discussed the program several times with the company, so as to adapt it to the needs of the Iraq Museum. Between 2004 and 2006, seventy operating staff and information technology specialists from the museum were sent to Jordan for database management training. Yet despite the equipment's arrival at the museum in Baghdad, work could not begin due to the deteriorating security situation in Iraq, which not only forced the sealing of the museum, but also caused a steep drop in the number of museum staff able to travel to get to work.

NEXT STEPS

General lessons can be learned from the experiences of the Iraq Museum in wartime, whether reviewing the conflicts of 1991 and 2003 or looking back to the Iran-Iraq War of the 1980s. It is essential that *all* museum administrators everywhere think of worst-case scenarios. Any museum could be the victim of looting in times of social unrest, especially given the current elevated prices for antiquities and works of art. Museums should have contingency plans to remove artifacts to safekeeping—perhaps even outside their countries, if practical—but at least to storerooms that are better constructed than is currently the standard in the Near East and elsewhere. Such transfers would entail a level of trust between cooperating nations and antiquities services. In light of the contention over unprovenanced Western museum holdings, this trust might be difficult to establish. However, UNESCO still has credibility in Near Eastern countries, and it might act as an enabling body for such agreements.

In any movement of artifacts from display, labels will be lost or confused. As such, personnel should develop a system that keeps information with the object. Some museums in the United States and Europe are beginning to use a barcode system for artifacts, but it is not clear yet how well that system will work.

No major museum we know of has a completely up-to-date, easily accessed record of its entire holdings. This is especially true of museums that act as repositories of all artifacts from excavations, such as national and provincial museums. Ideally, all excavation records, which are part of some museums' holdings, should be scanned and stored off-site as a backup.

Most museums are understaffed, especially in the records departments, and digitization of holdings is usually just being started. However, in the case of those that adopted computers early, their programs are now antiquated and in need of updating. Paper records, like the excellent ledgers of the Iraq Museum, serve very well if they are kept updated, but computer discs are much easier to transport and can be copied for transfer to safe and multiple locations. At a minimum, paper records should be photocopied or scanned with these duplicates deposited outside the country. Furthermore, there should be one or more internationally recognized depositories for duplicates of museum catalogs, photos, general records, and databases.

Museums need to photograph and otherwise document every item in their collections; otherwise, no law enforcement agency can do much to recover them. UNESCO should inaugurate a program for the digital documentation of collections so as to help museums in particularly vulnerable areas, such as the Middle East, and especially in countries that are currently under threat, such as Syria and Iran.

Funding should be provided for the hiring and training of local staff, the supply of adequate and appropriate equipment, and the furnishing of expertise. Such help should be available to any museum, either through international effort or national programs. In the United States there exists a governmental agency, the Institute of Museum and Library Services (IMLS), which gives grants for museum improvement. However, the grants are usually sufficient to begin programs but not sustain them.

In areas of special vulnerability, such as in the Middle East, database management programs need to be approached as emergency situations, with resources directed for the rapid creation of museum catalogs.

Beyond museums, there are standing monuments and archaeological sites that are part of every country's landscape, and UNESCO should play a role in documenting them. Only strongly committed governments can guard sites effectively, and Iraq, until 1991, had one of the best records for doing so. Even in the best situations, however, looting can still occur, as is clear from the many cultural heritage thefts in Italy, a country that aggressively acts to prevent and investigate them. With standing monuments there is a need for a comprehensive, well-documented database, complete with scale drawings, photographs, and other records.

The affixing of Blue Shield markings is essential, but all armies should be trained to recognize and respect them. However, even those markings will not guarantee the safety of cultural heritage. Unfortunately, the proviso in the Geneva Convention that excuses the destruction of cultural sites if they are used by fighting forces can be used as a loophole or an excuse to cover up such damage, even when looting takes place days or weeks after the cessation of battle, as happened in Baghdad.

For sites, especially the hundreds of thousands of mounds in the Near East, which can easily be mistaken as just hills, it is essential to know their precise location. Now, with the advent of GIS (geographic information systems), it is possible to provide that precision. In the past three years, the State Board of Antiquities and Heritage has had the cooperation of international bodies to train its staff in GIS techniques, including satellite imaging. The SBAH, working with the World Monuments Fund and the Getty Institute, is establishing a database for Iraq's approximately ten thousand locations officially recognized as archaeological sites. But this program cannot safeguard these and the thousands of other sites in Iraq, which are still being looted on an unprecedented scale. However, it does help to monitor the pace of destruction through the generation of new images. Imaging will also allow the documentation of the spread of looting over time. Such records will be essential when the State Board of Antiquities and Heritage undertakes an assessment of the damage done to Iraq's cultural heritage.

Involving locals in the protection of antiquities sites and monuments within their vicinities should result in their safeguarding in time of warfare, but even sites that have had the benefit of a long-term commitment of foreign or Iraqi expeditions show an inconsistent record. All long-term expeditions have guards on the sites, and in some cases these men held the sites against looters. Thus, the site of Uruk is still intact. The provision of a special bonus to the guards of the Japanese expedition at Kish seems to have helped protect that site, but the presence of a U.S. military unit on top of the ziggurat at Uhaimir probably had a greater effect. At Nippur, men arrived and cowed the two guards and dug for more than a month before police from the nearby town put an end to it. Now, new antiquities guards supplementing the expedition guards seem to be holding that site. Agreements with local tribal leaders may have some effect, but the cases of Umma, Umm-al-Aqarib, and other sites where the SBAH had left guards in place calls them into question. The day the war began, the agreements ceased to function and looters descended on those sites and drove off the guards. The local antiquities director and Italian forces in the province made repeated attempts to stop the looting of these and other sites, with some effect.

In the months before the Iraq war, a few academics in the United States and Europe furnished lists of sites to the U.S. and British military, and these sites were put on the no-strike list, along with more than one hundred standing monuments. As far as we can tell, none of these sites was hit deliberately. The military also had compiled a list of more than eighty buildings to secure in

Baghdad, of which the museum was ranked number two, but only one or two of the structures (not including the museum) were actually secured, and the listing did not prevent their looting by Iraqis while U.S. troops stood by.

The lesson to be learned here is that occupying forces should have real plans to protect cultural property, not only from their own troops but also from local looters. It would surely become a political issue if a country's antiquities officials were to make locations known to potential invaders, but it may be essential in the future for countries to list them in an international registry and take measures to mark their heritage sites not only to prevent bombing, but to make clear that they must be secured in the aftermath of fighting.

Personnel at museums and cultural ministries should also seek and expect help from their colleagues abroad. In the aftermath of the 1991 Persian Gulf War, and before, during, and after the invasion of Iraq in 2003, academics abroad were able to assist their Iraqi colleagues in a number of direct and indirect ways. From their own records, foreign archaeologists prepared lists and photos of objects that were taken, and assisted Interpol, the FBI, and other official bodies in identifying objects and preparing type-sheets for use at borders. Intimate knowledge of the country and the museum allowed foreign scholars to comment on TV coverage. And, probably most importantly, foreign scholars informed the general public of the significance of the country in terms of cultural heritage. The same would be the case for any other country involved in warfare. International scholars have an obligation to speak up for their fields, not just out of a sense of collegiality, but because they are a major core constituency of the world's cultural heritage.

THE WAY FORWARD

For Cultural Heritage NGOs

THE DEBACLE IN IRAQ MAKES CLEAR THAT IT WOULD BE FOOLHARDY TO ASSUME THAT governmental and international organizations can be relied on to do everything necessary to minimize the looting of cultural heritage in the aftermath of combat. Left to their own devices, they are likely to do very little indeed, and even with the force of international law, they may act ineffectively. Clearly, there is work to be done by nongovernmental actors, both indirect—through pressure on states to do the right thing—and direct—through self-generated initiatives of various kinds. This section describes what nongovernmental organizations devoted to the protection of cultural heritage have been doing to address the problem of postwar looting and offers suggestions for additional steps they should be taking before the next cycle of conflict begins.

CHAPTER 22

Preventing Looting after Armed Combat

The Way Forward for U.S. Nongovernmental Cultural Heritage Organizations

BONNIE BURNHAM AND STEPHEN K. URICE

UNLIKE OTHER INDUSTRIALIZED DEMOCRACIES, THE U.S. GOVERNMENT PROVIDES scant support for domestic[1] cultural affairs: the U.S. maintains no cabinet-level position equivalent to other nations' ministers of culture, funds no governmental department responsible for collecting and disseminating information about the cultural sector,[2] and provides negligible direct support for cultural organizations or activities.[3] Instead, as a matter of long-standing policy, the locus of cultural activity in the United States is the *private* nonprofit sector of the economy,[4] funded primarily with private dollars.[5] Accordingly, efforts within the United States to plan for and prevent the depredations that armed combat inflicts on cultural heritage will require the participation of nongovernmental organizations (NGOs). Supplemented by professionals working independently in the for-profit sector, NGOs possess the expertise, experience, capacity, and insights to act. What they will need, however, is a unified voice, a place at the table, and an established action plan. The first part of this chapter will describe U.S. NGOs that could assist in minimizing damage to cultural heritage in times of armed combat. The second part elaborates on a recommendation to assist NGOs to become more effective in achieving that goal, which emerged from "Protecting Cultural Heritage during Wartime: Learning the Lessons of Iraq," a conference sponsored by the Cultural Policy Center of the University of Chicago at the Rockefeller Brothers Fund's Pocantico Conference Center, August 11–13, 2006.

THE NONGOVERNMENTAL HERITAGE SECTOR AND ARMED COMBAT

The U.S. nongovernmental cultural heritage sector consists of four types of institutions: museums; colleges and universities; cultural service organizations and NGOs such as the American Association of Museums, the World Monuments Fund (WMF), and the Archaeological Institute of America (AIA); and philanthropic organizations such as the Getty Foundation and Getty Conservation Institute. It also includes independent scholars and professionals who practice privately in related fields, such as conservators, freelance curators and art historians, art dealers, archaeologists, preservation architects and engineers, and specialized lawyers. Many individuals, whether working within organizations or independently, have extensive dealings with their international colleagues. U.S. museums host exhibitions organized abroad, borrow from foreign institutions for their own exhibitions, and foster training and professional exchanges and collaborations; universities conduct overseas research programs, host international students, and participate in academic exchanges; service organizations share knowledge among counterpart groups internationally. Some foundations and other nonprofits support work directly benefiting foreign institutions and nationals in fields such as historic preservation and museum conservation. Supplementing this loose professional network are international consortia such as the International Council of Museums (ICOM), the International Council on Monuments and Sites (ICOMOS), and the International Institute for Conservation of Historic and Artistic Works (IIC), which have national counterpart organizations in many countries fostering local and global dialogue within their respective fields. This network and these consortia contribute to shared professional and ethical standards, enriching both knowledge and standards of practice internationally.[6]

Notwithstanding this rich array of institutions, professionals, and consortia directed toward common goals, no NGO has a specific writ or mission to engage and coordinate these resources in times of risk or catastrophe. Thus, a fundamental aspect of all cultural heritage institutions' missions—to protect and preserve the world's cultural heritage—remains unfulfilled. In the wake of natural catastrophes abroad and at home, the cultural sector has learned how to organize itself effectively to respond,[7] but in circumstances of war and civil conflict, individuals and cultural organizations have no role to play and very little opportunity to make a meaningful contribution.

Out of a sense of responsibility, some NGOs and professionals have begun to undertake their own activities in response to the risk posed to cultural heritage when armed combat is threatened or under way. These activities are by nature ad hoc, uncoordinated, and reactive and are not guided by established protocols: no governmental structure or organization exists to assist the cultural heritage sector through effective preparation for and response to armed combat. For example, the 1954 Hague Convention[8] provides protocols and procedures to be implemented by States Parties prior to and in the event of armed conflict but offers no framework for institutional or private action. (For more information on the 1954 Hague Convention and related Protocols, please see chapters 7 and 8.)

As early as the eighteenth century, legal theorists began to articulate principles to protect cultural property in times of war.[9] It was not until the American Civil War, however, that these concerns achieved expression in a clearly articulated military code of conduct.[10] Since then, such protection has been the sole province of multilateral treaties, military codes, and military tribunals.[11] Private organizations and individuals have played a minimal role or none at all. Indeed, not until World War II were professionals who had been trained in heritage-related fields specifically engaged in cultural property disaster preparation and mitigation through military service.[12] Since World War II, however, there has been little opportunity for cultural professionals to play a meaningful professional role in the military, nor have military authorities considered the protection of cultural property or sites to be a priority in the planning for and in the carrying out of combat operations.

At present, there exists no framework for dialogue or other interaction between the cultural sector and the military, and there have been very few situations in which plans have been made or implemented to protect cultural properties in the path of war.[13] During the Vietnam War, two internationally significant sites were substantially damaged by bombing—the heart of the Forbidden City in Hue, which was struck inadvertently by U.S. bombers targeting a nearby citadel during the Tet Offensive, and the Cham culture site of My Son, which was intentionally bombed because it was believed to be a munitions depot.[14] By contrast, the U.S. military successfully avoided bombing cultural sites in Iraq during the 1991 Persian Gulf War. Only a few important standing monuments—the Ctesiphon Arch and the site of Ur—received secondary damage, such as cracks and destabilization as a result of vibrations from explosions, during the 1991 conflict.[15] However, the looting of archaeological sites began with this destabilization and accelerated dramatically just prior to the 2003 invasion.[16]

Entities within the cultural sector have accomplished little other than advocating to their governments, and to the broader international community, for the protection of assets that are, in the words of the Hague Convention, "the cultural heritage of all mankind." This advocacy became a more overt international outcry at the time of the Balkan conflict, when the destruction of monuments as symbols of ethnic values became an overt strategy.[17] Since the Balkan conflict, this advocacy may have had an influence in advancing the current dialogue about creating better public policies, complemented with private sector efforts, to minimize cultural property losses in times of armed conflict and to provide financial and technical support for preventative actions prior to military engagement and postwar reconstruction.

THE POSTWAR PERIOD: UNCHECKED CULTURAL LOSSES IN
TIMES OF ARMED COMBAT

When the 1954 Hague Convention was drafted, western Europe and the Soviet Bloc were engaged in the reconstruction of key heritage sites damaged or destroyed during World War II. The Hague Convention sought to eliminate the prospect of this kind of cultural devastation in the future. At the same time, however, the Cold War was escalating. In the United States, the anticipation of a possible nuclear conflict and the increasing isolation between Communist and Western spheres of influence led U.S. decision-makers to conclude that the Hague Convention was unworkable or beside the point in the face of the global threat of mass destruction.[18] While military and intelligence activities focused on that urgent threat, conventional local conflicts continued to erupt, sometimes taking heavy tolls on cultural heritage.

At the time of the Biafra War (1967–1970),[19] cultural experts stood by aghast at their inability to stop highly important cultural objects from flowing across borders during times of chaos, and they were shocked at the lack of public awareness that entire cultures and the physical evidence of their history were being eradicated. The war of independence in Bangladesh in 1971,[20] the civil war that raged in Lebanon from 1975 to the mid-1990s,[21] and the unstable period following the Soviet invasion of Afghanistan in 1979[22] resulted in looting of museums and sites and a massive, disorderly exodus of cultural objects from their countries of origin. Significant parts of the architectural heritage of the cities of Kabul and Herat were destroyed in situ.[23] Looting of the Bamiyan caves, whose mural paintings are considered at least as artistically important as the Bamiyan sculptures, began during this period, and the area never restabilized. Long before the U.S. invasion of Afghanistan in October 2001, the lone voice of Nancy Dupree, founder of the Society for the Preservation of Afghanistan's Cultural Heritage (SPACH), warned that the Bamiyan caves were being systematically looted. But SPACH was able to do little more than report this depredation. These events attracted only marginal attention. They produced no lessons that were communicated within the field and resulted in no new codes or practices to guide military commanders.

With the Balkan War (1991–1992), cultural sites became key targets of aggression. Churches and mosques were destroyed specifically to trigger outrage among opponent factions, entire towns were razed because of their cultural history and significance, and at the height of the conflict, the historic cities of Dubrovnik and Split were shelled by Serbs hoping to break the Croats' spirit.

Bosnian Croats later deployed the same tactics by destroying the Mostar Bridge and leveling its historic center, a famed redoubt of Bosnian Ottoman culture. The blue shield of the Hague Convention, displayed on historic buildings in Croatia, was targeted by Serbian snipers who overtly flaunted the idea of respecting sites of international cultural significance in their pursuit of cultural genocide.[24]

And when the Taliban threatened to destroy the collections of the Afghan National Museum in Kabul (and eventually carried out their threat), last-minute efforts by museums in Europe and the United States to evacuate the museum's collection for safekeeping failed.[25] There was no international diplomatic protocol or private NGO through which these offers could be translated into practical action.

That framework is still lacking today.

THE 2003 IRAQ WAR

Prior to and during the 2003 war in Iraq, the nongovernmental cultural sector became proactive in efforts to protect cultural heritage. In meetings prior to the invasion, the sector provided information to decision-makers within the U.S. Departments of State and Defense regarding cultural sites and monuments at risk in the event of armed combat.[26] Additionally, international institutions that had conducted excavations in Iraq made efforts to secure sites where they had worked.[27] Information was widely diffused concerning suspected looting at renowned sites in Iraq such as Nineveh and Nimrud.[28] But all these attempts to rally professional resources, governmental attention, and public interest proved futile in the chaos that followed. The looting of the Iraq Museum was, in some ways, only a herald of wider destruction: as of this writing, no one can accurately estimate the damage, and since much of the destruction involves the looting of unexcavated antiquities, the losses will never be completely documented.

RECENT EFFORTS

Following the Iraq war, in an effort to repair the failure of the military to safeguard and protect key cultural heritage sites, Western NGOs undertook to redress the damage and to establish alternative, nongovernmental communications with Iraqi counterparts. For example, London's British Museum and New York's Metropolitan Museum of Art provided staff to help the Iraq Museum in Baghdad assess and begin to repair damage to the collections. The Oriental Institute of the University of Chicago set out to secure the Kish region where it had conducted archaeological research. Other academic institutions—such as the State University of New York at Stony Brook—established exchange programs to train Iraqi archaeologists and help rebuild Baghdad

University's capacity in archaeology.[29] These institution-to-institution efforts, which complemented official support offered to Iraq by foreign governments through UNESCO, sought to cut through bureaucratic red tape hindering public-sector reconstruction efforts. With funds contributed by donors representing the concerned citizenry, this private support was also intended to carry a message of goodwill, similar to the message accompanying charitable contributions in the aftermath of natural disaster.

GCI-WMF IRAQ CULTURAL HERITAGE CONSERVATION INITIATIVE: A CASE HISTORY

In 2004 the Getty Conservation Institute (GCI) and the World Monuments Fund (WMF)—two prominent, U.S.-based, international NGOs in the heritage conservation field—joined forces to assist in rebuilding a war-torn nation's capacity to manage monuments and sites. The GCI-WMF Iraq Cultural Heritage Conservation Initiative[30] focuses on three elements:

- the inventorying of sites to assess conditions and priorities so as to anticipate and prevent further damage to the archaeological record during postwar reconstruction
- short-term stabilization of war-damaged monuments
- training to build the capacity of the staff of Iraq's State Board of Antiquities and Heritage (SBAH)—the government agency with responsibility for monuments—so they could manage major monumental cultural heritage ensembles in the future.

During the isolation that occurred over the twenty-four years of Saddam Hussein's regime, Iraq had not trained specialized conservators or participated actively in international heritage conservation protocols such as UNESCO's World Heritage Convention.[31] After the fall of the regime, UNESCO and the Coalition Provisional Authority (CPA) immediately identified a tentative list of eight sites that were priorities for inscription on UNESCO's World Heritage List.[32] Under the terms of the convention, each would need a management plan to be eligible for inscription on the World Heritage List—easily a twenty-year exercise for a country currently lacking management-planning capacity for cultural heritage.[33] These sites are seen by the SBAH as focal points for rebuilding the country and interpreting its history to the international community. Therefore, their inscription is a high priority.

The initiative has developed a national heritage database and training courses in emergency condition assessment, and it is assisting the SBAH in the preparation of a management plan for Babylon, a key site in urgent need of protection, due to substantial modification during the Hussein regime and destructive military occupation since 2003. In addition to core support from

GCI, the initiative is supported by grants to WMF from U.S. governmental agencies (National Endowment for the Humanities and the Department of State) and U.S. private foundations, including the J. M. Kaplan Fund and the Annenberg Foundation. The initiative's training program for Iraqi personnel, conducted in Jordan, received support from UNESCO and the American Center for Oriental Research, expanding the partnership to include an intergovernmental organization and an "offshore" U.S. NGO, respectively.

The initiative has encountered many obstacles and can be considered only a partial success to date. Except for a small emergency project (to rebuild the shelter protecting the site of Nineveh), it has proven impossible for professionals working under the initiative to access cultural heritage sites in Iraq and carry out direct interventions. Additionally, there has been limited dialogue between international consultants and Iraqi trainees to evaluate the impact of the initiative's training programs or the accuracy of the field assessments conducted by those trainees. The database designed for preemptive evaluation of risks to the country's archaeological heritage cannot be deployed within Iraq because of the country's unstable security and infrastructure. Computers contributed by the initiative and records intended to be integrated into the database are sealed within the Iraq Museum, closed due to intensified security issues. A change of SBAH administration in the summer of 2006 produced delays as the international partners resubmitted credentials to new governmental appointees. Efforts to bring Iraqi professionals to the United States for training and consultation have been delayed by U.S. immigration requirements. While GCI and WMF remain committed to assisting professional counterparts in Iraq, it is becoming clear that an evaluation of the initiative's results cannot be achieved until security conditions in Iraq improve. Pending those results, it can still be said that two key lessons have been learned through the initiative: the importance both of working directly with host-country cultural heritage professionals to set priorities for action and of building local capacity for stewardship of cultural heritage.

RECOMMENDED CHANGES

The conference participants gathered at Pocantico concluded that the needs to aid in preserving cultural heritage in the aftermath of conflict are great, and they proposed that there may be opportunities to improve coordination in postconflict situations through the creation of an NGO that could develop the necessary linkages among institutions, individuals, governments, and the military in other conflicts.

The conference recommended the creation of a charitable, nonprofit organization to represent the interests and to assist the efforts of the U.S.'s cultural community in minimizing damage to the world's cultural heritage in times of armed combat or war. This section will describe one model for such an organization. The mission of the proposed new NGO would be to establish itself as the primary voice for the cultural community in assisting the U.S. government and military in matters related to the protection of cultural heritage in times of armed combat.

The organization would function as an umbrella[34] whose members would include NGOs, intergovernmental organizations (IGOs), and individuals with relevant missions or expertise. As will become clear, however, the functions of the new organization would necessarily expand beyond coordinating activities of its member NGOs to include service as the primary intermediary between its members and key individuals and offices within the U.S. government and military.

In addition to its own administration, the organization would have at least four operational activities: research and education, advocacy, coordination, and fund-raising.

Research and Education

To provide the information required by the organization's operational components, the new NGO would actively pursue a research agenda. That agenda would include activities such as the following:

- determining what data are currently available and what new data are necessary
- pursuing research to develop those needed data
- analyzing existing information and data sets for accuracy and dependability
- developing action agendas for known hot spots
- convening experts in working groups, conferences, and other venues

These activities would lead to new publications—technical, legal, informative, and advocacy-based—through which the organization would provide a new, independent voice of reliable information in advance of, during, and following conflicts or wars. These publications would take various forms, including research reports, briefing papers, informative pamphlets, and opinion pieces (op-eds), among others.

To increase the military's awareness of the need for and means of protecting cultural heritage, the organization would also develop curriculum offerings for the various military academies and provide speakers for conferences of military leaders.

Advocacy

The organization's advocacy capacity would enable it to complete the following:

- disseminate findings of its research
- conduct informational campaigns targeting policymakers, policy-influencers, journalists, public intellectuals, and the general public
- serve as an authoritative voice on key issues on which the government and the media would rely for objectivity, accuracy, and dependability

As an advocate for its members, the organization would identify and maintain lines of communication with key decision-makers within the government (especially the military) and the media. These relationships would enable the organization to bring its perspective into play quickly when circumstances warranted action.

Coordination

The organization's key role would be to coordinate the efforts of, and serve as the intermediary for, its members and the government (especially the military) and IGOs. By creating a practical interface between the interests of the cultural community and the U.S. government and military, the coordination efforts would fill a role completely lacking at present—that of providing a place at the table in discussions among key governmental and military decision-makers and facilitating access to areas of conflict for fact-finding and action.

In this capacity, the organization would work proactively to establish open lines of communication with key offices and individuals within the U.S. government and military. At times of reasonably foreseeable or active conflict, the organization would

- match the expertise and experience of its members with the risks presented
- assess IGOs' activities and determine how the organization and its members might best work to assist and expand those activities
- serve as an ongoing liaison between its members and governmental and military offices and personnel

The coordination function would be of equal importance to the organization's members, permitting them to obtain accurate, timely, and pertinent information from dependable contacts within the government and the military and allowing them to remain informed of the activities not only of the umbrella organization itself but also of its member NGOs. In this way, duplication of efforts would be minimized and appropriate efforts could be made available.

Fund-raising

A major hurdle in strategic planning for the organization is developing its own sustainability. Ostensibly, the organization would be supported primarily by fees charged to its members, grants from private foundations, and individual contributions. Given its purpose and organizational structure, support from governmental sources would not only raise potential conflicts of interest but also be unlikely. For the same reasons, corporate philanthropy could not be considered a likely source of funding.

Obviously, these functions interrelate and augment one another. And the audiences for the various activities also overlap. For example, the individuals and offices with which the organization would establish lines of communication through its coordination activities would be among the targets for the organization's advocacy activities and among those to whom its research would be made available.

THE BLUE SHIELD

While the U.S. Committee of the Blue Shield that is currently being formed (described in chapter 15 in this volume) may be able to perform some of the functions mentioned above, its focus on civil-military affairs, its quasi-governmental status and statutory restraints on membership, as well as its emphasis on education rather than research, training, and advocacy, limit its potential, at least at present. We believe that the Blue Shield should be supplemented and assisted by an umbrella group with a broader mandate and more freedom to examine possibilities and agitate for cultural heritage protection.

In the chaos during and following military conflict, significant aspects of a country's history are erased, dispersed, or irreparably damaged. These losses are widely decried by the public and create a sorry image for parties involved in the conflict. Repeatedly, combatants have demonstrated their incapacity to prevent wartime damage or to mitigate postconflict losses even when they express a desire to do so. The nongovernmental cultural sector can offer expertise and funding to complement and enhance governmental programs and policies to protect and preserve cultural heritage. However, this assistance cannot be provided without a mechanism that allows the cultural sector to work more effectively with militaries and governments: they alone can provide the requisite official approval and logistical support the sector requires to provide meaningful assistance. A nongovernmental organization, acting as a liaison among military authorities, governmental officials, diplomatic personnel, and the cultural sector would facilitate efforts to improve cultural heritage protection, conservation, and reconstruction. The creation of such an organization is warranted given recent history and the prospect of new conflicts, all of which have and will inflict a heavy toll on cultural heritage. A framework for such an organization is suggested in this chapter to stimulate discussion and, we hope, to encourage action.

NOTES

Acknowledgments. The authors thank Robin Schard, M.L.S., J.D., assistant library director for public services, University of Miami School of Law, for her assistance in tracking down and verifying citations provided in this chapter. Any errors in those citations, however, remain entirely the authors' responsibility.

1. International public (or "cultural") diplomacy is overseen by an undersecretary for public diplomacy and public affairs. See http://www.state.gov/r (accessed November 25, 2006).
2. However, the National Endowment for the Arts maintains a Research Division, for which limited documentation is available through http://www.nea.gov/research/ResearchNotes.html (accessed January 4, 2007).
3. In 1998, the federal government provided approximately 1.5 percent of the operating support of nonprofit arts and cultural organizations in the U.S. Cultural Policy and the Arts National Data Archive (CPANDA), "From What Sources Do Nonprofit Arts and Cultural Organizations Receive Financial Support?" http://www.cpanda.org/arts-culture-facts/artsorgs/support.html (accessed November 25, 2006). Substantial *indirect* government support is provided through charitable income, gift, and estate tax deductions.
4. Also commonly referred to as the "Third Sector" to distinguish it from the First Sector (governmental) and from the Second Sector (private for-profit).
5. The most recent available data (from the 1997 Census of Service Industries [Economic Census]) counted approximately 27,000 arts and cultural organizations that were active in the U.S. at the end of 1997. CPANDA, "How Many Arts and Cultural Organizations Are There?" http://www.cpanda.org/arts-culture-facts/artsorgs/howmanytotal.html (accessed November 25, 2006).
6. For example, ICOM promulgated its Code of Professional Ethics in 1986, amended it in 2001, and further amended and retitled it as Code of Ethics for Museums in 2004. http://icom.museum/ethics.html (accessed December 10, 2006).
7. There is no coordinating agency comparable to the Red Cross that, in the aftermath of catastrophic events, provides specialized assistance to preserve cultural heritage. However, cultural organizations can generally find a means to engage with civil authorities to obtain logistical support and coordination for their activities, and their contributions are warmly welcomed. Examples include the Committee to Rescue Italian Art, formed after the Florence flood in 1966; UNESCO's Private Committees Programme for the Safeguarding of Venice, established to coordinate the 1966 Venice flood rescue; the emergency response program organized by Heritage Preservation, a Washington, DC, nonprofit organization after the floods in the Midwest in 1993. In the last decade, many cultural institutions have planned for the contingency of natural disasters when they lie in zones of risk (cf. especially Getty Conservation Institute website [http://www.getty.edu/conservation] and Heritage Preservation website [http://www.heritagepreservation.org] and its publication, *Field Guide to Emergency Response* [Washington, DC: Heritage Preservation, 2005]).
8. "Convention for the Protection of Cultural Property in the Event of Armed Conflict," May 14, 1954, *Treaties and International Agreements Registered or Filed or Reported*

with the Secretariat of the United Nations, 249, no. 3511 (1956). "Regulations for the Execution of the Convention for the Protection of Cultural Property in the Event of Armed Conflict," May 14, 1954, *Treaties and International Agreements Registered or Filed or Reported with the Secretariat of the United Nations,* 249, no. 3511 (1956). "[First] Protocol," May 14, 1954, *Treaties and International Agreements Registered or Filed or Reported with the Secretariat of the United Nations* 249, no. 3511 (1956). "Second Protocol to the Hague Convention of 1954 for the Protection of Cultural Property in the Event of Armed Conflict," March 26, 1999, *International Legal Materials* 38, no. 4 (July 1999): 769–782. Texts of these documents are available at http://portal.unesco.org/culture/en/ev.php-URL_ID=8450&URL_DO=DO_TOPIC&URL_SECTION=201.html (accessed December 10, 2006) and http://www.icomos.org/hague/hague.convention.html (accessed December 10, 2006). For an analysis of the convention and an assessment of its current role, see Patrick J. Boylan, *Review of the Convention for the Protection of Cultural Property in the Event of Armed Conflict (The Hague Convention of 1954)* (London: Patrick J. Boylan, 1993).

9. See Emer de Vattel, *The Law of Nations, or, Principles of the Law of Nature Applied to the Conduct and Affairs of Nations and Sovereigns,* ed. Edward D. Ingraham (Clark, NJ: Lawbook Exchange, 2005), 365. For concise treatments of the precursors to the Hague Convention of 1954, see Kevin Chamberlain, "The Protection of Cultural Property—Historical Background" in *War and Cultural Heritage* (Leicester, UK: Institute of Art and Law, 2004), 7; and John Henry Merryman, "Two Ways of Thinking About Cultural Property," *American Journal of International Law* 80, no. 4 (October 1986): 831–853; reprinted in John Henry Merryman, *Thinking About the Elgin Marbles: Critical Essays on Cultural Property, Art and Law* (London: Kluwer Law International, 2000), 66. See also for a helpful summary Lawrence M. Kaye, "Laws in Force at the Dawn of World War II: International Conventions and National Laws" in *The Spoils of War: World War II and Its Aftermath: The Loss, Reappearance, and Recovery of Cultural Property,* ed. Elizabeth Simpson (New York: H.N. Abrams, 1997), 100.

10. *Instructions for the Government of Armies of the United States in the Field,* prepared by Francis Lieber, promulgated as General Orders no. 100 by President [Abraham] Lincoln, April 24, 1863, reprinted in *The Law of War: A Documentary History,* ed. Leon Friedman (New York: Random House, 1972), 158. The "Lieber Code" also appears in *The Spoils of War: World War II and Its Aftermath: The Loss, Reappearance, and Recovery of Cultural Property,* ed. Elizabeth Simpson (New York: H.N. Abrams, 1997), as appendix I at 272.

11. On the Nuremberg trial of Alfred Rosenberg for the Third Reich's appropriation and destruction of art and other cultural property, see John Henry Merryman, Albert E. Elsen, and Stephen K. Urice, *Law, Ethics and the Visual Arts* (London: Kluwer Law International, 2007), 16–22.

12. The most significant contribution involved the efforts of the Monuments, Fine Arts, and Archives program of the Civil Affairs and Military Government sections of the U.S.-led Allied armies from its founding in 1943 until 1946. For a description of the MFA&A's work, see Charles J. Kunzelman, "Some Trials, Tribulations, and Successes of the Monuments, Fine Arts and Archives Teams in the European The-

atre During WWII," *Military Affairs* 52, no. 2 (April 1988): 56–60; "Monuments Men and the Monuments, Fine Arts and Archives (MFAA) Section," *Wikipedia*, http://en.wikipedia.org/wiki/Monuments_Men_and_the_Monuments%2C_Fine _Arts%2C_and_Archives_%28MFAA%29_section (accessed January 4, 2007); Part 4: "Repatriations Following World War II," *The Spoils of War: World War II and Its Aftermath: The Loss, Reappearance, and Recovery of Cultural Property*, ed. Elizabeth Simpson (New York: H.N. Abrams, 1997); Lynn H. Nicholas, *The Rape of Europa: The Fate of Europe's Treasures in the Third Reich and the Second World War* (New York: Knopf, 1994) 234–*et seq.* and *passim*; and Robert M. Edsel, *Rescuing Da Vinci* (Dallas, TX: Laurel Publishing, 2006).

13. The only example of evacuation of cultural property under the banner of the Hague Convention occurred in 1970 prior to the Khmer Rouge takeover in Cambodia, at which time collections were moved from the Angkor Conservation Facility in Siem Reap to the National Museum in Phnom Penh (oral report from UNESCO Staff, Phnom Penh office). This did not involve transportation across national boundaries and this evacuation clearly did not provide any assurance of protection of the artifacts following the overthrow of the government by the Khmer Rouge. For more on the limited impact of the Hague Convention, see James A. R. Nafziger, "UNESCO-centered Management of International Conflict over Cultural Property," *Hastings Law Journal* 27, no. 5 (May 1976): 1051–67.

14. See www.unesco.org/vn and World Monuments Watch, "My Son," in *List of 100 Most Endangered Sites* (New York: World Monuments Watch, 1996).

15. See Richard L. Zettler, "Iraq's Beleaguered Heritage," *Archaeology* 44, no. 3 (May/June 1991): 38–43 and Paul Zimansky and Elizabeth C. Stone, "Mesopotamia in the Aftermath of the Gulf War," *Archaeology* 45, no. 3 (May 1992): 24–25.

16. Selma al-Radi, "The Ravages of War and Reconstruction," in *Looting of the Iraq Museum, Baghdad: Lost Legacy of Ancient Mesopotamia*, ed. Milbry Polk and Angela M.H. Schuster (New York: H.N. Abrams, 2005), 208–9. For a comprehensive assessment of Iraq's archaeological heritage between 1991 and 2003, see Friedrich T. Schipper, "The Protection and Preservation of Iraq's Archaeological Heritage, Spring 1991–2003," *American Journal of Archaeology* 109, no. 2 (April 2005): 251.

17. For an overview of the damage to Mostar and its postconflict conservation and revitalization see *Conservation and Revitalisation of Historic Mostar* (Geneva, Switzerland: Aga Khan Trust for Culture, 2004), http://www.akdn.org/hcsp/mostar.pdf (accessed January 10, 2007).

18. Although the U.S. is a signatory to the Hague Convention, it has never ratified it. Not until the Clinton administration did the president transmit the treaty to the U.S. Senate for advice and consent. Senate Treaty Document, Doc. No. 106-1 (1999).

19. See Arnold Rubin, "Looting of the African Continent of Its Sculptural Heritage, Particularly with Regard to the Nigerian Situation," *African Arts* 4, no. 2 (Winter 1971): 79.

20. Cf. Emanul Haque, "The Museums, Monuments, and Archaeological Sites in Bangladesh: The Situation After the War of Independence," *ICOM News* 25, no. 1 (January 1972).

21. See Selma al-Radi, "In the Aftermath of Civil War. Cultural Heritage in Lebanon" *Conservation* (Getty Conservation Institute Newsletter) XI, no. 1 (Spring 1996): 14–16.

22. "Soviet War in Afghanistan," *Wikipedia*, http://en.wikipedia.org/wiki/Soviet_war_in_Afghanistan (accessed December 15, 2006). Cf. also Ahmed Rashid, "Crime of the Century," *Far Eastern Economic Review* 158, no. 38 (September 21, 1995): 60–62.

23. Dan Cruickshank, "Afghanistan: At the Crossroads of Ancient Civilizations," BBC (September 1, 2002), http://www.bbc.co.uk/history/recent/sept_11/afghan_culture_01.shtml (accessed January 4, 2006).

24. World Monuments Watch, "Vukovar," in *List of 100 Most Endangered Sites* (New York: World Monuments Watch, 1996).

25. Philippe de Montebello, "Museums: Why Should We Care?" *The Opinion Journal from the Wall Street Journal Editorial Page*, June 1, 2005, http://www.opinion journal.com/la/?id=110006760 (accessed January 4, 2007); "Beyond Bamiyan: Will the World Be Ready Next Time?" (Panel discussion at Asia Society, New York, April 3, 2002) http://www.asiasource.org/culturalheritage/beyondbamiyan .cfm (accessed January 4, 2007). Agence France-Presse, "Pre-Islam Idols Being Broken Under Decree by Afghans," *New York Times*, March 2, 2001; Reuters, "New York's Metropolitan Makes Afghan Art Offer," March 1, 2001, circulated electronically by the Afghanistan Research Group as "News from Afghanistan" 01/015, March 2, 2001, cited in Finbarr Barry Flood, "Between Cult and Culture: Bamiyan, Islamic Iconoclasm, and the Museum; Afghanistan," *The Art Bulletin* 84, no. 4 (December 2002): 641–659.

26. See discussion in Lawrence Rothfield "Preserving Iraq's Heritage from Looting: What Went Wrong (within the United States)," *supra* 14–19. See also, unpublished reports to the International Coordinating Committee for Iraq, UNESCO, 2003–2005.

27. Ibid.

28. John M. Russell, "Loss of Wall Reliefs from Sennacherib's Palace at Nineveh, Iraq," *International Foundation for Art Research (IFAR) Reports* 17, no. 5 (May 1996): 6–7; John M. Russell, "More Sculptures from Nineveh on the Market," *IFAR Reports* 17, no. 10 (December 1996): 9–11; John M. Russell, "Looted Sculptures from Nineveh," *Minerva* 8 (1997): 16–26; John M. Russell, *The Final Sack of Nineveh* (New Haven, CT: Yale University Press, 1998). See also World Monuments Watch, "Nimrud" and "Nineveh" in *List of 100 Most Endangered Sites, 2002* (New York: World Monuments Watch, 2001).

29. See U.S. Agency for International Development—Iraq Higher Education and Development for Archaeology and Environmental Health Research (HEAD) Program, http://ws.cc.stonybrook.edu/usaidhead (accessed January 4, 2007).

30. See World Monuments Fund, "Iraq Cultural Heritage," http://wmf.org/iraq.html (accessed December 15, 2006) and the Getty Conservation Institute, "Iraq Cultural Heritage Conservation Initiative," http://www.getty.edu/conservation/field_projects/iraq/index.html (accessed December 15, 2006).

31. On UNESCO's World Heritage Convention of 1972, see http://whc.unesco.org/en/conventiontext (accessed January 4, 2007).

32. The sites are Nimrud, Samarra, the Ancient City of Nineveh, the Fortress of Al-Ukhaidar, the Marshlands of Mesopotamia, the Sacred Complex of Babylon, Ur, and Wasit. "Looting of Iraq's National Treasures," *World Heritage Newsletter* (June/July/August 2003): 5.

33. Iraq became a State Party to the 1972 Convention Concerning the Protection of the World Cultural and Natural Heritage in 1984. http://portal.unesco.org/la/convention.asp?KO=13055&language=E&order=alpha (accessed December 15, 2006). Two Iraqi sites are included on the World Heritage List: Hatra (1985) and Ashur (2003). UNESCO, *World Heritage List,* http://whc.unesco.org/en/list (accessed December 15, 2006).

34. A model mentioned at the Conference is InterAction, which describes itself as follows: "InterAction is the largest alliance of U.S.-based international development and humanitarian nongovernmental organizations. With more than 160 members operating in every developing country, we work to overcome poverty, exclusion and suffering by advancing social justice and basic dignity for all." InterAction, "About Us," http://interaction.org/about (accessed November 25, 2006). According to InterAction's most recently available informational tax return (2004 Internal Revenue Service Form 990), the organization had approximately a $5.3 million operating budget.

APPENDICES

International Conventions and Recommendations Related to the Protection of Cultural Heritage

THE LEGAL INSTRUMENTS PUT IN PLACE BY UNESCO ARE:

- Convention for the Protection of Cultural Property in the Event of Armed Conflict with Regulations for the Execution of the Convention, The Hague, May 14, 1954
- Second Protocol, The Hague, March 26, 1999
- Convention on the Means of Prohibiting and Preventing the Illicit Import, Export and Transfer of Ownership of Cultural Property, Paris, November 14, 1970
- Convention concerning the Protection of the World Cultural and Natural Heritage, Paris, November 16, 1972
- UNIDROIT Convention on Stolen or Illegally Exported Cultural Objects, Rome, June 24, 1995
- Convention on the Protection of Underwater Cultural Heritage, Paris, November 2, 2001 (not yet in force)
- Convention for the Safeguarding of Intangible Cultural Heritage, Paris, October 17, 2003 (in force since April 20, 2006 with 54 State Parties at the end of July 2006)

In addition there are the following:

- Recommendation on International Principles Applicable to Archaeological Excavations (1956)
- UNESCO Declaration concerning the Intentional Destruction of Cultural Heritage (2003)
- UNESCO, ISESCO, ALECSO, Doha Statement of the International Symposium of 'Ulamâ on Islam and Cultural Heritage, Doha, Qatar, 15–16 Shawwāl 1422, December 30–31, 2001

Excerpts from the 1954 Hague Convention and the 1954 First Protocol

EXCERPTS OF THE CONVENTION FOR THE PROTECTION OF CULTURAL PROPERTY IN THE EVENT OF ARMED CONFLICT, MAY 14, 1954

THE HIGH CONTRACTING PARTIES,

Recognizing that cultural property has suffered grave damage during recent armed conflicts and that, by reason of the developments in the technique of warfare, it is in increasing danger of destruction;

Being convinced that damage to cultural property belonging to any people whatsoever means damage to the cultural heritage of all mankind, since each people makes its contribution to the culture of the world;

Considering that the preservation of the cultural heritage is of great importance for all peoples of the world and that it is important that this heritage should receive international protection;

Guided by the principles concerning the protection of cultural property during armed conflict, as established in the Conventions of The Hague of 1899 and of 1907 and in the Washington Pact of 15 April 1935;

Being of the opinion that such protection cannot be effective unless both national and international measures have been taken to organize it in time of peace;

Being determined to take all possible steps to protect cultural property;

Have agreed upon the following provisions:

Chapter I. General Provisions Regarding Protection

ARTICLE 1. DEFINITION OF CULTURAL PROPERTY. For the purposes of the present Convention, the term "cultural property" shall cover, irrespective of origin or ownership:

(a) movable or immovable property of great importance to the cultural heritage of every people, such as monuments of architecture, art or history, whether religious or secular; archaeological sites; groups of buildings which, as a whole, are of historical or artistic interest; works of art; manuscripts, books and other objects of artistic, historical or archaeological interest; as well as scientific collections and important collections of books or archives or of reproductions of the property defined above;

(b) buildings whose main and effective purpose is to preserve or exhibit the movable cultural property defined in sub-paragraph (a) such as museums, large libraries and depositories of archives, and refuges intended to shelter, in the event of armed conflict, the movable cultural property defined in sub-paragraph (a);

(c) centers containing a large amount of cultural property as defined in sub-paragraphs (a) and (b), to be known as "centers containing monuments."

ARTICLE 2. PROTECTION OF CULTURAL PROPERTY. For the purposes of the present Convention, the protection of cultural property shall comprise the safeguarding of and respect for such property.

ARTICLE 3. SAFEGUARDING OF CULTURAL PROPERTY. The High Contracting Parties undertake to prepare in time of peace for the safeguarding of cultural property situated within their own territory against the foreseeable effects of an armed conflict, by taking such measures as they consider appropriate.

ARTICLE 4. RESPECT FOR CULTURAL PROPERTY. 1. The High Contracting Parties undertake to respect cultural property situated within their own territory as well as within the territory of other High Contracting Parties by refraining from any use of the property and its immediate surroundings or of the appliances in use for its protection for purposes which are likely to expose it to destruction or damage in the event of armed conflict; and by refraining from any act of hostility, directed against such property.

2. The obligations mentioned in paragraph 1 of the present Article may be waived only in cases where military necessity imperatively requires such a waiver.

3. The High Contracting Parties further undertake to prohibit, prevent and, if necessary, put a stop to any form of theft, pillage or misappropriation of, and any acts of vandalism directed against, cultural property. They shall refrain from requisitioning movable cultural property situated in the territory of another High Contracting Party.

4. They shall refrain from any act directed by way of reprisals against cultural property.

5. No high Contracting Party may evade the obligations incumbent upon it under the present Article, in respect of another High Contracting Party, by

reason of the fact that the latter has not applied the measures of safeguard referred to in Article 3.

Any High Contracting Party in occupation of the whole or part of the territory of another High Contracting Party shall as far as possible support the competent national authorities of the occupied country in safeguarding and preserving its cultural property

ARTICLE 5. OCCUPATION. 1. Any High Contracting Party in occupation of the whole or part of the territory of another High Contracting Party shall as far as possible support the competent national authorities of the occupied country in safeguarding and preserving its cultural property.

2. Should it prove necessary to take measures to preserve cultural property situated in occupied territory and damaged by military operations, and should the competent national authorities be unable to take such measures, the Occupying Power shall, as far as possible, and in close co-operation with such authorities, take the most necessary measures of preservation.

3. Any High Contracting Party whose government is considered their legitimate government by members of a resistance movement, shall, if possible, draw their attention to the obligation to comply with those provisions of the Convention dealing with respect for cultural property.

ARTICLE 6. DISTINCTIVE MARKING OF CULTURAL PROPERTY. In accordance with the provisions of Article 16, cultural property may bear a distinctive emblem so as to facilitate its recognition.

ARTICLE 7. MILITARY MEASURES. 1. The High Contracting Parties undertake to introduce in time of peace into their military regulations or instructions such provisions as may ensure observance of the present Convention, and to foster in the members of their armed forces a spirit of respect for the culture and cultural property of all peoples.

2. The High Contracting Parties undertake to plan or establish in peacetime, within their armed forces, services or specialist personnel whose purpose will be to secure respect for cultural property and to co-operate with the civilian authorities responsible for safeguarding it.

PROTOCOL TO THE CONVENTION FOR THE PROTECTION OF CULTURAL PROPERTY IN THE EVENT OF ARMED CONFLICT 1954 (FIRST PROTOCOL)

The High Contracting Parties are agreed as follows:

I.

1. Each High Contracting Party undertakes to prevent the exportation, from a territory occupied by it during an armed conflict, of cultural property as defined in Article 1 of the Convention. . . .

2. Each High Contracting Party undertakes to take into its custody cultural property imported into its territory either directly or indirectly from any occupied territory. This shall either be effected automatically upon the importation of the property or, failing this, at the request of the authorities of that territory.

3. Each High Contracting Party undertakes to return, at the close of hostilities, to the competent authorities of the territory previously occupied, cultural property which is in its territory, if such property has been exported in contravention of the principle laid down in the first paragraph. Such property shall never be retained as war reparations.

4. The High Contracting Party whose obligation it was to prevent the exportation of cultural property from the territory occupied by it shall pay an indemnity to the holders in good faith of any cultural property which has to be returned in accordance with the preceding paragraph.

II.

5. Cultural property coming from the territory of a High Contracting Party and deposited by it in the territory of another High Contracting Party for the purpose of protecting such property against the dangers of an armed conflict, shall be returned by the latter, at the end of hostilities, to the competent authorities of the territory from which it came.

Policy Recommendations as of August 2006

THE RECOMMENDATIONS BELOW WERE DEVELOPED BY PARTICIPANTS IN MEETINGS held in February and August 2006 under the auspices of the Cultural Policy Center at the University of Chicago. For more detailed discussions of these recommendations, and for other recommendations by individual contributors to this volume, see the chapters in part II.

I. UNESCO
   Establish policy to provide museum and site security assistance to countries whose cultural heritage is at risk for looting during and following armed conflict.
   A. Work with cultural heritage NGOs, foundations, governments, and private philanthropies to create a fund dedicated to the protection of cultural heritage from war-related damage, destruction, and looting.
   B. Create museum and site security assessment team with special expertise in securing buildings against unauthorized entry and deterring or discouraging intruders from sites.
   C. Establish list of countries at risk.
   D. Approach antiquities ministries in countries at risk with offers to produce a needs assessment.
   E. Assist local antiquities ministries in assessment after a conflict.
II. Other International Institutions
   Create cultural heritage departments affiliated with emergency response teams.

A. NATO should establish a cultural department and emergency response team.

B. The CCOE (CIMIC Centre of Excellence based in Netherlands) should implement its plans to set up a cultural heritage protection department.

III. Cultural Ministries, Departments, and Agencies Worldwide

If possible, act on specific recommendations provided by UNESCO assessment team, but at minimum:

A. Establish registry of items possessed by museums.

B. Prepare special storerooms and plans for storing most valuable items in a timely manner in the event of impending armed conflict.

C. Take steps to strengthen existing guard capabilities:
  1. weaponry
  2. communications systems (i.e., walkie-talkies)
  3. surveillance (i.e., guard towers)
  4. number of guards

D. Develop contingency plans with local guards, antiquities officials, and civil society authorities to mobilize community-based emergency cultural heritage site protection.

IV. Military Ministries Worldwide

A. Cultural heritage protection must be included in military planning for both active combat operations and postcombat stability and security operations.

B. Planners should establish a task force to develop concrete steps to be taken to address cultural heritage, based on the particular conditions to be faced in the conflict situation. That task force should include:
  1. An officer responsible for phase III active combat operation planning regarding cultural heritage protection. In the U.S. military, this officer would probably be detailed from Special Operations.
  2. Officers responsible for phase IV postcombat stability and security operations planning regarding cultural heritage protection. Because cultural heritage protection against looting requires a combination of guarding efforts (by regular soldiers, by military or paramilitary police, by antiquities ministry employees, by local civilian groups, etc.), planning efforts should include input from both civil-military and military policing officers.
    a. In the U.S. military, these officers would probably be detailed from Civil Affairs or from Combined Forces Command.
    b. Other countries or coalitions may be able to provide officers from national police units specializing in cultural heritage protection, such as the Italian Carabinieri or the Spanish Guardia Civil.

3. A liaison from the cultural heritage sector capable of representing the sector's concerns and of providing expertise to identify what needs to be protected, what needs to be known in order to do this most effectively, and how the cultural heritage community might be able to contribute in support of particular purposes.

4. A high-ranking military official or civilian war planner with budgetary resources to oversee the task force and provide for sufficient logistical support to properly implement its recommendations.

C. The task force should consider the following tactical options:

1. For active combat forces:

   a. Each sector's commander must be provided with a list of buildings, sites, and monuments whose protection should be a top priority.

   b. In the first wave of any attack, military forces moving past prioritized buildings should do whatever feasible to quickly secure them at least temporarily. Museum entrances and windows, for example, could be made inaccessible by being sprayed with sticky or slippery foam. Malodorants might also be used to deter damage and looting.

   c. As quickly as possible, field commanders should detail forces to take up positions protecting museums and other prioritized buildings.

2. For phase IV, stability and security operations:

   a. If the situation is sufficiently stable, use Civil Affairs personnel to liaison with antiquities ministries and distribute funding expeditiously to pay for guards, provide walkie-talkies, trucks, etc.

   Note: funding source for this purpose must be established pre-war for this emergency purpose and transport logistics worked out so equipment can be delivered promptly.

   b. During any transitional period, in the likely event that the antiquities ministry is unable to operate effectively without backup provided by a central authority, the military should take one or more of the following steps, after consultation with the antiquities ministry:

      i) Preclude road access to selected sites by sowing the road with tire-puncturing tacks.

      ii) If feasible, make a show of force at strategically selected sites, confiscating, disabling, or destroying a few of the vehicles used by potential looters as a deterrent to future potential looters.

iii) Prevent long stays at the sites by some combination of passive technological means (such as wire-tripped release of malodorants, sound, temporary infestation of nuisance or intimidating animals). Some combination might succeed in holding off looters for at least a period of time.

iv) Arrange to pay local civil leaders to provide site security. Appropriate intermediaries of this sort should be identified by archaeologists and antiquities officials well in advance if possible. Civil leaders should be informed that sites are being monitored by satellite and digging will be detected (even if this is not actually being done).

v) Establish military guard units at sites of greatest importance.

vi) Create monitoring system to identify sites under assault or threat of assault by looters, using:
- communications equipment for local antiquities officials to report,
- satellite imagery,
- onsite intruder detection technologies.

vii) Respond to monitor alerts by focusing further efforts on those sites.

V. Legislative Bodies Worldwide

    A. Ratify the Hague Convention and its two Protocols.

    B. Draft and enact legislation to outlaw the domestic sale of stolen cultural heritage.

    C. Fund law enforcement efforts against the illicit antiquities trade, both domestically and internationally.

    D. Encourage art trade to establish an enforceable code of conduct, and if such a code is not established voluntarily, enact one.

VI. Foreign Services Worldwide

    A. Establish and maintain up-to-date web-based organizational charts of cultural ministries to facilitate postconflict reconstruction efforts to be undertaken with help from these ministries.

    B. Identify and establish liaisons with key antiquities officials.

    C. Share information with military postwar stability and reconstruction planners.

VII. U.S. Cultural Heritage Community

    A. Form an umbrella organization to represent the interests of the U.S. cultural heritage community, modeling it on InterAction, an umbrella group for humanitarian NGOs, or other umbrella organizations representing diverse interests.

1. Organizational structure should include:
   a. A think tank component
   b. An advocacy wing
   c. A military-liaison wing
2. Organizational efforts should include the following steps:
   a. Create a draft training guide on cultural heritage for distribution to U.S. Department of Defense officials.
   b. Create an attractive and concise briefing pamphlet to hand out at meetings with Congressional staff and other governmental officials.
   c. Meet with representatives from several bureaus at the State Department to publicize conference findings: Bureau of Cultural Affairs, the Office of the Coordinator for Reconstruction and Stability Operations, the Near East Bureau.
   d. Create more public interest and support in the looting of cultural heritage through publications that will attract the attention of policymakers, including articles in journals such as *Foreign Affairs* and opinion pieces for major newspapers.
   e. Use the U.S. Committee of the Blue Shield's organization to liaison with military and other government representatives and institutions, with the goal of securing meetings with:
      i) Army Peacekeeping and Stability Operations Institute
      ii) Faculty of armed service academies
      iii) Training Commands
      iv) Civil Affairs
      v) U.S. Department of Defense/Joint Chiefs of Staff
VIII. International and Domestic Law Enforcement Agencies
   A. Actively seek funding from governments, cultural organizations, and foundations for investigative resources to recover looted objects.
   B. Build a more seamless international law enforcement infrastructure to enable investigators to undertake controlled deliveries of illicit cultural property and make simultaneous arrests of all involved individuals in several countries.

A Closer Look at
NATO CIMIC Doctrine

BOTH THE UNITED STATES AND MOST EUROPEAN COUNTRIES ARE NATO MEMBERS and therefore comply with NATO regulations. This is a common denominator that can be taken advantage of if the doctrine is used as a reference when implementing CIMIC/CA cultural and cultural heritage matters and that can offer opportunities to create a multinational team of militarized experts. The following are excerpts of CIMIC doctrine and how they could apply to cultural affairs.

Doctrine	Application
"CIMIC activities form an integral part of the Joint Force Commander's (JFC) plan, are conducted in support of his mission and are related to implementing the overall strategy and achieving a stable and sustainable end-state."	For Cultural Affairs this means that planners and commanders have to be made aware of the importance and value of cultural heritage. One can point out the economic impacts of tourism, the unifying effect on national identity, security concerns related to illicit trafficking that generates funds for insurgents. In addition, there are obligations for military deriving from international treaties and other documents such as the Hague Convention of 1907, the Treaty of Versailles of 1919, the Roerich Pact of 1936, the Hague Convention and First Protocol of 1954 and Second Protocol of 1999, and the World Heritage List of UNESCO. A commander can only determine if cultural heritage protection is in support of his mission if he gets all the information needed about the cultural situation in his area of responsibility (AOR) to make a decision. The commander must be trained and counseled in matters related to culture to interpret this information.
"The Commander's CIMIC staffs are fully integrated into his Headquarters (HQ) and have full vision of and are authorised to coordinate CIMIC activities in the Joint Operations Area (JOA), theatre or region."	In this case, an international military cultural heritage expert team or individual experts should temporarily be added to a commander's CIMIC or CA staff as augmentee(s) with a reach-back capability outside of theatre. In other words the experts are lent out by their ministries of defense or an organization such as NATO following requests and make use of a (virtual) back office of civilian experts that can supply additional and also more specific information if needed.
"In co-operating with a potentially wide range of civilian bodies, NATO forces will, as far as possible and within military means and capabilities, accommodate and support the activities of these bodies, providing this does not compromise the mission."	If the situation permits it and civilian experts are available, it is recommended to have them on the ground instead of militarized or military experts.
"CIMIC activities are carried out with a view to timely transition of those functions to the appropriate civilian organisations or authorities."	Military cultural experts should not stay in-theatre longer than necessary and should hand over their activities and project information to civilian

organizations or succeeding militaries before leaving. However the following situation can also occur: military forces from a certain country redeploy before the situation is stable enough to hand over to the proper civilian bodies and agencies. Procedures have to be developed to properly hand over cultural rescue activities in case such events occur.

"CIMIC is applicable to both Article 5 Collective Defence and Non-Article 5 Crisis Response Operations (CROs). In both scenarios commanders are increasingly required to take account of social, political, cultural, religious, economic, environmental and humanitarian factors when planning and conducting military operations. Furthermore, commanders must take into account the presence of large numbers of IOs and NGOs with their own aims, methods and perspectives, all of which may have to be reconciled with those of NATO. The context and profile of CIMIC will alter according to the nature of the crisis or operation. In combat operations, the focus of CIMIC is likely to be narrower than in other operations. In a CRO, the focus of CIMIC will be broader and more complex, enabling a commander to play his part in what is likely to be a composite, multi-functional approach to a complex political emergency."

Cultural Affairs supplies information and guidance concerning the above mentioned. This concerns both cultural awareness as well as cultural heritage matters. CIMIC/CA Cultural Affairs always aims to cooperate with NGOs, IOs and local civilians wherever and whenever possible. It must be noted that there are not many NGOs and IOs dealing with this so it will be likely that Cultural Affairs will be called upon more often than other CIMIC branches.

"Relationships with the Civil Environment. Challenges will be enhanced by the presence of the media and the expectations of both the international and local communities. Therefore effective relationships with a wide range of civilian organisations as well as local populations, governments and military forces will be essential in future conflict resolution. These relationships may include joint planning mechanisms at the strategic level. CIMIC is the Commander's tool in establishing and maintaining these relationships."

Cultural and cultural heritage matters have proven to be quite effective door-openers in attempts to bring parties together in times of minor conflicts. Also, the protection of cultural heritage is good for the PR of organizations involved, including military.

Technologies for the Protection of Cultural Property

Appendix E. Technologies for the Protection of Cultural Property

	EFFECT ON INTRUDERS						CHARACTERISTICS OF TECHNOLOGY								WARTIME USE			
	Effective vs. unprepared intruder	Effective vs. professional intruder	Inhibits intruder movement	Potentially harmful to intruders	Potentially kills intruders	Labels intruders for later identification	Barrier, short-term	Barrier, longer-term	Expensive to purchase / implement	Easy to apply / use	Auto-activated	Easy to counteract	A risk to cultural property	Keeps artifacts in place	Has been used in wartime	Potentially effective in wartime	Legal in military operations	Legal in domestic peace operations
Delay and Denial Foams																		
sticky	Y	?	Y	?	N	N	Y	N	N	Y	Y	N	?	Y	Y	Y	Y	Y
slippery	Y	?	Y	?	N	N	Y	N	N	Y	Y	N	?	N	N	Y	Y	Y
fast-hardening	Y	?	Y	?	N	N	Y	Y	N	Y	Y	N	?	Y	N	Y	Y	Y
Visual Obscurants																		
smoke grenade	Y	Y	Y	Y	N	N	Y	N	N	Y	N	?	Y	N	Y	Y	Y	Y
cold smokes	Y	Y	Y	N	N	N	Y	N	N	Y	Y	?	?	N	Y	Y	Y	Y
riot control agents (CS/OS)	Y	Y	Y	?	N	N	Y	N	N	Y	Y	N	?	Y	Y	?	N	Y
residual agents	Y	Y	Y	?	N	?	Y	N	N	?	Y	N	?	Y	Y	Y	N	Y
Physical Impediments																		
barbed wire	Y	N	Y	Y	N	N	Y	N	N	Y	N	N	N	Y	Y	Y	Y	Y
transportable barriers	Y	N	Y	N	N	N	Y	?	?	Y	?	Y	Y	Y	Y	Y	Y	Y
remote-controlled portable barriers	Y	Y	Y	N	N	N	Y	Y	N	?	Y	N	N	Y	Y	Y	Y	Y
Illumination																		
nighttime security lights	Y	Y	N	N	N	N	N	N	N	Y	Y	?	N	N	Y	Y	Y	Y